2-13-2023

Lou,

This story about my grandpa is a favorite of our mutual friend, Myrle Carner. As we are reviewing production in a limited series, would you be interested in hearing more about this? Best Jimmie's Granddaughter Stephanie

UNDAUNTED

THOMAS WILLIAM SIMPSON
with Garrison Scarbrough

THE EXTRAORDINARY
STORY OF THE FIRST AVIATOR
TO ATTEMPT A SOLO FLIGHT
AROUND THE WORLD

UNDAUNTED

VEGA RISING

©2022/Cloud Country, LLC

All rights reserved. No part of this publication may be reproduced or transmitted in any form or by any means, electronic or mechanical, including photography, recording, or any information storage and retrieval system, without permission in writing from the author.

Imprint: Vega Rising

Library of Congress Control Number: 2021940640
Paperback ISBN 978-1-7373661-0-2
Hardcover ISBN 978-1-7373661-1-9
eBook ISBN 978-1-7373661-2-6

There is no sport equal to that which aviators enjoy while being carried through the air on great white wings.

WILBUR WRIGHT

Houston, Tranquility Base here. The Eagle has landed.

NEIL ARMSTRONG

For Pattie & Joy

CONTENTS

INTRODUCTION	1
PROLOGUE	9
CHAPTER ONE	11
CHAPTER TWO	19
CHAPTER THREE	27
CHAPTER FOUR	37
CHAPTER FIVE	47
CHAPTER SIX	57
CHAPTER SEVEN	69
CHAPTER EIGHT	79
CHAPTER NINE	91
CHAPTER TEN	101
CHAPTER ELEVEN	113
CHAPTER TWELVE	125
CHAPTER THIRTEEN	135
CHAPTER FOURTEEN	143
CHAPTER FIFTEEN	153
PHOTO ALBUM	161
CHAPTER SIXTEEN	213
CHAPTER SEVENTEEN	221
CHAPTER EIGHTEEN	231
CHAPTER NINETEEN	239
CHAPTER TWENTY	249
CHAPTER TWENTY-ONE	259

CHAPTER TWENTY-TWO	269
CHAPTER TWENTY-THREE	277
CHAPTER TWENTY-FOUR	287
CHAPTER TWENTY-FIVE	297
CHAPTER TWENTY-SIX	307
CHAPTER TWENTY-SEVEN	317
CHAPTER TWENTY-EIGHT	325
CHAPTER TWENTY-NINE	333
CHAPTER THIRTY	341
EPILOGUE	347
AFTERWORD	351
ACKNOWLEDGMENTS	353
TRIBUTES	355
JIMMIE MATTERN AVIATION RECORDS*	361
JIMMIE MATTERN HONORS AND AWARDS	363

INTRODUCTION

It is the greatest shot of adrenaline to be doing what you have long wanted to do so badly. You almost feel like you could fly without the plane.

Charles Lindbergh made this comment soon after completing his solo, transatlantic flight from New York to Paris on May 21, 1927.

During the Golden Age of Aviation, flying was not so much a vocation as a passion. Early aviators frequently spoke of a *need* to fly, a *desire*, a *hunger*, a *yearning*.

Some flew for accolades, others for records, still others for cash prizes. But few flew without a fervor bordering on fanaticism.

Lindbergh.
The Wright brothers.
James Doolittle.
Wiley Post.
Noel Wien.
Amelia Earhart.
Louis Blériot.
Alberto Santos-Dumont.
Howard Hughes.
Glenn Curtiss.
Bessie Colman.

Beryl Markham.
Blanche Noyes.
Louise Thaden.
James Joseph Mattern.

These are just a few of the brave men and women who climbed into heavier-than-air flying machines, raced down a dirt or grass runway, lifted into the air, and went aloft.

Orville and Wilbur Wright are generally credited with the first powered flight on December 17, 1903.

Just sixty-six years after their twelve-second flight, Neil Armstrong and Buzz Aldrin landed on the moon, stayed most of a day, and returned safely to earth.

Thousands of pilots, designers, engineers, mathematicians, mechanics, and scientists made possible the extraordinary leap from that twelve-second flight to a successful lunar landing. Some who participated in this rapid development of aviation attained fame and even fortune, but the vast majority of those individuals who made flight possible, and eventually commonplace, pursued their dreams and were soon forgotten.

Conquering the skies, leaving earth behind, provided all the incentive they needed.

Undaunted chronicles the life of one mostly forgotten aviation pioneer who flew with intense passion and incredible courage. He was born at the dawn of powered flight in March of 1905 and lived through most of the twentieth century. He lived to see, and often directly participate in, an astonishing number of aviation triumphs and milestones, including a number of firsts.

First across the English Channel.
First across the continental USA.
First across the Atlantic.
First across the Pacific.
First around the world.

INTRODUCTION

First to the moon.

James Joseph Mattern knew the men and women who set these records. He was, after all, one of them. Over the course of his lifetime, he was well acquainted with three distinct generations of aviators.

In the '20s and '30s, he knew Lindbergh and Post, Earhart and Doolittle. He even dined with the incomparable Frenchman Louis Blériot.

In the '40s and '50s, he knew the combat flying aces Richard Bong, Gregory "Pappy" Boyington, and Bob Hoover, as well as Chuck Yeager, the first flier to break the sound barrier.

And in the '60s and '70s, he mentored the men who conquered space: Alan Shepard, John Glenn, Wally Schirra, Scott Carpenter, Buzz Aldrin, and Neil Armstrong.

Jimmie Mattern's career in aviation spanned these decades and the accomplishments of these intrepid aviators. His life in many ways both portrays and symbolizes the birth and rapid growth of aviation.

Undaunted is Jimmie's story.

JIMMIE MATTERN, 1905–1988

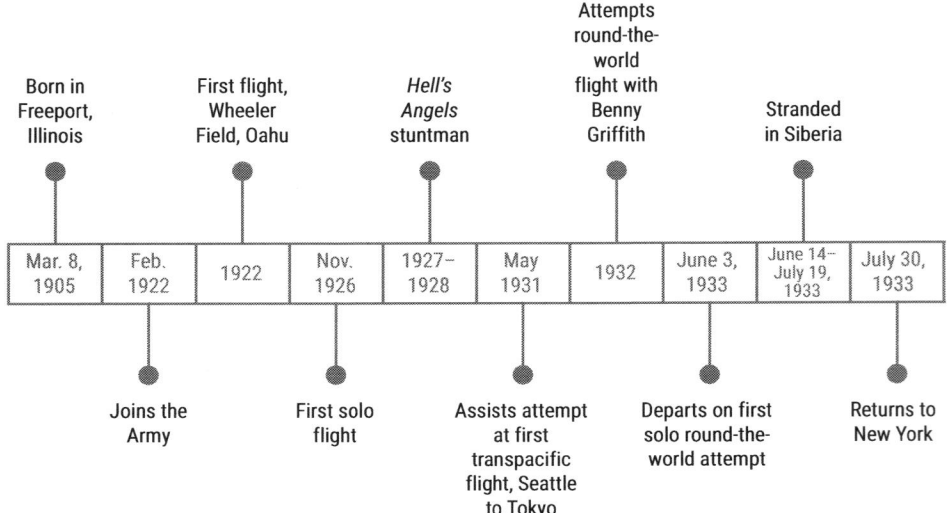

WORLD EVENTS AND AVIATION MILESTONES, 1903–1988

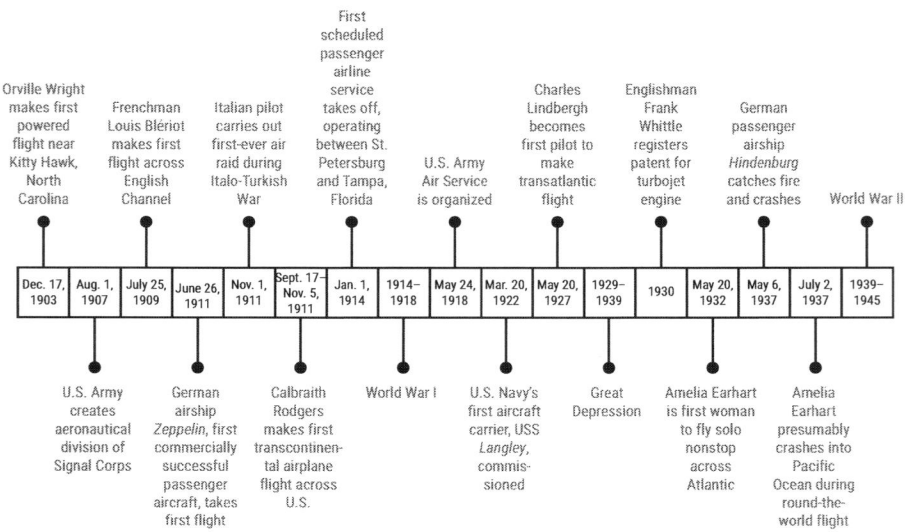

INTRODUCTION

JIMMIE MATTERN, 1905–1988

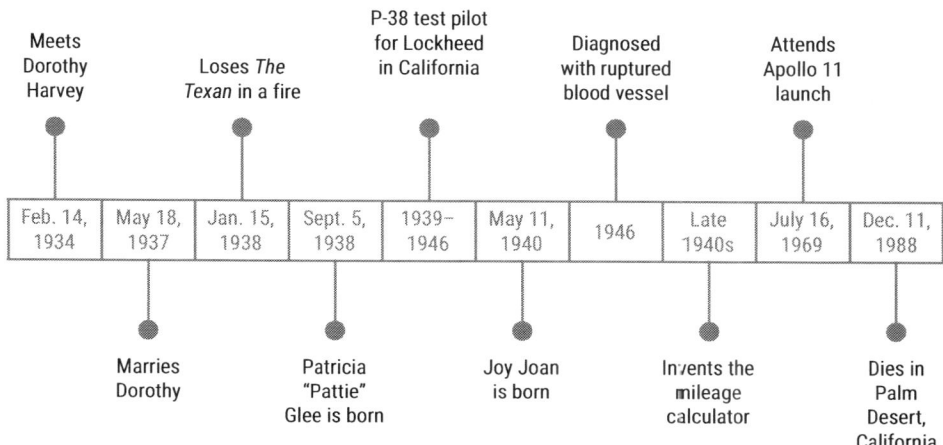

WORLD EVENTS AND AVIATION MILESTONES, 1903–1988

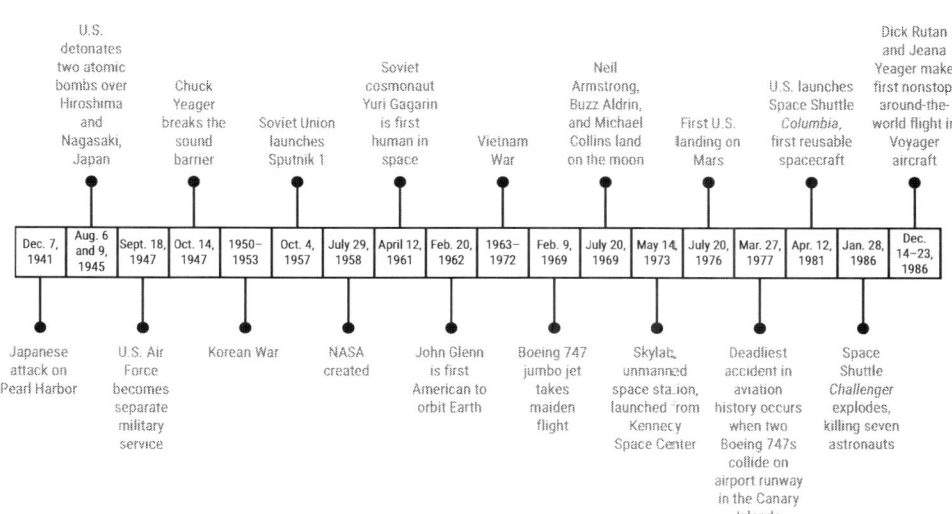

INTRODUCTION

JIMMIE'S ROUTE AROUND THE WORLD

PROLOGUE

In the dim, predawn light, he could see his airplane parked at the far end of the runway. Amidst the shadows, it looked like an apparition, and for just a moment he thought he might be dreaming. But this consideration quickly passed, as he rarely spawned a dream that did not soar.

In the dissolving darkness, he had to admit his airplane looked small against the vast coastal landscape. Inconsequential. Insignificant.

Still, despite its paltry size, he knew his airplane could do big things. Great things. Things that would change the world.

He had a lot riding on that airplane—including his life. He planned to fly that airplane around the world. Solo. Hopefully, breaking distance and speed records along the way.

If he could do it, if he could cover the sixteen thousand miles and arrive home safely in one piece, he would be the first. And he would be, like Lindbergh, lionized.

Standing in the dark hangar, looking out the window at his Lockheed Vega in the distance, a sizeable crowd gathering on the tarmac, he had his concerns, his doubts, his fears.

What rational human being wouldn't? The task ahead was daunting.

Would the plane hold up? Would *he* hold up?

Did he have sufficient food? Sufficient water? Sufficient fuel?

Would the Vega even lift off the ground carrying such an excessive quantity of fuel?

What if his instruments failed?

Or his Pratt & Whitney Wasp? Engine failure at five thousand feet over the Atlantic would be catastrophic.

Did he possess the navigational skills needed to fly around the world?

Navigation, Howard Hughes had told him years earlier, was not a science but an art.

And the weather—the weather was a constant source of anxiety. More than any other single factor, the weather was the one thing over which he had absolutely no control.

Still, he believed in blue skies and tailwinds. An eternal optimist by nature, he possessed the ability to conquer his fears and vanquish uncertainty. It was this unerring character trait that made him exceptional, and why he was destined to become one of the great fliers in the history of aviation.

CHAPTER ONE

Floyd Bennett Field
Long Island, New York

5:00 a.m.
June 3, 1933
Clear skies, 62°F, 6-8 knot westerlies

Jimmie Mattern walked out of the hangar at Floyd Bennett Field on Long Island with a strut in his step and a broad smile on his handsome face. In his leather flight suit and silk scarf, goggles and leather helmet under his arm, he looked every bit the jaunty airman.

He exuded confidence and good cheer.

And when the horde of newspapermen and aviation enthusiasts swarmed around him, their flashbulbs exploding, their questions flying at him like darts from all directions, Jimmie answered with witty ripostes and snappy retorts.

"What are you most worried about, Jim?"

"My tea getting cold."

"What about food?"

"An overrated luxury."

"How long will it take you?"

"Not as long as Post and Gatty."

"You gonna beat Lindy's time to Paris?"

"I'd better. I have an eight o'clock dinner reservation at Maxim's."

This drew a laugh, and then, "Where's Benny?"

"Benny who?"

Benny was Bennett Griffin, the decorated aviator with whom Jimmie had attempted an around-the-world flight the previous summer. In preparation for this flight, Jimmie had led the press to believe the two fliers would again be setting off together. Jimmie had engaged in this mischievous act of misinformation partly to keep Wiley Post off guard. Post, who already held the around-the-world record with Harold Gatty, was also preparing to solo. Jimmie did not want his old pal Wiley to know of his own plans.

But the overriding reason Jimmie kept his solo attempt secret was this moment unfolding right now. Jimmie Mattern was a natural showman. He loved the spotlight and he knew the press would go wild when they found out he intended to go it alone.

"What do you mean, 'Benny who'?" they shouted over each other. "Benny Griffin! Your old pal Benny!"

"Oh right, Benny. Sure. Benny can't make it," Jimmie joked. "He has an appointment with his dentist."

Reporters from all the major papers stood on the tarmac—*The New York Times*, *The Boston Globe*, the *Los Angeles Times*, the *Chicago Tribune*, *The Times* of London, plus dozens of reporters from small papers all over the country. It was, after all, the Golden Age of Aviation. Aviators were hailed as heroes, celebrated for their pluck and derring-do. Especially those aviators like Lindbergh and Post and Mattern, who took off into the wild blue yonder in single-engine planes made mostly of plywood and fabric.

"What are you talking about, 'his dentist'?" the reporters demanded.

"Caps and crowns."

"Come on, Jimmie, what gives?"

"I just felt like getting away by myself for a few days."

"Seriously, Jimmie! Is this on the level?"

"What do you boys want me to say?"

"Are you going solo?"

The first faint traces of dawn began to appear in the eastern sky over Long Island. Jimmie Mattern knew it was time to go. He would soon be burning daylight. But it was tough to pull away from the spotlight—this was just too good. More than anything, he loved to fly, but this banter with the boys came in a close second.

He ran his fingers through his thick, wavy brown hair, smiled devilishly, and said, "You boys should've had a closer look at the Vega."

"How could we get a closer look, Jim? You've had her locked up in that hangar like Anne Boleyn in the Tower of London."

"Come on, boys, she's been out and about. And had you taken a closer look, you would've noticed a serious lack of space for a copilot. Heck, there's barely room for *me* inside the *Century of Progress*. Whole blasted inside of that airplane's nothing but a giant fuel tank. A bunch of fuel tanks, actually."

"How much fuel, Jimmie?"

"More than the weight of the airplane, by God. She'll probably never get off the ground."

"You'll get her up, Jim!"

Jimmie smiled. "I'll do my best, boys. I'll give it my all."

And with that, Jimmie turned and headed for the car that would drive him to the end of the runway where his Lockheed Vega sat idling. His mechanic, Fred Fetterman, had topped off the fuel tanks and started the engine so it would be warm and ready to fly.

Jimmie opened the passenger door of the sedan. Before sliding inside, he called over his shoulder, "I'll see you boys right back here in a few days."

"We'll be waiting, Jim!"

"Try not to forget about me."

And then he gave a wave, ducked into the car, and slammed the door.

Jimmie Mattern's Lockheed Vega, *Century of Progress*, was an amalgam. The original *Century of Progress*, which Jimmie and Benny Griffin had used for their around-the-world attempt in 1932, had crashed in the Soviet Union and never flown again. The Soviets, however, had shipped the broken aircraft back to Jimmie in early 1933. He salvaged what he could, including the engine, a 420 hp Pratt & Whitney Wasp. One of the finest airplane engines of its day, the Wasp could cruise at 130 mph with a trailing breeze, burned little oil, and was reasonably fuel efficient. Most importantly, the Wasp was a workhorse. Kept in good tune, it rarely suffered mechanical failure.

Nevertheless, Jimmie had Pratt & Whitney perform a complete overhaul on the pistons and camshafts. They "supercharged" the engine, giving it an additional 100 hp, increasing its top speed to 140 mph under optimal conditions. When traveling more than sixteen thousand miles, an extra ten miles per hour would add up to some significant savings.

Upon completion of the overhaul, Fred Fetterman looked the overhauled engine over and deemed it "better than new."

Lockheed first manufactured the Vega in 1927. At that time, it was a technological marvel, a design unlike anything seen before. A high-wing monoplane, the Vega had an enclosed cockpit to protect pilot and passengers from the elements. Originally, Lockheed engineers Jack Northrop and Gerard Vultee designed the Vega to carry passengers and cargo on short flights of a few hundred miles or less. Transportation via airplane was at that time in its infancy. The Lockheed Aircraft Corporation, formed in 1926 by Northrop and Allan Lockheed, first envisioned itself as an airline, not an airplane manufacturer. This all changed, however, with the success of the Vega and later the famous combat fighter, the P-38 Lightning.

Jimmie's *Century of Progress* was pure Lockheed Vega, but it carried parts from half a dozen different airplanes. The engine and some of the controls were from the plane he had crashed in the USSR the summer before. The fuselage and wings came from a junked Vega owned by Standard Oil Company of New Jersey. Standard Oil's head of aviation, Ed Aldrin, strongly believed in Jimmie Mattern's skill and resolve to circumnavigate the globe solo. Aldrin convinced his bosses to offer the company's vast resources to assist the young aviator in his mission.

The *Century of Progress* had a new Hamilton controllable-pitch propeller. Jimmie's original Vega had a basic wooden propeller that worked well but had several limitations, including the need for someone to physically grab the blade and give it a spin to get it started. The Hamilton propeller could be started by flipping a switch on the instrument panel inside the cockpit. The pilot also had the ability to adjust the propeller up and down to aid in takeoff and landing and to improve fuel economy during level flight.

The instrument cluster from the original *Century of Progress* was repaired and updated by the Bendix Aviation Corporation, free of charge. The basic instruments—airspeed indicator, altimeter, turn and bank coordinator, heading indicator—were enough to allow Jimmie to "fly blind" in bad weather and at night. The *Century of Progress* was not, however, equipped with a basic air-to-ground radio, deicing equipment, or even a rudimentary automatic pilot. These flying aids were still in early stages of research and development. Their reliability was questionable at best and their install costs extremely high.

At the end of the runway, Jimmie stepped out of the car and noted the wind direction, an old habit for such a young flier. He walked slowly around his airplane. She was a beauty with her fresh sky-blue paint job and the striking red image of a fierce eagle adorning the fuselage and wings. Jimmie chose an eagle to show his patriotism and to let people know he flew for America.

He strode around his airplane, checking the propeller, tires, landing-gear struts, wings, wing flaps, and tail.

Satisfied, he held a brief conversation with Fred Fetterman, who assured him everything he had requested had been stowed on board: two Thermos bottles (donated by Wiley Post and Amelia Earhart for good luck), hunting knife, fishing line, revolver, fleece-lined flying suit, mosquito netting, a special box camera, and a miniscule food supply of three oranges, two sandwiches, and three chocolate bars.

In each Thermos he had his favorite hot tea with sugar.

"Tanks topped off?" Jimmie asked his mechanic.

"Absolutely, Jim."

"Hundred percent?"

"Hundred percent. Not to worry. Everything's been taken care of."

Jimmie smiled. "You know my motto, Fred. Proper preparation paves the road to success."

Jimmie had guts, but he also had brains and, for a young man just twenty-eight years old, good sense. Prior to the flight, he had done everything in his power to get his plane and his body in the best possible shape. He'd purchased the best equipment, hired the best mechanics and engineers, eaten a healthy diet, run three miles a day, done a hundred or more pushups daily, and tried to get plenty of sleep.

Jimmie did not like to leave things to chance.

He slapped Fred on the back, thanked him for everything, and stepped onto the starboard wheel pants of his Lockheed Vega. The wind gusted. Jimmie caught the salty fragrance of the sea. It made him think of his days on Oahu, his carefree Army days playing trombone and drums in the bugle corps.

But this, he knew, was no time to be thinking of the past. Jimmie knew that for the next several days he needed to laser focus on the present. The journey he was about to embark upon would put life and limb in danger. He would need all his skills, determination, and concentration to achieve success and return safely.

He waved to Fred and to the newspaper boys back on the tarmac and then climbed into the cockpit. It was not a spacious compartment—anyone susceptible to claustrophobia would wither quickly.

Once settled into the padded wooden seat, Jimmie had little room to maneuver. A six-footer with long legs and broad shoulders, he filled that cockpit practically from starboard to port and from stem to stern. Legroom was especially cramped, since the fuselage narrowed considerably as it funneled toward the nose.

His feet had nowhere to rest except on the pedals. The stick that operated the plane stuck up between his legs, forcing him to remain more or less in the same position for hours at a time on these long-haul flights. The instrument panel pushed right up in his face, not even an arm's length away.

What made this constrained space tolerable was the abundance of glass. A tall windshield and wraparound windows allowed the world into the cockpit, lessening the sense of restriction and isolation.

Still, the cockpit of a Lockheed Vega was an inhospitable place. It was a rare flier who could stay aloft for any length of time, let alone a journey clear around the world.

CHAPTER ONE

Relentless engine noise, persistent turbulence shaking and rattling the fuselage, the harsh smells of oil and gasoline—all of this took their toll on the aviator. Only a special person with tremendous grit and the ability to overcome extreme physical discomfort would attempt long-distance flying in a Lockheed Vega.

Jimmie closed and secured the overhead hatch. He knew he would likely not be getting out to stretch his arms and legs for at least twenty hours. Perhaps longer.

But just as it was no time to reflect on the past, it was also no time to be contemplating the future and its potential miseries.

Dawn opened on the eastern horizon.

The time had come to fly.

Once in action, Jimmie was not a man to worry. But as he settled into the cramped seat, his legs straddling the stick, he could not help but think about all the weight he would soon be asking the little Vega to lift off the ground. She ran twenty-eight feet from nose to stern with a wingspan of just over forty feet. Her fuselage and wings were nothing more than sheet plywood covered with woven fabric and held together with steel fasteners and aviation glue. Her landing gear was fixed, and though shock cords had been added and the struts lowered to aid in rough landings, Jimmie was a realist. He knew a hard jolt on a rocky or potholed runway might knock the landing gear clean off the fuselage.

A Lockheed Vega weighed, on average, without oil, gas, or passengers, right around 3,500 pounds. Without modifications, she could stay aloft for approximately five hours and cover, under optimal conditions, around 750 miles.

The *Century of Progress*, however, was not a typical Lockheed Vega. Jimmie had modified the small plane considerably with seven additional fuel tanks, extending its range to more than thirty hours and nearly five thousand miles. But all that gasoline was heavy—in excess of 4,200 pounds.

Would she get off the ground? The time had finally come to find out.

Jimmie knew he had plenty of runway, almost four thousand feet. Normally, a Lockheed Vega needs less than half that distance to get airborne. Once, on a short runway with a stiff headwind assisting lift, Jimmie had gotten airborne in less than a thousand feet. But that was with an airplane carrying just a few hundred pounds of fuel and no passengers or cargo. This bird idling on the runway was a whole different animal.

Jimmie took a few deep breaths and told himself to remain patient. *Remember to use the entire runway*, he thought. *All four thousand feet of it if necessary.* Otherwise, he knew he might well wind up in Sheepshead Bay, rapidly ending his dream of first to fly solo around the world.

His Vega did not have brakes, so the moment Jimmie opened the throttle, the plane began to roll forward. He could feel the weight as she bumped down the reasonably smooth grass runway and slowly picked up speed. No thoughts beyond the business at hand went through Jimmie's head. He had learned to fly by touch and feel, and all that training served him well as he made small corrections with his pedals and stick to keep the *Century of Progress* rolling dead straight in those final seconds before takeoff.

Jimmie felt the wings lift the fuselage. He knew she was ready to fly!

He pulled back on the stick. The nose rose. A smile crossed his face as the Vega left the earth behind, crossed low over a marsh covered with cattails, then ascended quickly into the early-morning sky streaked with orange as the sun lifted out of the Atlantic.

Before heading northeast across Long Island and out over the Sound, Jimmie circled the airfield and dipped a wing to the crowd of newspapermen and aviation enthusiasts waving and shouting below.

And then the aviator was alone and on his way.

CHAPTER TWO

March 1905–February 1922

James Joseph Mattern was born March 8, 1905, in Freeport, Illinois. His parents, Philip Mattern and Caroline Kennedy Mattern, shortly thereafter began calling him "Jimmie," a nickname he would carry throughout his life.

Aviation was in its infancy at the time of Jimmie's birth. Just over one year had passed since Orville Wright had piloted the Wright Flyer on a twelve-second flight covering 120 feet over Kill Devil Hills, North Carolina, on the morning of December 17, 1903. This was the first successful flight to use a gasoline-powered engine to assist in lift and speed.

James Joseph Mattern and the Age of Powered Flight had arrived practically simultaneously at the beginning of the twentieth century. The two would grow up together.

Freeport was a small city a hundred miles west of Chicago with a population of approximately twenty-five thousand residents. It was a quintessential midwestern town founded and settled by European immigrants from Germany, Holland, Sweden, and Norway. Surrounded by some of the most fertile farmland on the planet, Freeport was also home to a variety of prosperous businesses. The Illinois Central Railroad had its headquarters there, as did the Henney Motor Car Company, at that time one of the world's major manufacturers of hearses.

The largest building in Freeport was a massive brick factory ten stories high that housed the W. T. Rawleigh Medical Company. Rawleigh made a variety of "medicines," but their bestseller by far was a medicated salve the company claimed cured head colds, croup, earaches, headaches, aching joints, muscular pain, insect bites, cuts, burns, mouth sores, and fever. It could be used internally or externally and, according to the label, "should always be applied liberally and rubbed in vigorously."

Jimmie's father, Philip, was born in Mannheim, Germany, and immigrated to America with his parents in the early 1880s at age twelve. Philip was an excellent athlete, and for a time played semi-professional baseball in Illinois, Indiana, and throughout the Midwest. He dreamed of playing ball professionally and traveling the country, but in the end his father convinced him to settle down and take up the family vocation, shoe repair, and in this manner Philip earned a respectable living and cared for his family.

Jimmie's mother, Caroline Kennedy, was born on a freighter in the middle of Lake Ontario, though her birth was registered in Cleveland, Ohio. She grew up in a loving home and received an adequate public-school education. Reading was a particular passion. She married Philip Mattern in the summer of 1892 at age sixteen.

Philip and Caroline had four children: Philip Jr., born 1893; Gertrude, born 1895; Roy, born 1897; and James Joseph, born 1905. Jimmie was not particularly close to his siblings, due in part to the fact that Philip, Gertrude, and Roy were all quite a bit older. But also, Philip and Roy, as older siblings are inclined to do, frequently used young Jimmie for sport, teasing him and calling him a mama's boy. This caused some bad blood. But all the teasing ended before Jimmie reached middle school. By then, his brothers and sister had moved out of the house to pursue higher education and employment.

Jimmie was close with his parents, as he was the only child living at home for several years. Like his father, Jimmie excelled at athletics. He ran like the wind and could hit a baseball a country mile. His father encouraged Jimmie to play sports, but even more he encouraged him to study hard and prepare for the future. Philip wanted his youngest son to follow him into the shoe business, and he often spoke with Jimmie about the family owning a string of shoe stores that would stretch from Freeport to Chicago and beyond.

Jimmie, however, had little interest in shoes. He was a dreamer. From an early age, he looked into the sky and dreamed of open spaces and far-off lands.

Still, he was a good son. He respected his parents, completed his chores without complaint, and performed reasonably well in school. But what he really liked to do was run free. He loved the outdoors. He hated being cooped up inside almost as much as he hated being told what to do. He liked to jump on the trolley with his buddies and ride from one end of Freeport to the other. The boys ran wild through the woods on the edge of town, played baseball and football in the town parks, and climbed on the tall monument that marked the location where Lincoln had debated Douglas back in 1858.

In the summer, Jimmie liked to swim in the Pecatonica River that ran through town. In the winter, he skated on that same river. He dreamed of skating all the way to Chicago. He dreamed of taking the train to New York.

Jimmie dreamed of seeing the world.

Even as a young boy living a quiet life in a small midwestern city, Jimmie Mattern simmered with wanderlust.

In the summer of 1919, at age fourteen, Jimmie had his first close encounter with aviation. He had on occasion seen airplanes fly overhead, but that summer he physically put his hands on an airplane for the first time.

A World War I flying ace named George Rideout flew into Freeport early one morning in a Curtiss JN-4 "Jenny" biplane with an OX-5 motor. George was barnstorming the country, flying from town to town, offering three-minute plane rides for $3.

Jimmie didn't have three dollars, and no way was his father coughing up the cash for such a silly indulgence, but George allowed young Mattern to sit briefly in the cockpit.

While Jimmie fiddled with the stick and played with the pedals and pretended to fly, George regaled the young lad with his exploits over France, knocking German Fokkers and their cocky pilots out of the sky.

That was all it took to ignite the flame. Right then and there, Jimmie decided he would one day be a flier.

He was excited to tell his parents about his career decision, but before he could say a word, his father launched into a hard criticism of airplanes and aviators, insisting the whole enterprise was a "terrible waste of time that would never amount to a hill of beans."

"Really?" asked Jimmie.

"If man were meant to fly," Philip Mattern thundered, "God would have given him wings."

Jimmie clammed up. He did not want to argue with or disappoint his father, despite the fact that he thought the man was dead wrong. The Wright brothers of Ohio had proved man could fly, and every year brave pilots flew higher and faster and farther.

Still, Jimmie did not want to go against his father, so he kept his dream of one day being an airman to himself.

Just one year later, in late May of 1920, Philip Mattern, age forty-nine, passed away after suffering for some time with failing kidneys. Before he passed, Philip called Jimmie into his room. "Son, your brothers and sister have grown and gone. I'm afraid it's up to you. I know you're young, and I am sorry for leaving you so soon with this burden, but I need you to promise me you will take good and proper care of your mother."

Jimmie, confused and sad and right on the edge of tears, assured his father he would do his duty. He would most assuredly take good care of his mother.

And so right from that fledgling and formative age, James Joseph Mattern faced an age-old dilemma thrust upon so many young men: duty or desire, domesticity or adventure. He was a boy just bumping up against manhood who understood his responsibilities but who also dreamed of freedom and wide-open spaces.

It was a dilemma that would trail him well into adulthood.

The family grieved following Philip's death, and thereafter suffered financial hardship. The Mattern Shoe and Shoe Repair Shop at 95 Stephenson Street in Freeport was sold off to a local competitor. Debts, however, had piled up, and any profit from the sale of the business was soon exhausted. The family house was sold, and Jimmie and his mother packed up their few remaining possessions and moved north to Calgary, Alberta, to live with Jimmie's sister, Gertrude, and her new husband.

As money was in short supply, Jimmie had to go to work. He took a job as a cowboy on a large ranch a few miles east of Calgary near the town of Cheadle. Jimmie had never ridden a horse before, but he took to it like a retriever to water. His first mount was a wild pinto pony Jimmie rode bareback and had to break himself. In no time, he could ride and rope and spend hours in the saddle without tiring. Jimmie enjoyed riding all day and sleeping under the stars with his saddle for a pillow and the ground for a bed. But the other aspects of cowboy life, the mundane chores of mending fences and grooming horses and cleaning stalls, along with often sleeping in smelly, noisy bunkhouses, were not so much to Jimmie's liking.

The older, more experienced cowboys pushed him around the same way his older brothers had pushed him around, so Jimmie quit, went back to Calgary, and took a job with Gertrude's husband. He did not even have a driver's license, but here he was, driving a limousine.

This employment proved short-lived, however, as the limousine broke down frequently, leaving Jimmie's passengers stranded and in foul moods.

Next came a gig as a window washer at the Palliser Hotel in downtown Calgary. The Palliser was the city's premier lodging establishment, an ornate ten-story brick-and-glass hotel financed by the Canadian Pacific Railway. Jimmie, young and wiry, was sent to the top floors, where he had to crawl out onto the narrow ledges, and with squeegee in hand, remove the dust and grime from the tall double-hung windows.

Less than a decade in the future, Jimmie would willingly and confidently fly over oceans and mountains in a single-engine airplane. But standing on those narrow brick ledges with nothing but air between himself and the sidewalk a hundred feet below made young Mattern squeamish. After just a few days on the ledge, he thanked the manager very much for the employment opportunity but handed over his squeegee.

The manager understood young Mattern's reluctance, liked the cut of Jimmie's jib, and so sent him out to the Banff Springs Hotel, another Canadian Pacific Railway hostelry, where Jimmie was hired as a busboy. Banff Springs was a colossal wood-frame hotel with spectacular views of the Canadian Rockies. Jimmie had never seen such incredible scenery. He'd grown up in the flatlands of the Midwest, and Calgary had been more of the same. But Banff was a mountain town where tourists flocked to hunt and fish and hike.

There were also plenty of girls, good-looking young girls who came to Banff with their parents on holiday. Jimmie, with his handsome features, broad smile, and easy demeanor, quickly discovered that girls found him appealing, especially after he learned to dance.

Every week, Jimmie sent money down to Calgary to help his mother with expenses. Every few weeks, he took the train down to pay her a visit. It was a good life for a young man and Jimmie enjoyed the freedom and independence.

In fact, Jimmie might well have kept his job at the Banff Springs Hotel, except for one small inconvenience—the weather. Summer and autumn were outstanding seasons, but when winter hit, watch out. The mercury fell below freezing by Thanksgiving, below zero by Christmas, and in late January the temperature plunged to almost thirty degrees below zero.

That kind of cold was more than Jimmie could take. He hated to leave, but the young man needed a warmer clime.

He made his way west to British Columbia on a cattle train, but in Victoria he could not find work. With the few remaining dollars in his pocket, Jimmie bought a ticket on the ferry bound for Seattle. His idea was to get back to the States, enroll in school, find a part-time job, and finish high school.

But broke, hungry, and with no place to lay his head, these plans were quickly waylaid when an Army recruiter found Jimmie sitting forlornly on a park bench on the edge of Discovery Park, a stone's throw from Puget Sound.

"You look like you could use a helping hand, young feller," the recruiter said to Jimmie.

"Maybe," said Jimmie.

"Ever consider the Army?"

"Nope."

CHAPTER TWO

"The United States Army could sure use a helping hand from a strapping young buck like yourself."

"The Army, huh?"

"Yes sir. What do you say we help each other out?"

The recruiter promised a crisp new uniform, a comfy bed, and lots of hot chow, all Jimmie could eat. It was February 1922. Cold and raw. Jimmie's clothes were in tatters, and he hadn't eaten a decent meal in days. He'd been sleeping outside and waking up half frozen.

So Jimmie signed up, and lied about his age to do so. He was still just sixteen years old, a month shy of seventeen.

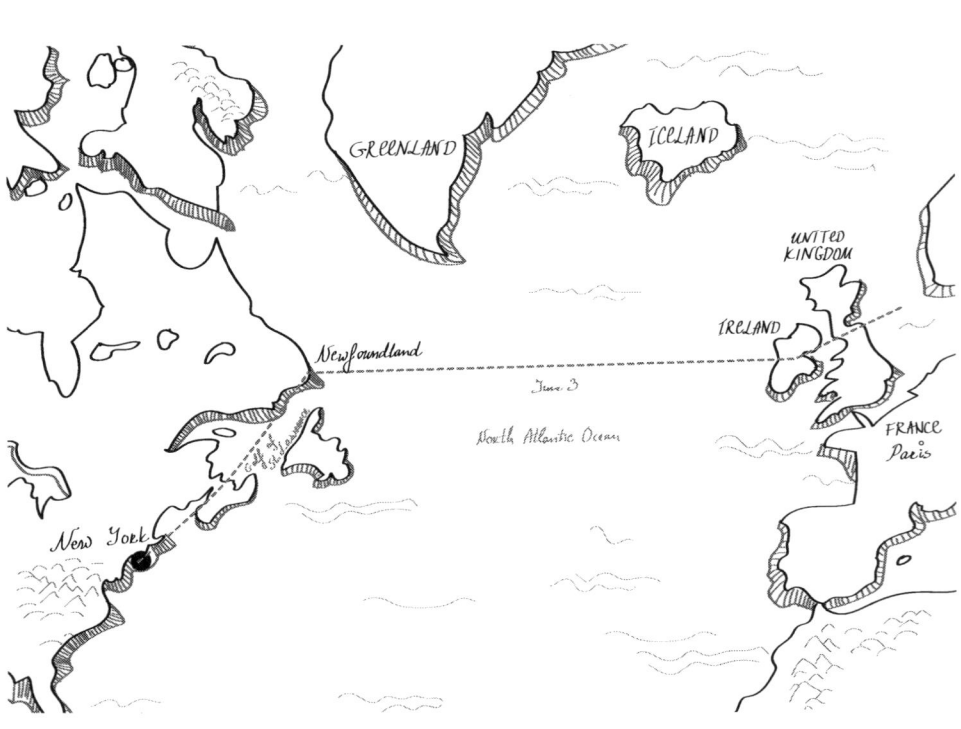

CHAPTER THREE

Over the Atlantic

June 3, 1933
Clear skies, 66°F, winds variable out of the east
Altitude 5,000 feet

After crossing Long Island Sound and reaching Rhode Island near Newport, Jimmie followed the coastline to the northeast. The skies remained clear and the winds light. Jimmie found calm air and settled in at an altitude of around five thousand feet above sea level. He flew over the eastern end of Cape Cod and briefly descended below one thousand feet, where he dipped his starboard wing to a group of sunbathers waving on the beach near Wellfleet. From there, Jimmie flew due north over Cape Cod Bay. He could see Boston to the west, then, in quick succession, Gloucester, Portsmouth, and Portland, Maine.

At this early stage of his long journey, all felt calm and familiar. This was the same route he and Benny Griffin had flown a year earlier on their attempt to beat the around-the-world record set by Wiley Post and Harold Gatty in 1931. Jimmie and Benny had also taken off from Floyd Bennett Field and flown up the coast before landing in Newfoundland to refuel.

Floyd Bennett Field and all those pushy newspapermen with their cameras and pads and pencils and questions stood a couple hours and a few hundred miles back to the southwest. Jimmie, as always, had enjoyed the verbal jousting with those newspapermen, but the business of flying his Lockheed

Vega, *Century of Progress*, while hauling four thousand pounds of fuel in eight different tanks, now demanded his full attention.

Out over the Gulf of Maine, the weather close to perfect, Jimmie relaxed a bit. He drank some warm tea, ate an orange, and allowed his thoughts to drift. He pushed aside a brief twinge of loneliness by reminding himself that he was not really alone. Sure, he piloted the Vega alone, and would do so for the next few days, maybe a week or more, but Jimmie really believed he had the support of the entire nation. Interest in aviation had soared ever since Lindbergh had soloed the Atlantic and landed in Paris. People had started to realize air travel could make the world a much smaller and hopefully more civilized and peaceful place. Jimmie wanted to be the first to fly solo around the world, but he also believed his flight offered something more important than individual accomplishment. A severe economic depression had swept the country and left one of four workers unemployed. The stock market had collapsed. Wages had hit rock bottom. People felt trapped and desperate. Jimmie believed his flight, if successful, would give people hope. It would offer them a glimpse into the future.

People asked Jimmie all the time, "Why do you do it, Jim?"

"Are you crazy?"

"Do you have a death wish?"

Jimmie usually just shrugged and offered his toothy grin. "Smiling Jimmie Mattern," that's what the press called him. It came naturally. He'd been blessed with a pleasant, optimistic, easygoing disposition.

"Come on, Jim. Why do you fly? Give us a clue. Why do you risk your neck?" Reporters asked these questions over and over.

"Why did Columbus set sail into the unknown?" Jimmie would answer on those occasions when he felt reflective. "Why did Magellan have the gall to attempt to sail around the world when so many still thought the earth flat? Francis Drake. Amerigo Vespucci. Marco Polo. Lewis and Clark. Amundsen. Hillary. Lindbergh. Post. Earhart. Come on, fellas, as long as we walk the earth, there'll be men and women trying to conquer what hasn't yet been conquered. Most folks don't hanker for adventure, but some, thank God, do. Some folks are content with the status quo, but those with the curiosity and the right stuff, well hell, they're going to plow forward into the unknown. Tell us it can't be done"—and here Jimmie would smile—"and we'll show them it can. And that's the thing with flying, you know. They told Orville and Wilbur they were wasting their time, they were out of their gourds, but those boys didn't listen. They persisted. And good God, look at the door they swung wide open. Santos-Dumont, Louis Blériot, J. W. Dunne, Lucky Lindy, Wiley and Harry Gatty—the critics and cynics and naysayers all told those men they were crazy fools, wasting time and money. Man flying like an eagle—ridiculous. How arrogant to think it was even possible! They parroted the old cliché: If man were meant to fly, God would have given him wings."

No question, like many a rebellious son before and after him, Jimmie took great motivation from what his father had disparaged and found trifling. And so, on occasion, when the mood struck, Jimmie could pontificate on the gospel of exploration and powered flight. But he always did so with an ease and grace that never offended. He was a zealot when it came to flying, a man built physically, psychologically, and spiritually to go aloft in small airplanes and accomplish feats mankind had not previously accomplished.

And if his father's dismissal of the whole enterprise helped fuel Jimmie's ambitions . . . well, so be it.

Jimmie's reverie over the Gulf of Maine and then the Gulf of St. Lawrence ended abruptly when he spotted the southeast coast of Newfoundland. He knew it was Newfoundland because a year earlier he and Griffin had made their first pitstop at the airstrip outside St. John's. The weather had been atrocious—fog as thick as pea soup, making it difficult for Jimmie and Benny to even see the Vega's propeller. They'd flown around half lost for hours before the fog finally lifted and they could land.

This time the weather was flawless—clear skies with light winds. But Jimmie had another problem, a potentially major problem.

He did not need to land. The whole purpose for all those fuel tanks and all that fuel was to permit the *Century of Progress* to fly and fly and fly— all the way, God willing, from Floyd Bennett Field on Long Island to Le

Bourget Field on the outskirts of Paris, where Lindbergh had touched down after his historic flight.

Jimmie's first goal on this solo flight around the world was to set the New York-to-Paris speed record. But sighting the coast of Newfoundland as he crossed the Gulf of St. Lawrence did not bode well for the success of this initial triumph. He knew immediately any chance of setting a speed record to Paris was suddenly in serious jeopardy. In fact, the entire flight might well be in jeopardy.

Why?

Because the route Jimmie had plotted and planned for months did not include the coast of Newfoundland. He was off course, north and west, by several degrees.

And he had no idea why.

Jimmie pushed aside a brief moment of panic. All was well with the plane, after all. The Vega was intact. He had plenty of fuel. The weather could not be better. He could be on the ground in St. John's in minutes if need be.

But the last thing Jimmie wanted to do was land his airplane. Or turn back. He had been thinking about this flight for years, practically since he'd first sat in the cockpit of George Rideout's JN-4 Jenny at the grass airstrip in Freeport. And he had been in full-time preparation for this flight since he and Benny Griffin had returned from their aborted around-the-world attempt the previous July.

Turn back?

Not a chance.

Jimmie didn't have any turn-back in him. He was a man focused on the future. He just had to stay calm and figure out why his compass had gone awry and slowly pushed him to the north and west.

By this time, Jimmie knew, he should have been far to the east over the North Atlantic.

He studied his instrument panel. All gauges appeared to be working normally.

CHAPTER THREE

But something was messing with his compass. Fetterman had checked it for accuracy just a day or two ago and it had easily hit dead reckoning.

Jimmie's eyes fell on the Thermos bottles stowed under his feet. They were made of metal. Could they be the culprits?

He picked one up and passed it back and forth in front of the compass. The needle did not stray.

Jimmie sighed and looked around his small, cramped cockpit. That's when he remembered the camera Beau Collins of Pathé News had given him to record his trip on film. It was a big, heavy box camera. Jimmie had been reluctant to haul it along, but Pathé News had sponsored the flight, along with Standard Oil of New Jersey, Lockheed, Pratt & Whitney, Bendix, and several other generous companies. Jimmie had felt obligated to carry the camera. But was the metal body of the camera causing his compass to malfunction?

With some difficulty, Jimmie reached back over his head to the small storage compartment aft. He pulled out the camera and held it in front of the compass. Sure enough, when he passed the camera back and forth in front of the compass, the needle swung in unison.

"I'll be damned!"

It was the first time Jimmie had heard his voice since leaving New York.

Months of meticulous preparation, and then done in by a camera he didn't even want on board.

Jimmie knew without question the camera had to go. But it was enormous. It didn't come close to fitting through the small sliding window. He tried to dismantle it in the hopes of tossing it out the window piece by piece, but to no avail. The big box camera with its fixed lens was a solid chunk of steel and glass.

Jimmie sighed and gave in to the hard reality that he was married to the camera until he could land and slide open the cockpit door, a task he dared not do while in flight. At this speed and altitude, the door might rip right off the fuselage. The only solution was to keep moving the camera from one side of the cockpit to the other every few minutes, thereby maintaining a reasonably steady course.

Jimmie, despite his adventurous nature and courageous bearing, was a bulletproof realist. He knew his chances of finding Paris were suddenly just about nonexistent. *France* would be difficult to find, let alone the City of Lights. In fact, as Jimmie flew what he hoped was due east, he knew he'd be lucky just to hit the European continent.

An hour later, the Pathé News camera turned into a minor problem.

Ever since leaving Floyd Bennett Field, the winds had been calm and sky clear, not so much as a cloud in sight. But Jimmie had been flying long enough to know not to trust weather this fine. It was too good to be true. He knew, eventually, he'd pay for weather so perfect.

And sure enough, a couple hours later, as afternoon wore into evening, Jimmie spotted real weather on the eastern horizon. By his calculations, he was now at the point of no return, that point being approximately halfway over the Atlantic between North America and Europe.

The storm ahead looked formidable. It stretched from north to south as far as he could see. Extraordinary bolts of lightning flashed from swirling black clouds.

Jimmie knew he would be in the middle of the storm within minutes unless he took evasive action immediately. He could do a 180 and try to outrun the tempest, but such a course offered no guarantees beyond quite possibly putting an end to his mission.

Seconds later, the storm, roaring with ferocity and menace, swept over the tiny airplane. A classic North Atlantic nor'easter, she moved like an express train. The winds tossed the *Century of Progress* around like a beachball on a frothy sea.

Rarely in his flying career had Jimmie Mattern felt fear. But for the next several hours, as the storm raged and darkness descended, Jimmie experienced full-fledged terror. He did everything in his power to hold the stick steady and keep the plane from tumbling into a tailspin and plunging into the frigid North Atlantic.

But despite these efforts, Jimmie feared his time had come; death was definitely at hand. He would die all alone out here over the cold dark ocean.

CHAPTER THREE

His thoughts turned to Della, his wife of almost six years. They had married when Jimmie was still just a boy, not quite twenty-two years old. He had loved her fervently. But before too much time had passed, Jimmie's other love began to impose itself upon their union. Jimmie needed to fly. He needed to fly like an alcoholic needs a drink. When not flying, he dreamed of flying. This battle between flight and marriage waged for several years before finally coming to a breaking point when Jimmie set off on his around-the-world attempt with Benny Griffin in July 1932.

The marriage survived that flight, but in the past year Jimmie and Della had spent very little time together. For the press, Della performed admirably as the loving wife sitting home alone by the radio, stoically awaiting the return of her valiant, heroic husband. But in truth, the marriage was all but over, all that youthful passion used up and burned out.

But right at this moment, fearing death, already feeling the grip of the icy Atlantic, Jimmie wished he could embrace his wife. He wished he could apologize for his insensitivity and selfishness, for putting his ambitions above their marriage, for not understanding what might really matter in life.

His reverie waned when he began to feel the weight of the Vega pulling him out of the sky. Exceptional pilots, especially pilots from those early years of aviation, possess a variety of skills that set them apart. Courage, of course, and audacity. But also uncanny navigational capabilities and an innate ability to communicate with their aircraft. The *Century of Progress* weighed in excess of 3,500 pounds, and at that point in the flight, it still carried at least 2,000 of fuel. Fifty-five hundred pounds flying through a deafening, tumultuous nor'easter, but still Jimmie could sense additional weight, especially out on the wings of his airplane.

Ice! The storm was slowly but most assuredly depositing ice on the wings and fuselage. The plane did not have deicers—they had only recently come into existence, and the *Century of Progress* was not so equipped. Ice, Jimmie knew, would plunge his airplane into the Atlantic even faster than the gale-force winds howling over the fuselage.

He needed warmer air. Already at almost 6,500 feet, Jimmie did not dare go higher. In his unpressurized cabin and without oxygen, his breathing would quickly become compromised if he gained altitude.

He needed to descend. And quickly. But just as he pushed the stick forward, he heard a loud *snap*!

His starboard wing had cracked. Jimmie froze. He felt certain the entire wing would fail, and soon thereafter he would just be another flier lost at sea.

There had been so many. Far more pilots had died trying than had actually achieved success crossing the Atlantic.

Why did he think his fate would be any different?

Half a minute passed. A minute.

Two minutes.

Five slow, agonizing minutes passed. He waited to hear another snap and then feel his airplane begin to tumble.

But to his enormous relief, the canvas fabric covering the wing held it firm.

He flew on.

He pointed the nose down in the hope of finding warmer, perhaps calmer air. At 5,000 and then 4,000 and then 3,000 feet, the ice continued to accumulate. Finally, at 2,000 feet, the air began to warm considerably.

The ice began to melt. The plane lightened.

But still, for safety and his own sanity, Jimmie descended even lower. He went to 1,000 feet and leveled. The air was warmer, but still the winds wailed. He dropped even lower—700 feet, then down to 500.

Jimmie knew the Atlantic was just under his wings, practically lapping at the landing gear, even though the storm and the black of night impeded his visibility. The only thing he could see beyond the cockpit glass was the propeller spinning manically.

Inside the cockpit, Jimmie shivered in his flight suit. The combination of cold and fear took its toll.

He decided to go even lower in search of warmer air and maybe an end to all his teeth-chattering and uncontrollable shivering.

He flew on through the night, just two hundred feet above the cold, churning, white-capped North Atlantic. Jimmie Mattern was not a religious man, but nevertheless he asked God to see him through this maelstrom and to please spit him out in one piece on the other side.

CHAPTER FOUR

February 1922–November 1926

Just twenty-four hours after a recruiter approached him on that park bench overlooking Puget Sound, Jimmie enlisted in the United States Army. Immediately thereafter, he became a private first class in the 7th Infantry Regiment. His new home was Camp Lewis, just a few miles southeast of Tacoma, Washington. Camp Lewis was a sprawling military base encompassing nearly 90,000 acres. It owed its existence to the First World War, as the U.S. Congress, back in 1916, had deemed it necessary to construct "a modern and technologically advanced military compound on the west coast with easy access to the Pacific Ocean."

This is where young Jimmie Mattern, still a few weeks shy of his seventeenth birthday, did his basic training. Despite his youth and sturdy build, Jimmie did not fare well during those twelve grueling weeks of physical exertion. The first several weeks, in particular, hit him pretty hard. Due to poor nutrition and general homelessness over the preceding month or so, Jimmie was not in very good shape. The long runs and endless calisthenics imposed by the drill sergeants wore him to a frazzle. He fell into bed each night trembling with exhaustion and petrified he would not be able to rise in the morning to do his duty. But slowly his conditioning improved, and as it did, Jimmie assured himself he would never again neglect his body.

He quickly concluded, however, that the Army was the pits, nothing but a boot camp run by power-hungry guards posing as drill sergeants. Within weeks of his enlistment, he started looking forward to the end of his three-year tour of duty.

But Jimmie's attitudes toward Army life took a 180-degree turn soon after he finished basic training at Camp Lewis. He and some of his mates were loaded onto a troop carrier and transported out of Puget Sound and down the Pacific coast to the Presidio in San Francisco.

The Presidio occupied the whole northern tip of the peninsula between San Francisco Bay and the Pacific Ocean. It had been a Spanish fort as far back as 1775; the U.S. Army had been there since 1848. Jimmie drilled and did guard duty, and at least twice a week earned a pass that allowed him access to the city and its entertainments. In his crisp uniform, and with money in his pocket, he could saddle up to the bar and, despite his age, buy himself a beer. The girls smiled at his youthful good looks and Jimmie held their attention with his natural gift of gab.

Suddenly, Army life didn't seem too shabby. He had a comfy bed, three squares a day, pretty easy duty, and money in his pocket. And every week he sent some of that money back to his mom, who was now living in Vancouver with Gertrude and her husband and their new baby.

A buddy suggested he join the bugle corps. The corps was highly sought after because its members did a lot of practicing, which meant a whole lot less marching and guard duty. Jimmie liked the sound of that, so he tried out for the drums, partly because he'd had a few lessons back in Freeport and partly because no one else wanted the job.

And a sweet job it was. Led by Captain Troy "Mac" McAdams, the bugle corps was attached to the 19th Infantry Regiment. McAdams believed practice made perfect. His boys rehearsed hours and hours every day. They practiced so much there was just no time left for drilling or standing guard duty.

McAdams also had a deep love of exotic ports and an uncanny ability to manipulate military protocols. Before spring turned to summer, McAdams finagled a transfer of his bugle corps to the island of Oahu in Hawaii. On July 4, 1922, seventeen-year-old Jimmie steamed into Pearl Harbor aboard the USS *Omaha*. He would spend the bulk of his Army enlistment there, over two years, at Schofield Barracks, a U.S. Army base nestled in the foothills of the Waianae Mountains a dozen or so miles northwest of Honolulu.

Schofield Barracks housed the U.S. Army Pacific Command. In those halcyon days between the world wars, the soldiers at Schofield had little to do but enjoy the exceptional year-round weather while performing their routine duties. The base had a bowling alley, a swimming pool, a golf course, a riding stable, tennis courts, and a boxing ring. And, just a few miles away, the practically deserted pristine beaches of the Pacific.

Back in San Francisco, the bugle corps had a small handful of musicians who performed primarily at reveille, taps, and during parades. But here on Oahu, the corps swelled to more than fifty musicians. Jimmie played drums and trombone and even did a little conducting.

Several members of the corps formed a marching band and played at dances and performed concerts all over the island. On a few occasions, they even played wedding receptions. During these shows, Jimmie played with a full set of drums, including snare, bass, toms, and cymbals. He became quite accomplished and was a much sought-after entertainer.

It was during this two-year stint on Oahu that Jimmie Mattern first took to the air.

In addition to Schofield Barracks, the United States military also had a naval base at Pearl Harbor and an Army Air Service base at Luke Field. The Air Service was attached to and commanded by the Army. It was not until after World War II that the United States Air Force became a separate branch of the military.

Luke Field on Ford Island, adjacent to Pearl Harbor, was commissioned in 1917. Initially it was staffed by just fifty fliers and mechanics with a dozen aircraft, mostly single-engine Curtiss HS-2L flying patrol boats. By 1921, those numbers had grown exponentially, and soon thereafter the brass determined another airfield was necessary. Wheeler Field was built in 1922 on land contiguous with Schofield Barracks, just a short distance from Private Mattern's bunk. Jimmie watched construction of Wheeler Field and saw the first planes land on the brand-new asphalt runways in the spring of that year.

Despite peace around the globe, with the exception of the Irish War of Independence, the U.S. military continued to build its presence on Oahu. By the summer of 1922, the Air Service on the island had grown to several thousand enlisted men and officers managing nearly three hundred aircraft. Those aircraft included the JN-4 Jenny, the DB-1 Gallaudet daily bomber, the AO-1 Atlantic, used primarily for observation and reconnaissance, and the GA-1 Boeing, used for training and ground attack.

Jimmie, often looking skyward, couldn't take his eyes off those planes swooping down out of the clouds, circling overhead, and dropping onto the runway. First chance he had, Jimmie walked over to Wheeler Field to get closer to the action. He stood on the tarmac and watched young fliers practice their takeoffs and landings.

A fresh-faced second lieutenant who didn't look a whole lot older than Jimmie sauntered up with his thumbs hooked inside his britches. "Ever been up, kid?"

Jimmie shook his head. "Nope. Never."

"Thought as much. You got that look in your eye."

"What about you?" asked Jimmie. "You ever been up?"

"Oh hell yes I've been up. I'm Army Air Service, buddy. What do you think?"

"I think you're a lucky man."

"Damn straight." The young officer pointed into the morning sky. "You see that?"

"See what?"

"That Jenny coming in hard at three o'clock?"

"I see her."

"After she's refueled, I'll take her up and wring her out."

"That right?"

"Damn straight."

"What do you mean, 'wring her out'?"

"Put her through her paces, kid. You know, loops, rolls, spins, hammerheads."

"Actually, I don't know," said Jimmie. "But I'm sure excited to find out. I think I'll stand right here and watch."

"I got a better idea," said the second lieutenant.

"Yeah, what's that?"

"That Jenny, she's a trainer. A two-seater. Fore and aft. Why don't you come up with me and have a spin?"

Jimmie heard that invitation and came near to passing out with excitement. He could feel his heart blasting away inside his chest. "Seriously?"

"Never more so."

Just half an hour later, one of the greatest fliers in the history of aviation climbed into the rear cockpit of that JN-4 Jenny, sped down the runway, and lifted into the air for the first time in his life.

It was an inauspicious beginning.

That officer had his wings, and was, in fact, a pilot in the Army Air Service, but his skills with the stick and pedals needed some fine tuning. When the engine suddenly conked out and the propeller quit spinning, that flyboy quickly lost his cool. At an altitude of just two hundred feet, he likely could have glided in and made a landing, had he kept his head.

Instead, he overworked the pedals and swung the stick around like Grandma stirring the Thanksgiving gravy after a little too much sherry. The aircraft went instantly into a steep nosedive, and mere seconds later crash-landed in a cane field. Fortunately, just before impact, the copilot, on his maiden flight, sitting aft, was thrown out of the plane. Jimmie flew through the air, and before he knew what had hit him, he lay sprawled on the ground on a soft mound of just-dug dirt. He rose, dazed, and after a time wandered over to the plane with its nose half buried in that sugar field. Others came running and shouting.

They pulled the second lieutenant from the wreckage. He was injured but able to stand and walk under his own power.

Someone yelled, "There were two fellows in that plane when it took off! Anyone seen the other guy?"

Someone else hollered, "He must be tangled up in the wreck. Probably half dead or dead by now."

That's when Jimmie, wobbly on his feet and the color of freshly fallen snow, managed to mutter, "Uh, I'm the other fellow who was in that plane."

Seconds later his knees gave way and he collapsed to the ground. They placed him on a stretcher and rushed him to the hospital. Thankfully, for both Jimmie and the cocky second lieutenant without the skills to back up his boasting, they had escaped serious injury beyond a few bumps and bruises and a terrible fright.

Within a couple days, Jimmie was out of the hospital and back at Wheeler Field. A pilot had stopped by the hospital and given Jimmie some advice. "Kid, if you're going to fly, you're going to crash. Just the nature of the enterprise. And I know right now you're shook up. But first chance you get, go back up. Climb aboard and get in the sky. It's like riding a horse, kid. You fall off, best thing to do is get right back on."

Jimmie's second flight was on an old Keystone light bomber left over from the Great War. They took off at dusk. This time, Jimmie had the seat up front in the glass nose of the plane. From that vantage point, he could see practically the entire island of Oahu. Wide-eyed, he watched the lights of Honolulu snap on and illuminate the city as darkness fell.

It was a beautiful, inspiring, providential moment. He couldn't articulate it, but he felt like he had aviation fuel running through his veins and arteries. Flying was what he wanted to do with his life.

But flying would have to wait.

Jimmie managed to finagle a seat on a few more flights while stationed in Hawaii, but faster than he might have preferred, his enlistment wound down and in the late autumn of 1924, the bugle corps was shipped back to the States. The corps returned to the Presidio shortly after Christmas, and in early February, Jimmie was handed his honorable discharge papers and $300 cash in severance pay. It felt good to be free and—at least in the eyes of a nineteen-year-old who had never held that much money before—rich.

Jimmie thought that money would last a lifetime.

CHAPTER FOUR

He took the train north to Vancouver, British Columbia, where he visited his mother, sister, and young niece Naomi. Jimmie stayed for several weeks, but, unable to find work, he traveled south to Seattle in search of a job. His severance was fast disappearing. He had given his mother $100 and had spent lavishly on his niece. Back in Seattle, he counted his remaining cash and realized he likely wouldn't make it to the end of the week.

Jimmie found a job at a service station, cleaning up and helping the mechanics. He took a room at the local YMCA. On the night of his twentieth birthday, March 8, 1925, Jimmie heard music coming from the basement. He went down to investigate and found four men around his age pumping out some pretty snappy tunes. They had a real nice sound playing piano, violin, clarinet, and saxophone.

When the young men paused, Jimmie said, "You're missing something."

"Oh yeah," they asked, "what's that?"

"Percussion," answered Jimmie. "You fellas need a drummer."

Well, as fate would have it, the quartet had been searching for exactly that. They marched straight up to Jimmie's room, where a full kit of drums from his Army days sat in a corner. Those boys carried the entire outfit down to the basement, set it up, and welcomed Jimmie into the band. They played deep into the night.

And when not playing, they talked about where they might find work as musicians.

Jimmie had an idea. "I came down by ferry from Vancouver a few days ago. Lots of action at the port. It might be a long shot, but what say we take a walk over there tomorrow and see what we can drum up? No pun intended."

The following afternoon, the boys walked across town to the offices of the Pacific Coast Steamship Company on the Bell Street Pier. Jimmie, never shy or afraid of rejection, walked straight up to the woman at the front desk, smiled, and said, "Ma'am, we'd like to talk to the executive in charge of hiring folks to work on the ships."

The woman said, "I'm sorry, young man, the *Admiral Evans* sails tomorrow for Alaska, but she has a full crew."

"We're not sailors, ma'am," Jimmie countered. "We're musicians."

Mr. Dave Olsen, in charge of hiring for the steamship company, just happened to step out of his office at this opportune time. "Musicians, huh?"

"That's correct, sir."

"Are you any good?"

"The absolute best, sir. I just spent three years in the Army playing drums and trombone for the bugle corps. I'm a professional."

Dave Olsen was impressed. He rubbed his chin and looked the five young men over. They looked clean enough and earnest and reasonably well dressed. He thought it might just work. "So, do you boys have your own instruments?"

"We sure do, sir," replied Jimmie. "Well, with the exception of Ken Fredericks here. He's our piano player, so his instrument is a little tough to carry around."

"Tomorrow morning," said Olsen.

"Tomorrow morning, sir?"

"That's right. Eight o'clock sharp. The *Evans* sails at noon. Be on board and bring your instruments."

Jimmie, listed on the program as "J. J. Mattern, Band Leader," and his four brand-new bandmates—Wyn Griffin (no relation to Bennett), Jack Haines, Ken Fredericks, and Bill Fleetham—steamed north to Alaska the very next day. They had their own staterooms, access to the bar and restaurant, and freedom to wander the decks, all in exchange for playing a few tunes. They played on the foredeck during embarkation and when the *Admiral Evans* arrived at ports of call—Ketchikan, Juneau, Seward, Sitka, Kodiak. In the evening they played during dinner, and they played at night for entertainment and dancing. They played light jazz, mood music, swing. They played "Westward," "I May Be Dancing with Someone Else," "On a Quiet Evening at Home," "Sumatra," and many other popular tunes of the day.

The live music was a huge hit—never before had the Pacific Coast Steamship Company featured a band on board. Jimmie and his mates made the Alaska run several times over the next year, and when not playing for Pacific Steamship, they signed on with other carriers. They plied the West

Coast from San Diego to Seattle on the *H. F. Alexander*. These voyages made stops in Portland, San Francisco, Santa Cruz, and Los Angeles.

When the coast grew monotonous, the boys signed on with the Dollar Steamship Company, more colloquially known as the Dollar Line. Dollar had recently acquired a massive cruise ship christened the *President Grant*. For Jimmie and the boys to get invited to play on board this first-class cruiser was a very big deal. The *President Grant* toured the Orient with ports of call in Kobe, Yokohama, Shanghai, Hong Kong, Manila, and Honolulu, where Jimmie visited some of his old Army pals.

From March of 1925 until November of 1926, Jimmie and his bandmates spent nearly all their time on the high seas. While it was a rollicking great adventure filled with friendship and romance and exotic destinations, Jimmie still dreamed of flying nearly every day. He would stroll the decks, but his eyes would always drift skyward when he heard the drone of a passing airplane, and he would wonder, *When am I going to take to the skies?*

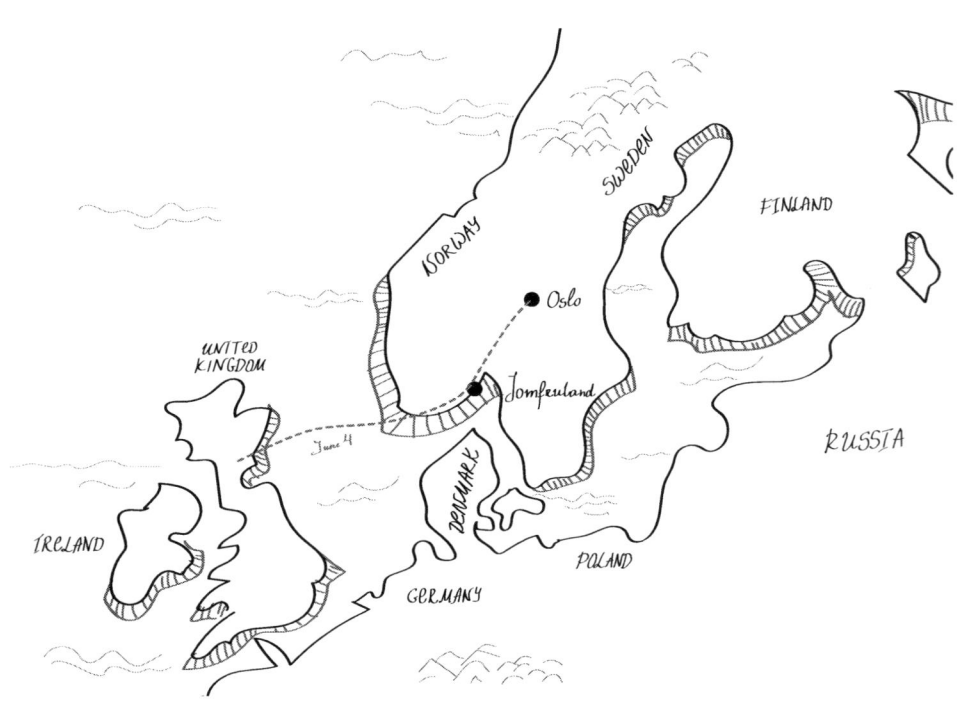

CHAPTER FIVE

The Norwegian Coast

June 4, 1933
Stormy skies, 49°F, 15-20 knot easterlies
with gusts up to 40 mph
Altitude 800 feet

At Le Bourget Field in Paris, the world waited for Jimmie Mattern. More than a hundred journalists from America and Europe anxiously watched the skies for the arrival of the *Century of Progress*. Paris, after all, was Jimmie's first planned stop on his around-the-world flight. He had left Floyd Bennett Field on Long Island almost twenty-two hours earlier with the hope of reaching Paris by noon the following day, thereby eclipsing Charles Lindbergh's transatlantic time by almost ten hours.

The skies over Le Bourget were fair with light breezes out of the southwest and a few high cumulus clouds. There was no sign, however, of the American flier.

And as journalists are inclined to do, those reporters at Le Bourget lost patience and began to speculate. They sent dramatic cables back to their anxious editors in New York and London and Washington and Boston, conjecturing that the *Century of Progress* had very possibly gone down somewhere over the North Atlantic, perhaps never to be heard from or seen again.

Within hours, bold headlines on newspapers around the world announced:

MATTERN FEARED LOST

FAMOUS AVIATOR MISSING AT SEA

AROUND-THE-WORLD FLIER VANISHES

MATTERN OVERDUE!

Sensational headlines sell newspapers, especially in this case with literally millions of people following Jimmie's flight with great anticipation. There had been no verified sighting of the *Century of Progress* since the previous afternoon over Newfoundland. Reports had come out of Londonderry, Belfast, and Glasgow that a small monoplane had been sighted, but there was no firm confirmation this plane had been piloted by Jimmie Mattern.

The world held its collective breath.

The fact was this: Jimmie Mattern, due to a compass gone askew and a North Atlantic storm that raged for hours and battered his tiny ship, was almost a thousand nautical miles off course. But the intrepid aviator, despite the adversity, was still flying, still navigating, still hopeful he would spot land and put down the Vega before she ran out of fuel.

The fuel supply was just another in a long litany of problems Jimmie had to combat as he flew east through the stormy night and foggy dawn. When the fuel ran low on one of eight separate tanks, Jimmie had to manually switch to another tank. This was a relatively simple procedure that involved cutting fuel to the engine for a few seconds while the wobble pump engaged and pulled gasoline from the next tank in line.

This procedure had gone off without a hitch until Jimmie attempted to engage his smallest and final tank of fuel. This seventy-gallon starboard wing tank had been a gift from Amelia Earhart, who had told her young friend, "Jimmie, you never know when a few extra gallons might come in handy and get you out of a jam."

Well, if Jimmie had any chance at all of getting free of this relentless storm, finding land, and putting the *Century of Progress* back on the ground, he needed those seventy gallons.

And he needed them *now*.

He flipped the wobble pump switch back and forth several times.

Nothing happened.

And then the engine, starved for fuel, quit. Without power, at just over eight hundred feet, he would not stay aloft for long. "Come on, come on, come ON!" he shouted, repeatedly ordering the wobble pump to engage and pull some gasoline out of that last tank.

Seven hundred feet.

Five hundred feet.

He felt the plane begin to fall out of the sky. It wouldn't be long now, mere seconds, before he hit the water.

He pounded the dash with his fist and gave that switch one last off-and-on toggle.

And that's when she caught. The baffle opened. Fuel began to flow. The engine coughed, sputtered, and roared back to life.

His heart pounding, adrenaline rushing, Jimmie flew on.

It had been, by any measure, a long, tough night. Fear, doubt, loneliness, and despair had all swept over young Mattern as the minutes slowly passed. More than once, he had given up hope and felt the grip of death upon his shoulder. But he had kept flying, and eventually the longest night of Jimmie's life began to fade with the darkness.

First the rain stopped. Then the winds abated and the fog and clouds lifted. Moments later, blue skies appeared for as far as Jimmie could see.

A sigh of relief spilled from Jimmie's dry mouth. Every tense muscle in his body relaxed for the first time in hours. And not long after, his famous smile flashed wide when, sure enough, he spotted land dead ahead.

What land he didn't yet know, he wasn't absolutely sure, but no matter, land was land, and now he just needed to find a flat level strip long enough to put the plane down. He had been in the air almost twenty-six hours.

At first glance he thought it might be Ireland, but the land looked far too rugged, the mountains too high. Plus, he felt certain he should be farther to the east. Scotland, perhaps, up around Inverness. But upon closer inspection of the steep mountains and narrow fjords, Jimmie realized he had flown all the way to Norway.

"A long way from the City of Lights," Jimmie announced out loud.

They'll be wondering where I am, he thought. *Della will be worried about me . . . or will she?*

He didn't have time to dwell on any of this. He needed to put the Vega down, and soon, as the plane was rapidly running out of fuel. He banked left and banked right. Nothing but mountains and rivers and lakes. Still, he felt sure Oslo could not be far to the northeast, a hundred miles at most. But did he have a hundred miles left in Amelia's tank?

He wasn't confident he did. Plus, once he reached the city, he would still need time to find the airport.

Jimmie decided he did not have time to waste. He had come too far and endured too much to crash for lack of fuel. Time to put the *Century of Progress* back on the ground.

Suddenly he found himself over open water again. It had to be Skagen Channel, separating Norway from Sweden. Oslo would be due north. Jimmie flew in that direction. He descended to under one hundred feet. He flew up the coast, almost skimming the treetops of the towering Norway spruce and wych elms. He spotted a narrow island running north and south. The southern tip of the island looked barren and wide open, plenty of room to land.

Jimmie made a pass. He spotted close to half a mile of open beach—but the rocks! Rocks as big as footballs!

Jimmie decided he had no choice. There couldn't be more than two or three gallons left in Amelia's tank. The Wasp would soon be running on fumes.

After several long, deep breaths, Jimmie swung the plane around to the north and brought the Vega in flying south, his speed as low as he dared. Moments later he hit the ground. It was easily the bumpiest landing of his flying career, but finally, after almost twenty-seven hours in the air, the *Century of Progress* was back on terra firma.

CHAPTER FIVE

Jimmie pushed open the cockpit hatch, uncurled his hunched form, reached his arms to the sky and stretched. His body felt exhausted. The muscles of his back and neck ached from the long hours in the same position. It felt good to inhale some of that cool, fresh air blowing out of the north.

A light drizzle fell from a leaden sky.

Jimmie pulled out the step and carefully climbed down onto the wheel pants. All around him large rocks littered the ground. It was a miracle he hadn't hit one upon landing and destroyed the landing gear.

A quick inspection of the Vega offered two blown tires and a busted tail from the hard landing. Plus the wing that had splintered out over the Atlantic was nearly broken in half. But all in all, not too bad. He knew his plane could easily be at the bottom of the ocean or completely demolished here on this rocky beach.

Next he checked his fuel tanks. Nothing in any of them but air and fumes. Even the Amelia Earhart tank was almost bone dry, not even a gallon left. It would have been a disaster had he tried to make Oslo.

A young couple hurried across the beach. To Jimmie's joy and astonishment, they spoke excellent English. He soon learned he had landed on the Norwegian island of Jomfruland, just seventy-five miles south of Oslo. Another few gallons of fuel and he would have made it.

Jomfruland was a resort island where Norwegians and Swedes came on holiday. The island also had exceptional soil and served as an agricultural center. Aksel and Leah Weiburg were farmers and innkeepers, as well as extraordinarily kind and generous people. They listened intently while the stranger from the sky explained that he was an aviator from America trying to circumnavigate the globe. He had gotten off course, run into a storm, run low on fuel, and put down here on this rocky beach. It was easily the most astonishing story they had ever heard.

Jimmie showed them the flat tires, the broken tail, the cracked wing. Also, the empty fuel tanks.

The Weiburgs alternately nodded and smiled and looked concerned. Finally, Aksel, a strong, sinewy young fellow with a full beard, said, "You are not to worry. You need food and rest, for you tell us you have been up for many hours without sleep. You go now with Leah. Not far. Just off the beach. She will feed you and give you a bed to sleep. The rest"—and here Aksel swept his arm in the direction of the *Century of Progress*—"you leave to me. I know what to do."

Jimmie was not at all sure about leaving his plane in the hands of this gentleman, though a fine and pleasant gentleman he obviously was. But hunger and exhaustion are powerful motivators, and soon thereafter Jimmie found himself crossing that boulder-strewn beach with Aksel's lovely young wife, Leah. Picking his way carefully among the rocks, Jimmie did not fail to acknowledge and appreciate his great good fortunate at having made it to this place at this time with these outstanding folks.

He knew he could have suffered a far worse fate.

Leah fed him eggs, lamb, grilled salmon, biscuits, and *kumla*, a delicious Norwegian potato ball made with lots of garlic, salt, and salt pork. Jimmie thought it might be the tastiest thing he had ever eaten. For dessert, Leah cut him a thick slice of *krumkake*.

Jimmie ate until he could eat no more and then retired to a bedroom on the second floor of the couple's small guest house. He pulled off his boots and socks and unzipped his flight suit. He fell asleep on the soft bed before he could fully remove the suit. There Jimmie lay, without moving, for the next several hours.

When he finally came around, he needed a minute to regroup and get his bearings. It all felt like a dream, like he couldn't possibly be lying here on this bed in this guesthouse on an island in Norway. He was supposed to be in France. In Paris! Answering questions and having his picture taken for the morning papers.

But all of that, Jimmie knew, as he rose and dressed, his body stiff and sore from head to toe, would have to wait.

Back at the beach, after another meal, Jimmie saw the *Century of Progress* had been pulled onto a smooth grassy knoll by a pair of plow horses, where it was much easier to perform repairs. A bevy of workers surrounded his small monoplane.

Jimmie hoped they knew what they were doing.

Upon reaching the plane, he saw both tires had been replaced with new rubber. A young lad worked hard filling those tires with air, using what looked like a heavy-duty bicycle pump. Jimmie asked Aksel where the tires had come from and how much they had cost, but the rugged Norwegian just smiled and slapped Jimmie on the back. "You fly around the world! I take care of tires!" Then Aksel grabbed the American aviator's arm and led him to the rear of the airplane. Both the rudder and the vertical stabilizer had been repaired and appeared in perfect working order.

It was Jimmie's turn to pat Aksel on the back. "How can I ever repay you? You have saved my flight from certain failure."

"It is nothing," the Norwegian said, leading Jimmie to the port-side wing. The cracked wing had been bound with heavy fabric and glue. "We did not dare attempt to replace the broken part of the frame," he explained. "We feared the entire wing might collapse."

Jimmie agreed. He could not believe these men had taken it upon themselves to repair the *Century of Progress*. He felt as though his forced landing on this remote, rocky beach was somehow preordained. Jimmie did not typically have thoughts like this, but under the circumstances—Aksel and Leah, the food, the bed, the tires, the repairs, the exceptional kindness—how could he not? He believed more than ever that this flight was about something far greater and more distinguished than his individual ambitions.

A few minutes later, a seaplane appeared off the coast and landed on the water just beyond the small breakers. Jimmie and Aksel watched as the seaplane plowed through the waves and taxied up onto the beach. Aksel walked over, splashed through the shallow water, and climbed up onto the wing. The cockpit door swung open and the pilot stepped out. The two men shook hands and spoke for a few minutes.

Aksel turned and pointed at Jimmie. The pilot waved. Jimmie returned the gesture. The pilot then pulled two five-gallon containers of fuel from his cockpit. Aksel climbed off the wing and the pilot passed down the containers.

Aksel waded back to shore. The pilot waved again, climbed back into the cockpit, taxied out to calm water, and took off in a northerly direction.

Jimmie just stood by in awe at this outpouring of humanity. Despite his navigational glitches and hard luck over the Atlantic, he felt more determined than ever to complete his around-the-world adventure.

Jimmie had arrived on Jomfruland in the late morning. He had slept for several hours, most of the afternoon. By the time he climbed back into his airplane it was close to 7:00 p.m., but the sun still hung high in the sky. In Norway, this time of year, early June, the sun does not set until almost midnight, and it rises again just after 3:00 a.m. Jimmie hoped to get airborne, shoot up to Oslo, and get his plane serviced and fuel tanks filled first thing in the morning.

The Amelia Earhart tank accepted the ten gallons of gas delivered by seaplane. Then came the task of figuring out how to get the Vega safely airborne on this boulder-strewn strip of hard, damp sand.

Plus, Jimmie had noted that not only were there enormous rocks everywhere, but potholes large enough and deep enough to make a cow disappear littered the beach.

Nevertheless, he'd landed. Now he needed to get back in the air.

As the Vega did not have brakes, she just rolled to a stop, sometimes with the help of a swing-turn ground loop. But brakes were handy when runway space was limited. The pilot could apply the brakes, rev the engine high, build the RPMs, then release the brakes and fly down the runway, instead of gradually picking up speed.

Unfortunately, Jimmie did not have this advantage.

Aksel came up with a solution.

The small plane was pulled back out onto the beach by the two plow horses and aimed into the wind. Large rocks were placed in front of each wheel. Sturdy ropes were tied around the rocks. Aksel explained that the rocks would hold the plane in place while Jimmie revved the engine. When he was ready to go, he would give a signal and the rocks would be pulled away.

"Pure genius!" declared Jimmie.

"First let's see if it works," cautioned the Norwegian.

Jimmie said thank you a thousand times before climbing up into the cockpit of the *Century of Progress*. Back behind the stick, his feet on the pedals, Jimmie felt the pull to be on his way. Yes, he had missed Paris and breaking Lindbergh's transatlantic flight time, but he was still hours ahead of the mark set by Post and Gatty back in '31. But to maintain that edge he needed to keep moving, keep flying.

He warmed the engine, checked the rudder, the flaps, the gauges. Everything appeared in perfect working order. He had plenty of fuel to reach Oslo. Ready to roll, he pushed the throttle forward. The RPMs slowly increased.

The propeller spun.

The engine roared.

Jimmie stuck his hand out the cockpit window and gave the signal.

His spotters yanked the rocks away.

The Vega shot across the beach.

With Norwegians everywhere pointing out extra-large rocks and deep potholes, Jimmie wove his way through that minefield until he had just enough speed to lift the nose of the *Century of Progress* and reach for the sky.

Once aloft, he circled back, dipped a wing in salutation and appreciation, and then flew on through the gathering dusk to Oslo and beyond.

CHAPTER SIX

November 1926–July 1927

When not out on the Pacific, Jimmie and his bandmates stayed with Wyn Griffin's mom, who was the house mother at the Alpha Gamma Delta sorority house at the University of Washington in Seattle. The boys slept in the basement, as far from those pretty college girls as Mrs. Griffin could get them.

One day at dinner, Jimmie met Professor Alan Brown. Like Jimmie, Professor Brown was an aviation enthusiast. When the professor learned of Jimmie's desire to fly, he called a friend and lined up an opportunity for young Mattern to join the Army Air Corps. This meant leaving the band, but Jimmie knew he had to pursue his dream.

A few days later, Jimmie crossed Puget Sound and reported to the military base in Bremerton. He and three other young hopefuls spent the day taking aptitude tests and performing various physical exertions. By now, Jimmie was in excellent physical shape and so aced those parts of the entry exam. He also did well on the aptitude tests. But at the end of the day he was told he would not be accepted as a cadet because he did not have two years of college.

The news first depressed and then angered young Mattern who could, on occasion, possess a short fuse and a fiery temper. "Then why did you waste my time coming over here?" he demanded of the officer in charge of the examinations.

The officer, oblivious to Jimmie's disappointment, shrugged and said, "Tough luck, kid. Get yourself educated and come back to see me."

Jimmie simmered. He knew acceptance into the Army Air Corps Training Center in San Antonio, Texas, was a passport to a career in aviation. A lesser man might have packed it in right then and there. Given up.

Not Jimmie.

One of the other boys trying out that day told Jimmie about a flight school that had recently opened in San Diego. Jimmie knew it was now or maybe never. So he said so long to his bandmates, sold his drums, packed his gear, and a few days later headed down the coast.

"Flight school" might have been a slight exaggeration. At a small airfield north of San Diego, T. Claude Ryan and Frank Mahoney had started an airline. Its sole aircraft was a Standard J-1 World War I trainer modified to carry a pilot and four passengers. It shuttled between San Diego and Los Angeles at a cost of $14.50 one way and $22.50 round trip.

The Ryan Airline Company was the very first airline to offer regular air service in the United States.

In addition to their San Diego/L.A. run, Ryan and Mahoney offered flight lessons as a way to raise revenue. Interest in aviation was picking up and lots of young men like Jimmie Mattern wanted to learn to fly.

Jimmie had money in his pocket from his recent stint as bandleader on the *President Grant*. He had no qualms spending that dough on flight lessons. His instructor was Doug Kelly, who had clocked more than five hundred hours of flight time. He instantly became Jimmie's hero.

They took to the air in a vintage Jenny with fore and aft cockpits. Jimmie sat in the rear and struggled to hear Kelly's instruction; the combination of engine roar and wind noise made hearing extremely difficult. Mostly, Jimmie peered over Kelly's shoulder and watched his instructor operate the controls.

After exactly four one-hour in-air lessons, Doug Kelly declared James Joseph Mattern, age twenty-one, ready to solo.

"Solo!" shouted Jimmie. "Are you out of your mind?"

"You're ready, kid."

"I'm not."

"Trust me, kid, you are."

"I don't think so."

"You got the three things needed to succeed as a pilot."

"Oh yeah?"

"You got brains, a steady hand, and most of all, you got grit."

"Grit?"

"You got moxie, Mattern. So let's roll, climb aboard. Take her up. Make a couple passes, then bring her in gently."

"You're serious?"

Kelly nodded. "One hundred percent dead serious. Just don't smash her up, kid. She's the only one I've got."

Anyone who has ever flown an airplane knows the feeling of that first solo flight. Nothing else compares to the terrifying adrenaline rush of being up there for the first time all by yourself with no instructor to bail you out.

But Doug Kelly knew his student. He was dead right: Mattern had moxie.

The young man went calmly through his preflight checklist—oil and fuel levels, landing gear, instruments. Then he made himself comfy on the cloth-covered seat, opened up the throttle, used most of that grass runway, pulled back lightly on the stick, and lifted that old Jenny off the ground like a veteran of the skies.

Jimmie was home. This was where he belonged.

The sky was the limit that morning—clear and blue for as far as Jimmie could see. He made several passes over the airfield, dipping a wing at his instructor each time he passed overhead. Only when he saw Kelly scowling and wildly gesticulating to bring her down did Jimmie prepare to land. He could have flown forever.

Most pilots on their first solo flight suffer from ground shyness. That is, they're afraid to put those wheels on the ground. Half a dozen passes are sometimes needed before they find the courage to hit the runway and roll out.

Not Jimmie. He swooped out of the sky on his very first try and put that trainer down on the grass just as gently as a new mother putting her baby to bed.

Kelly came over, hot under the collar. "I told you to make a couple passes and bring her down, kid! What the hell was all that?"

"Huh?"

"You were up there over half an hour!"

"Was I? Seriously? Golly, that was something. Felt more like a couple minutes. Greatest couple minutes of my life."

Kelly shook his head. "You got it, kid. You got the grit."

In February of 1927, after Jimmie had been taking lessons for several weeks, a young flier showed up at the airfield. He hung around for a few days and had many lengthy chats with Ryan and Mahoney. Rumor had it the young pilot was negotiating with the two gentlemen about construction of a small single-seat, single-engine, high-wing monoplane.

Jimmie had a brief discussion with the youngster, who looked even younger than Jimmie, though he was actually three years older.

"You're a pilot, huh?" asked Jimmie.

The young man nodded.

"Been flying awhile?"

He nodded again.

"How long?"

The young man shrugged, his expression, like his general demeanor, taciturn.

"What kind of flying do you do?" asked Jimmie.

"Mail delivery mostly," answered the young man in a voice so soft Jimmie almost missed it.

The pilot's name was Charles Lindbergh. He was in San Diego to order the *Spirit of St. Louis* so he could compete for the Orteig Prize, a $25,000 purse for the first aviator of any Allied country to successfully fly solo across the Atlantic from New York to Paris or Paris to New York.

On that day in February, Lindbergh, like Mattern, was just another young buck who loved, more than anything else, to go aloft. Just four months later, his transatlantic flight a success, young Charles Lindbergh would become one of the most famous men in the world, a designation he would spend the rest of his life trying to vanquish.

CHAPTER SIX

Doug Kelly had too many students—Jimmie was lucky to get an hour in the air every few days. The time had come to move on. He searched high and low for an advanced flight training school, but aside from the Air Corps Training Center in Texas, such a thing simply did not exist anywhere in the States.

Jimmie decided the only way to build up his flight hours and gain experience was to buy his own plane. To this end, he ventured up to Los Angeles, where the friend of a friend owned a Waco (pronounced "wah-co") dealership. Jimmie looked over the various models and decided he could afford a Waco 10 with a Curtiss OX-5 engine. Total cost with engine and prop installed came to $2,625.

With his few remaining dollars, Jimmie caught the train east to Troy, Ohio, where the Waco factory was located. He had high hopes of taking possession of his new airplane and flying solo back to California. But when executives in the front office took one look at the rambunctious, fresh-faced kid barely out of knickers, they said, "No way. You'll kill yourself on takeoff and Waco will take the heat."

They argued back and forth. The deal nearly fell through. A refund check made out to J. J. Mattern for $2,500 ($125 withheld for clerical purposes) was processed. But before the check changed hands, a pilot named Freddie Lund showed up and agreed to fly the plane, and its new owner, back to California. Jimmie had heard of Lund. He was the most famous stunt pilot in the country and renowned for his daredevil antics in the sky.

Lund being at the Waco factory in Troy at the same time as Jimmie, and offering to fly the Waco 10 back to California, felt to young Mattern like fate had intervened. It was a feeling Jimmie would experience numerous times in his life. If Freddie Lund had shown up a day later or not at all, Jimmie would've been back on the train with his tail between his legs.

The very next day, they fueled up and set off. All went well, if slowly. The Curtiss engine had just 90 hp, and with a full load of fuel and two adult men aboard, she flew—but not sprightly. To navigate, Freddie mostly followed westbound railroad tracks.

"The Iron Compass!" he called back to Jimmie. "You find tracks, son, and rest assured those tracks will take you somewhere there's food and folks."

The trip was an incredible experience for young Mattern. The entire journey west was one long flight lesson. Freddie taught Jimmie how to read the wind, how to deal with turbulence, when to change altitude, the importance of coordinating your hands and your feet. Freddie put Jimmie up front and let the youngster fly.

And when they reached Los Angeles, after much beseeching from Jimmie, Freddie taught the novice aviator how to perform rolls, dips, and dual-wing spins, which Jimmie attempted but could not quite complete. Freddie had to keep taking over from the rear seat, often just seconds before they hit the ground.

"You got guts, kid," praised Freddie. "I'm not sure what you got between your ears, but you sure got guts."

His brief, fortuitous tenure with Freddie Lund turned Jimmie Mattern into a seasoned pilot in short order. Everything he learned from Freddie would serve him well, and even save his life, in the daring and adventurous years ahead.

A movie crew advance team showed up at the airport on the morning Freddie intended to head back east. The guy in charge said they were making a movie about air combat during World War I and they needed seasoned pilots.

Freddie gave Jimmie a little shove. "Here's your man, fella. As I am now headed east, he's the best damn pilot on the West Coast."

Jimmie signed on and was told to report to Caddo Field in Van Nuys the next morning at seven sharp.

"Should I bring my plane?"

"What kind you got?" asked the production crew chief.

"A Waco 10."

"She fight in the war?"

"Nope. Brand new."

"Then we can't use her, kid. Boss demands authentic World War I flying machines only."

CHAPTER SIX

The film was *Hell's Angels*, produced and directed by Mr. Howard Hughes.

By the time Jimmie came aboard in the late spring of 1927, the film had already been in production for several months. In those days, Van Nuys, several miles northwest of Los Angeles, was mostly farmland—lemons and oranges. Hughes had purchased several hundred acres of land in preparation for the making of his World War I epic. He built an airfield, hangars, a control tower, and a whole film studio right on site.

Jimmie arrived to find a scene that looked like nothing but mass confusion. It was only 6:30 a.m., so there were no planes in the sky yet, but literally hundreds of people swarmed over the tarmac between the grass runways and the buildings. Actors, directors, technicians, cameramen, carpenters, writers, gaffers, grips, drivers, and pilots all coalesced into one constantly moving organism Jimmie immediately found to his liking. He was a rare bird: a young man who loved to be alone, just him and his plane shooting across the sky, but he was also a very gregarious fellow who flourished in the company of others.

Jimmie soon had his bearings—and the knowledge that filmmaking was a slow, ponderous business with much jawboning and standing around. In fact, that whole first day not a single plane went into the sky.

"No clouds," was the reason given. "The boss likes clouds."

"How come?" Jimmie asked.

"Boss says blue skies are boring. No contrast."

The boss was Howard Hughes. Jimmie didn't know a whole lot about the young millionaire other than he was rich, liked to fly, and was born, like Jimmie, in 1905. He was only twenty-one years old and here he was making a massive motion picture. With his own dough.

Jimmie was plenty impressed.

He was also impressed with the planes Hughes had purchased to make his movie. He had nearly a hundred planes, all authentic aircraft that had survived aerial combat during World War I. There were British Sopwith 7F.1 Snipes, Thomas-Morse S-4 Scouts, and plenty of German Fokkers—Spins, Eindeckers, and V.42s.

Jimmie and the other pilots stood around for hours, marveling over and inspecting the large collection of planes Hughes had accumulated for his movie extravaganza. But what those boys really wanted to do was fly.

And fly they did. Over the next sixteen months, Jimmie spent hundreds of hours in the skies over Southern California. He flew Snipes. He flew Scouts. He flew Fokkers. He wore the uniforms of British fliers, American fliers, and German fliers. Hughes demanded everything be 100 percent authentic, right down to the buttons on their jackets and the laces in their boots. "Anything less," he lectured, "and the illusion of reality is destroyed."

Originally, the female lead in the film was played by Norwegian actress Greta Nissen, but Greta was a silent screen star. Hughes had conceived of *Hell's Angels* as a silent film, but a year or so into production the advent of sound became a reality, and Hughes immediately decided to make his epic a talking picture, damn the cost. So Nissen, who had a thick Norwegian accent, was replaced with an unknown platinum blonde bombshell named Jean Harlow. Harlow was only eighteen years old at the time, without a single screen credit to her name.

Hell's Angels would catapult her to Hollywood stardom.

Jimmie came to know Miss Harlow, as well as many of the other stars of the film, including Ben Lyon, James Hall, Lucien Prival, and John Darrow. He had his own airplane, after all, and soon the dashing young pilot was providing aerial taxi service between Santa Monica Airport and Caddo Field for members of the cast and crew.

Jimmie tried more than once to convince Miss Harlow to accompany him on a night out on the town, but the beautiful, up-and-coming starlet was more aloof than an Austrian princess. Jimmie did pal around with Lyon and Prival and Hall and some of the other actors in the cast. He was an aviator, and in those days aviators were marked as heroes and so they fit in well with the glitz and glamour of Hollywood.

Around this time, Jimmie started to see one girl exclusively. He had been going out with a different girl practically every night of the week, but all that ended abruptly after one very special night with a pretty girl from Walla Walla.

CHAPTER SIX

Her name was Della Huffey Leo. Jimmie and Della had first met over a year earlier up in Vancouver. Della had been at the house visiting Jimmie's sister, Gertrude, when Jimmie arrived to see his mother and niece. Right away Jimmie and Della hit it off, making eyes at each other and joking around. But Jimmie was still playing drums aboard cruise ships, so it did not prove a very opportune time to start a romance.

Several months later, they ran into each other again in Seattle, just before Jimmie shoved off for San Diego to pursue his flying career. They again made eyes at each other, even went out dancing, but the timing was simply not right. However, when fate threw them together a third time outside a speakeasy on Sunset Boulevard in Hollywood one warm night in early July, the die was cast. Jimmie could not resist. Nor could Della.

She was several years older than him. She had been married twice before, and she definitely knew her way around. Born and raised in the small town of Dixie just east of Walla Walla, Washington, Della had spent most of her life in the Pacific Northwest and had lived in Seattle for several years, where she'd worked at various jobs including waitress, receptionist, and saleswoman. She was petite and pretty and fetching with her short dark bob and big blue eyes.

Jimmie, still just a kid of twenty-two, was smitten.

Jimmie didn't spend all his time with Della that summer; he still had to go to work. And the work was often stressful. Stunt flying was no walk in the park, and Mr. Howard Hughes could be a very difficult and demanding boss. There were days when Hughes had sixty or more "combat" planes in the sky at one time, plus another dozen airplanes with film crews aboard to capture all the aerial action. The battle scenes would be choreographed in great detail down on the ground, but inevitably, once airborne, all the fine planning often went awry. There were crashes, and more than one pilot lost his life during the making of *Hell's Angels*.

Jimmie first met Howard face to face when he volunteered to perform a particularly audacious maneuver. Hughes wanted a British Snipe to fly through the open doors of a large barn and fly out the other side. Several pilots had a look at the barn and passed. The wheels of the plane would be just inches off the ground, and the tips of the wings barely fit through the open doors. There wasn't more than a foot to spare on either side.

"Goddammit!" snarled Hughes. "I want this shot!"

Jimmie stepped forward. It was an impulsive step. "I can do it."

Hughes grabbed the young flier's hand and gave it a hearty shake. "Atta boy! That's the spirit I'm looking for. Let's roll, people!"

Jimmie didn't have time to consider the madness. He was airborne minutes later, and minutes after that, heart pounding and adrenaline flowing, he came in low and fast and swept through that old barn in about the time it takes to snap your finger. Cameras caught both the entry and the exit, and the stunt was immortalized on film forever.

Later, Hughes slapped Jimmie on the back and said, "Nice job out there today, kid."

"Thanks, Mr. Hughes." Jimmie felt funny calling a guy his own age "mister," but what was he supposed to call him? Howard?

"Glad to see somebody on this crew has a decent set of balls."

Jimmie smiled and nodded but found it kind of big-headed that a twenty-one-year-old guy, even if he *was* a millionaire, had the nerve to call him "kid."

A week or so later, Hughes again sought a volunteer for a particularly dangerous stunt. He wanted a pilot to go up in a Thomas-Morse Scout and put the plane into a death spiral as though headed for a crash. Obviously, the pilot would pull out of the spiral before the Scout hit the ground, but still Hughes had a hard time getting a volunteer. The reason for all the hesitation was the Scout's Le Rhone rotary engine. The Le Rhone was a powerful and extremely reliable engine, but it was not fixed. It rotated with the propeller, so it pulled mightily to the right and the pilot had to constantly battle against this impulse. Putting the Scout into an intentional death spiral was asking for trouble, as it might prove impossible to pull out once the spinning commenced.

Hughes shouted at his pilots and called them cowards. He threatened to fire them all and bring in some "real" men.

His threat did nothing to produce a volunteer, so Hughes announced he would perform the stunt himself.

Jimmie tried to talk the boss out of it even while Hughes, right out on the runway, changed into the uniform of a British flier and marched toward the Thomas-Morse. Jimmie did his best to explain the dynamics of the rotary engine.

Hughes shrugged, gave instructions to his camera crews on how to shoot the sequence, and climbed aboard.

Sure enough, not five minutes after taking to the air, young Howard Hughes found himself plummeting toward the earth, his Thomas-Morse Scout spinning like a top, and all his efforts to pull out and gain altitude to no avail.

Hughes nosedived into the ground but somehow survived, though not without a concussion and a sizeable facial gash that demanded surgery and three days in the hospital.

Jimmie visited the boss each day but never once said, "Hey kid, I told you so."

In late July of 1928, in a simple ceremony attended by just a couple of friends as witnesses, Jimmie and Della became husband and wife. Prior to the nuptials, several friends had quietly told Jimmie he was making a mistake marrying an older divorcée, but Jimmie just smiled and shrugged.

Nor did it unsettle him in the least that Della had a flush savings account at the Farmers and Merchants Bank down on Main Street in Los Angeles, a consequence of her divorce from Mr. George Leo of Seattle.

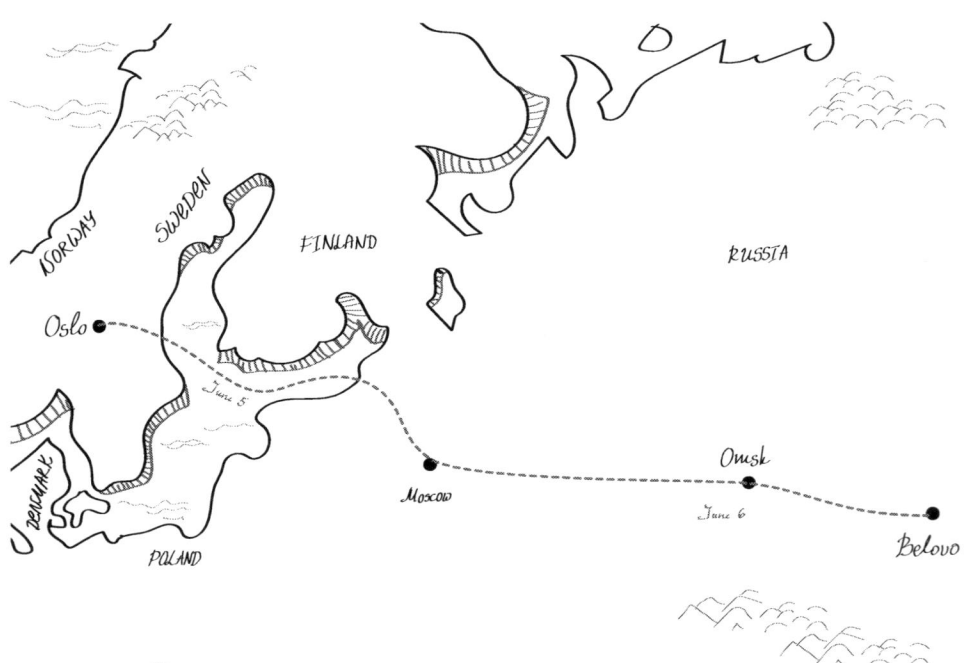

CHAPTER SEVEN

Oslo to Belovo

June 5, 1933
Clear skies, 58°F, light winds
Altitude 3,000 feet

Jimmie did not stay long in Oslo. His lengthy and unexpected stop on the island of Jomfruland had taken most of a day. He was still ahead of the Post/Gatty around-the-world flying record, but any additional unplanned stops and his lead would quickly dissipate.

He landed at the military airdrome outside Oslo just as the sun began to rise. Personnel at the airdrome had been alerted to his arrival. They could not believe the American aviator had flown nonstop all the way from New York, but one look at his plethora of fuel tanks and they realized how he had accomplished the spectacular feat.

They set about refilling the tanks on the *Century of Progress* at once. It was a laborious process that could take well over an hour.

While the gasoline flowed, mechanics changed the oil and cleaned the filters. The new tires installed on Jomfruland were balanced and properly inflated. Adjustments were made to the rudder and stabilizers. Jimmie never left the field other than to use the bathroom, grab a bite to eat, and send a few cables back to the States. He also removed the compass-confounding box camera from the cockpit and asked the airport manager to please ship the equipment back to Pathé News in New York City.

The Norwegians had a thousand questions for Jimmie about his flight around the world. For a while he did his best to answer. After all, they had been kind enough to offer their assistance and expertise. But soon his patience grew thin. He needed to get airborne and be on his way. His flight had been delayed long enough.

At 8:57 a.m., now nearly forty-eight hours after leaving Floyd Bennett Field on Long Island, Jimmie thanked his Norwegian hosts and streaked into the sky. Minutes later he reached Sweden, and an hour or so after that, the Baltic Sea. He knew this would be his last open-water flying until he crossed Siberia and reached the Bering Sea on his return to North America. Flying over open water did not worry Jimmie the way it did some long-distance pilots, but he was still happy to have the Atlantic and now the Baltic to his rear.

Soon the *Century of Progress* was over land again, this time along the border between Latvia and Estonia. Next stop, Moscow.

Back in the States, word began to circulate that Mattern was alive and still flying somewhere over Northern Europe. He had flown off course and missed Paris, but Norway had welcomed him with open arms, and he was now purportedly on his way to the Soviet Union, still several hours ahead of the Post/Gatty time.

Headlines filled the afternoon papers on June 5 and the morning papers on June 6:

MATTERN FLIES ON

AROUND-THE-WORLD PILOT SAFE

MATTERN OVER EUROPE

SOLO FLYER ALIVE & WELL

CHAPTER SEVEN

News of Jimmie's flight spread via newspaper and radio. The only other news of note was Pres. Franklin D. Roosevelt taking the United States off the gold standard. But no one cared. The Great Depression was in full swing and so the last thing anyone wanted to read about was economic news. Everyone wanted to read about Jimmie Mattern, the handsome, daring midwesterner flying all by himself around the world. Just yesterday he'd been given up for dead, more than likely drowned somewhere in the North Atlantic. But no, he'd battled bad weather, a damaged aircraft, and low fuel, and still managed to reach Scandinavia.

Everywhere you went you heard folks talking about Jimmie and his flight. At newsstands and the corner store, at home and at the office, at the barbershop and beauty salon, up at Yankee Stadium and out at Wrigley Field, talk turned to the young flier risking his neck to become the first pilot to fly solo around the world. Some thought him brave, some thought him mad, some thought him heroic, and some thought him thoroughly out of his mind, but virtually everyone held an opinion on Jimmie Mattern and his bold attempt. He was the talk of the town, the talk of the country, the talk of much of the world.

Jimmie was not oblivious to the newsworthy nature of his flight. In fact, he was extremely savvy when it came to publicity. He knew a successful flight might well be parlayed into both fame and some measure of fortune. Rich and famous were not labels he had anything against. But right now, none of that mattered. All that mattered was keeping the *Century of Progress* in the air for a few more days and completing his mission. If he could succeed, fanfare, adulation, and endorsement would follow. It was failure that was not an option.

As Jimmie swept into Soviet airspace just a few hundred miles northwest of Moscow, he reminded himself that he was first and foremost a flier. A pilot. An aviator. A man trying to do something that had never been done before. And his singular goal, above and beyond his personal ambitions, was to circumnavigate the earth, thereby symbolically making the world a smaller and hopefully safer and more hospitable place.

All looked well—clear skies, light tailwinds out of the west, fuel tanks full, compass working correctly again, all systems go. Jimmie decided he could sit back and relax for a bit. All the way to Moscow, he held steady at 2,500 feet and enjoyed the view of endless farmland and rolling hills. Far below, farmers in their fields stopped plowing and hoeing and took a moment to look into that clear blue sky, remove their hats, and wave.

Jimmie dipped a wing to return their greeting. From up here they weren't Norwegians or Swedes or Latvians or Russians. They were just people, living their lives, trying to make a living, taking care of their kids and elderly parents.

The thought made him think of his mother back in Vancouver. He revered her. As a little boy, Jimmie had regarded his mother as the most beautiful woman in the world. He began calling her "Cleopatra," then "Cleo" for short. Cleo had given her youngest son her reluctant blessing for this around-the-world flight, but Jimmie knew it had been with a heavy heart. He hoped she was not worrying too much.

Late in the afternoon on June 5, a light rain beginning to fall, Jimmie touched down at Khodynka Aerodrome, a few miles north of Moscow. He had now completed the first third of his around-the-world flight.

His arrival at Khodynka was expected and planned in advance. Jimmie had needed to seek permission from the Soviet government to use their airspace and facilities. Money had already been paid for fuel and service.

So, while mechanics topped off his fuel tanks and serviced the engine of the Vega, Jimmie discussed his flight plans with several Soviet pilots. He had decent maps of Western Soviet Union, but beyond the Urals and all the way across Siberia, the maps looked sketchy at best and showed little more than mountains, rivers, and larger settlements. More than one of the pilots conveyed to Jimmie, through an interpreter, the need to refuel and change the engine oil at every opportunity, as foul weather was guaranteed and the probability of getting lost highly likely.

The interpreter did not translate every word the pilots uttered, but Jimmie felt certain his fellow aviators were predicting he would never make it back to America.

Jimmie knew he had a long leg ahead, so he grabbed a few hours' sleep on the floor of the pilots' locker room. When he awoke, he was happy to learn the mechanics had repaired his broken wing. It was as good as new.

The mechanics also took great interest in the Lockheed Vega's Hamilton propeller. Not only were they impressed that it could be started from the cockpit, they also marveled at the way its pitch could be altered for takeoffs, landings, and level flight.

Jimmie was sure Soviet planes would soon be using similar technology. He had complex feelings about this, as a year earlier he and Bennett Griffin had crashed near Minsk and been badly treated by Soviet authorities. They had been accused of being spies. Jimmie considered the USSR a potential enemy of the United States, but nevertheless, he wanted their aviators, and aviators across the world, safe in the skies. He hoped the Hamilton propeller, or a similar design, would soon be standard on all aircraft.

Before departing Moscow, Jimmie sent another batch of cables to *The New York Times* and several other newspapers indicating his present location and providing a general outline of his itinerary across the Soviet Union and Siberia. He ended by saying he might be out of communication until he reached Nome, Alaska, hopefully in just a couple days. The distance from Moscow to Nome was over five thousand nautical miles, more than a thousand miles farther than the distance from New York to Paris. Most of the trip would be over barren, inhospitable terrain. It was the leg of the journey Jimmie most dreaded, though he kept his dismay to himself.

Jimmie ate an evening meal with the pilots and mechanics, went over his plane one last time, then climbed aboard the *Century of Progress* to continue his flight. By the time he taxied to the end of the runway and prepared for takeoff, it was just after midnight on June 6.

The flight went well as Jimmie flew across the Russian steppes east of Moscow. Clear skies and light tailwinds gave him hope of reaching Omsk by midmorning or earlier. Unfortunately, as he approached the foothills of the Urals, the sky turned inky black, and soon the *Century of Progress* was being punished by a terrific thunderstorm. Lightning snapped at the wings as earsplitting claps of thunder rocked the fuselage.

The Urals range in altitude from three thousand to five thousand feet, with a few peaks reaching over six thousand. Jimmie knew these highest peaks lay farther to the south. He climbed to just under five thousand feet and managed to escape the worst of the storm's wrath. But it had been a stressful encounter both on the Vega and its pilot.

Following the tracks of the Trans-Siberian Railway, Jimmie finally reached Omsk just before noon, after almost twelve hours in the air.

It had been a rough flight, but more significant was the toll the overall journey was starting to exert on Jimmie's body and mind. He was in excellent physical shape, but all those long, stressful hours in that cramped cockpit demanded a reckoning. As much as he wanted to refuel and fly on, he knew he needed a break.

What he desperately needed was rest. A full night's sleep would have been pleasant, but no way did he intend to waste all that time. He asked a local pilot to please wake him in just a couple hours. When he awoke, groggy and still exhausted, he ate a hearty meal and relaxed in a hot sauna for half an hour.

He nodded off in the sauna, but quickly came awake.

While all this went on, Soviet mechanics filled his fuel tanks and did a few minor repairs necessitated by the Vega's passage through that intense mountain thunderstorm.

Finally, around 7:00 p.m., Jimmie got underway again. His fatigue lingered but he felt bolstered by the fact that Omsk was geographically the midway point of his journey. Young Mattern was now halfway around the world and on his way home.

Omsk to Irkutsk, near the border with Mongolia, was the next leg of Jimmie's journey. With good weather, relatively uncomplicated terrain, and the Trans-Siberian Railway as a navigational aid, it should have been smooth sailing.

And it would have been if not for Jimmie's growing exhaustion.

CHAPTER SEVEN

Three or four hours into the flight, not yet halfway to Irkutsk, Jimmie felt himself nodding off. He kept falling asleep. No matter how hard he tried, he couldn't keep his eyes open. And then his head began to throb. A pounding headache flashed behind his eyes. For several minutes he flew on, but the effort proved impossible.

Moments later, he passed out.

When he came around, the plane was in a steep dive and less than a minute from crashing nose first into the earth. Jimmie shook himself awake and pulled back hard on the stick. The plane leveled and disaster, at least temporarily, was averted.

The trouble was Jimmie's head. The pounding had grown so severe he thought his skull might explode. And his stomach—he felt terribly nauseous. He began to retch but struggled to hold himself together. A cockpit filled with vomit would be a bleak environment. Jimmie pushed open the small window and tipped the plane on its side to allow a greater stream of fresh air to enter the small, cramped space.

This provided some relief, but still Jimmie's head pounded. He knew something other than exhaustion had caused him to black out. That's when he caught a faint whiff of gasoline. Fumes were somehow leaking into his cabin.

Immediately he sought level ground and a place to land his airplane.

He found a farmer's field. All went well on the landing until just before coming to a stop, he hit an unseen stump with the rear of the plane and damaged the horizontal stabilizer.

Gasping now for fresh air, Jimmie opened the cockpit door, climbed down the fuselage, and dropped to the ground. He lay there for several minutes breathing deeply and trying to clear the gas fumes from his head and lungs.

The retching soon started and continued unabated until the weary pilot collapsed and again passed out.

When he came to, he found himself surrounded by Siberian peasants. Some had their broad, brown faces just inches from Jimmie's face. Others had climbed up into the cockpit and were busy fiddling with the controls.

He struggled to get up and tried to shoo them away. But he was too weak and soon found himself back on the ground, stomach heaving, head swimming.

Moments later, to his astonishment, a man bent down at his side and said in perfect English, "Rather peculiar seeing you here, young man."

Jimmie looked up and saw a bearded man in his fifties who held a remarkable resemblance to President Ulysses S. Grant.

"Who are you?" asked Jimmie.

"I am Viktor. And you?"

Jimmie tried to explain, to tell this man his story, but overcome with weakness, he found it difficult to speak.

Viktor had no such problem. He squatted there on the grass next to the sick aviator and told his story. He was Russian but had spent several years in Montana just before World War I, trying to organize miners into labor unions. After a stint in a Helena jail, he'd returned to his country and now was the foreman of a metal refining plant here in Belovo in the heart of Siberia. It was not his dream job, but under socialism the individual set aside his personal ambitions for the good of the masses.

All this Viktor told the sick pilot while Jimmie lay there flat out on the ground, laboring to breathe and head swimming.

Then, with a broad smile on his weathered, bearded face, Viktor added, "But not to worry, comrade. Despite you being an American imperialist, I am happy to help you."

Viktor drove the peasants away from the plane and had a couple of his factory workers act as guards. Jimmie managed to get to his feet and inspect the Vega. He soon found the small leak in the gas line running from the fuel tanks aft to the engine up in the nose. He pointed the leak out to Viktor, who assured him it would be fixed.

Next, Jimmie inspected the tail. The horizontal stabilizer was badly damaged. No way would the airplane be able to fly a steady course.

Jimmie felt pretty sure *he* would not be able to fly a steady course either. He soon thereafter went back down on his knees and retched for several minutes.

CHAPTER SEVEN

Viktor helped Jimmie to a small hut on the edge of the field. Jimmie removed his boots and jacket and slumped onto a hard, narrow bed. It felt glorious to lie down and pull a scratchy wool blanket over his trembling body.

Jimmie slept and slept. He had no idea how long he slept.

And when he finally came around, he still felt lousy—his head continued to pound and his stomach churned. But he was losing precious time. He needed to fly. He needed to get back in the air.

Jimmie pulled on his boots and jacket and, still wobbly on his feet, stepped out of the small hut into pouring rain. A deluge. Rarely in his life had he seen it rain this hard. He plodded through thick mud back to his airplane. It was now guarded by armed, uniformed members of the Soviet military.

The tail of the *Century of Progress* was being repaired by the chief engineer of the airport at Novosibirsk, thirty or so miles to the west. Using sheet metal and other materials from Viktor's factory, the engineer and his small crew of mechanics patched the tail and repaired the damaged horizontal stabilizer.

Jimmie could only stare in awe. This felt like Jomfruland all over again. Everywhere he went, people of different cultures speaking different languages wanted to help. Maybe that, he wondered, was the true purpose of his flight—international cooperation.

For hours and hours in that downpour, the Soviets worked on the small Vega. Jimmie was anxious for them to finish so he could be on his way, but getting the horizontal stabilizer to function properly proved problematic. Jimmie had little choice but to be thankful and remain patient. Flying without fully functioning stabilizers was impractical and dangerous.

Jimmie did what he could to assist, but mostly he stayed out of the way. Twelve and then eighteen hours passed. For the first time, Jimmie had to admit that his chance to beat the around-the-world flight time of eight days, fifteen hours, and fifty-one minutes set by Wiley Post and Harold Gatty might slowly be slipping away. But he quickly reminded himself that, with a little luck and some nifty flying, he could still be the first to solo around the world. Wiley Post, as far as Jimmie knew, had still not left New York on his solo attempt.

Finally, on the morning of June 8, now almost five days after leaving New York, the *Century of Progress* was again ready to fly. Jimmie still felt rotten, and every time he tried to eat, the food came right back up. Nevertheless, he donned his flight suit and prepared to go.

But Jimmie wasn't going anywhere. The rain had stopped but the muck lay ankle deep, and the field where Jimmie had emergency landed more than thirty-six hours earlier had turned into a sodden, muddy mess. Getting the *Century of Progress* to roll even a few feet forward proved difficult; thoughts of actually taking off were nothing but a fool's folly.

Jimmie, dejected and depressed, returned to the small hut on the edge of the field. There was nothing he could do but rest and wait.

CHAPTER EIGHT

October 1928–May 1931

Jimmie had a fine time flying for Howard Hughes and making *Hell's Angels*. He had made friends with several excellent pilots like Frank Clark, Roy Wilson, and Roscoe Turner. He and Della had gone out on the town with such Hollywood luminaries as Spencer Tracy, Jimmy Stewart, Robert Taylor, and Colleen Moore. But by late October of 1928, the aerial footage of *Hell's Angels* had mostly been shot and Jimmie's paychecks began to dry up.

He knew, and Della agreed, that if he wanted to make a living flying, the time had come to seek greener pastures.

One morning in early November, while hanging around Caddo Studios waiting to hear if he might be needed to do some stunt flying later that day, Jimmie ran into Eddie Stinson. Stinson was a towering figure in those early years of aviation. No one had accumulated more hours in the air than Eddie, estimated at that time to be well over ten thousand.

Recently, Stinson had started his own airplane manufacturing company. He had come to see Howard Hughes about building the millionaire a custom airplane. Before going into their meeting, Eddie spent a few minutes talking with Jimmie, a fellow flier. Jimmie, never shy, an upfront and direct midwesterner, asked straight away if Mr. Stinson needed pilots for his new venture.

Stinson had one simple question: "Kid, can you keep an airplane in the sky when the going gets tough?"

Jimmie answered without hesitation. "Sir, I'm at my absolute best when the going gets tough."

Stinson looked the young pilot up and down. "You've been flying for Hughes?"

"Sixteen months, Mr. Stinson. I've performed every stunt Mr. Hughes threw at me, and then some."

Stinson grinned. He had short-cropped hair and a prominent gap between his front teeth that made him look like a little boy. "Ever been to Texas, kid?"

"Can't say I have but I sure would like to go."

That night he talked it over with Della, who was keen for a new adventure.

By Thanksgiving, the Matterns were about as far south in the continental United States as it is possible to go. Brownsville, Texas, lies just across the Rio Grande from Matamoras, Mexico, and at that time had a population of around twenty thousand. Jimmie and Della found an apartment off McKenzie Road, not far from the Brownsville airfield.

All Jimmie knew about his new job was he and two other pilots would be flying brand-new Stinson Detroiters equipped with 225 hp Wright Whirlwind engines, the same engine Lindbergh had used to fly from New York to Paris. The three pilots would not be flying directly for Mr. Stinson, but rather for some obscure and nameless Texas millionaire who had recently set up a business hauling fresh fish from La Pesca, Mexico, north to Brownsville. The fishing at the mouth of the Rio Soto la Marina, where it emptied into the Gulf of Mexico near La Pesca, was, to say the least, robust. Saltwater trout, grouper, snapper, and yellowfin tuna as big as a twelve-year-old boy practically jumped into the ice-packed fuselages of those specially equipped Stinsons.

Once a day, six or seven days a week, Jimmie and his two flying buddies made the 175-mile run down the coast of Mexico to pack their planes with fish. It was good money, and with four or five hours a day in the air, Jimmie rapidly built up his flight time. He was becoming a bona fide aviator, a professional pilot, and still just twenty-three years old.

The job, however, did not come without hazards. On occasion, Mexican *bandidos* on horseback would descend upon the Detroiters during the loading of the fresh fish. This particular area of Mexico was still a mostly lawless backwater. More than once, Jimmie had to put his plane in motion and skedaddle, with only half a load of fish and the rear cargo doors still wide open and fish flying everywhere.

Another hazard was the weather. Fog so thick a flier couldn't see the nose of his airplane would roll in off the Gulf of Mexico without warning. The three pilots, fearing they might one day run into one another during their north/south jaunts, made a pact to have the southbound flights follow the coast at an altitude of fifty feet, whereas the northbound flights would stay offshore several hundred yards and fly at an altitude of one hundred feet. This way they could safely stay out of each other's flight path.

It worked well until one morning, while flying south in some pea soup fog, Jimmie, hugging the coastline, just about had his starboard-side wing torn off by a northbound plane.

Hot under the collar, Jimmie made a 180-degree turn and followed that airplane all the way back to Brownsville. He fully intended to rip that pilot up verbally and maybe even slug him in the jaw. The second he was back on the ground, he sprinted toward the other plane. That's when he saw it wasn't one of the Stinson Detroiters but a Ford Trimotor. And the pilot wasn't one of his fellow fish-haulers but, by God, Charles Lindbergh, now easily the most famous aviator in the world after his successful transatlantic flight the previous May. He was flying back from Mexico City after visiting his fiancée, Anne Morrow, whose father was the U.S. ambassador to Mexico.

The two pilots stood talking on the tarmac for half an hour or so about their chance meeting in San Diego when Lindbergh had been in town to purchase the *Spirit of St. Louis*. Jimmie asked about the famous transatlantic flight. Charles replied that the freedom over the Atlantic had been unlike anything he had ever experienced. Jimmie said he hoped to do something similar someday, and soon thereafter the two men shook hands, climbed into their airplanes, and flew off in different directions.

Just after Christmas 1928, Jimmie was given a fresh challenge. Some big shot in the Mexican military was into raising chickens. But the local chickens he kept getting were inferior in both size and taste. The general wanted American chickens.

"How many chickens does the general want?" Jimmie asked his boss.

"Ten thousand," was the answer.

"Ten thousand!"

"That's correct, Mattern. Ten thousand. But they're just chicks, barely hatched. I understand the general tried receiving American chickens, mostly Rhode Island Reds, first by truck and then by rail, but both loads arrived with virtually all the chicks dead or dying. So we're going to try flying the damn birds down there. You in?"

"Absolutely," answered Jimmie. He was not a man to ever say no to a fresh adventure.

The next morning, Jimmie flew to a hatchery thirty miles north of Brownsville. One hundred boxes were loaded into the cargo hold of his Detroiter. Each box contained one hundred peeps that had only just hatched within the past few hours. Jimmie took off and flew south to Tampico, where he landed to refuel before his final leg to Mexico City.

While taking on gas and having the oil checked, he went aft to check on his chicks. Right away he thought they looked unwell. In fact, he thought they looked dead. The peeps just lay there, unmoving. Jimmie, quickly growing frantic, checked one box after another. He started to fear he had ten thousand dead chickens on board.

"I show up in Mexico City with this load," he muttered aloud, "and that general will have my head."

He quickly pulled the boxes out of the hold and onto the ground to get the air circulating around the newly hatched chicks. Seconds later those peeps started to pop like kernels of popcorn. It had been cold in the cargo hold at altitude, and those newborn chicks had shut down. But now, back on the ground, warm and toasty, they all at once came roaring back to life. Within a minute or so, Jimmie had ten thousand rambunctious peeps running around his airplane and scattering across the ground as fast as their tiny feet could scamper.

CHAPTER EIGHT

"Gosh-darn chickens!" Jimmie shouted. "This could be worse than them being dead."

He ran around trying to collect the chicks, quickly realized he needed help, and soon had a virtual army of Mexican boys in his employ. They scooped up peeps by the hundreds and put them back in their boxes.

Jimmie landed in Mexico City a few hours later. It was estimated he delivered 9,500 healthy chicks. A few had died and the rest had earned their freedom back in Tampico.

Upon returning to Brownsville, Jimmie decided he'd hauled enough fish and fowl. He was sick of flying in the fog and dodging bandidos.

He heard Mr. Stinson was opening a distributorship up in Fort Worth, so Jimmie applied for a job and Eddie's manager, Randy Page, hired him on the spot.

Jimmie and Della left Brownsville without looking back.

Jimmie's new job involved flying airplanes and demonstrating those airplanes to potential buyers. He and several other pilots flew their Stinsons to airports in Texas, Mexico, Oklahoma, and Louisiana, where buyers could have a look, kick the tires, and, if interested, go up for a spin. Jimmie got to fly a wide range of aircraft, including the biggest plane he'd ever flown: an eight-passenger Detroiter with a massive 425 hp Wasp motor.

One day in Oklahoma, Jimmie met a gentleman who would change his life. His name was Levi Smith, a bigwig at Big Lake Oil Company. Big Lake at that time was pumping more oil out of the ground in Texas than any other outfit. Jimmie took Smith up in the Detroiter. Within minutes, Smith, a man who had a reputation for knowing his mind, took a liking to the airplane. He tipped back his hat and said, "Son, I'll buy her."

Jimmie was plenty shocked. He'd been on the payroll a couple months but had yet to make a sale. He had a few pending, but no done deals.

"You will? Seriously?"

Smith nodded. "On one condition."

"Sure, Mr. Smith, what's that?"

"You come along in the deal as my private pilot."

Jimmie, even more shocked now, wanted to jump at the chance but he also didn't want to disappoint Eddie Stinson or Randy Page, who had only recently given him a job. When Jimmie told Page about the offer, Randy said, "You gotta strike when the iron's hot, kid. And hell, if it don't work out, you just come on back."

Della, too, was all in with the new job, as it did not entail another move and the salary was a bit more generous.

And so that's how Jimmie's career as a pilot for some of the most successful wildcatters in the history of the oil business literally got off the ground.

Jimmie first flew for Levi Smith, but Levi's boss, Michael Late Benedum, took a liking to young Mattern, so before long, Jimmie was his full-time, on-duty pilot. Benedum owned Big Lake Oil but he also owned Benedum-Trees Oil Company, which some years earlier had made him one of the four or five wealthiest men in the world. The man had single-handedly invented wildcatting. It was said Mike Benedum could walk across a barren field in West Texas and smell crude a mile underground.

Benedum proved to be a demanding boss. He did not take time off. In fact, he claimed he'd never taken a vacation in his life. Jimmie was on call around the clock. Benedum did not do business on the phone or via the mail.

"Face to face, Jimmie," he would tell his pilot. "Look a man in the eye and you'll know in an instant if he's telling you the truth. Forget the contracts, the promises, the lawyers. It's in the eyes, Jimmie, the eyes, I tell you."

Based out of Pittsburgh, Benedum-Trees did business all over North America. Jimmie flew back and forth between Pittsburgh and Texas, as well as trips to New York, California, Canada, Mexico, Louisiana, Montana, and Arizona. He felt like he was in the air all the time, always coming or going. It allowed him to amass an enormous amount of flight time.

It did not, however, make for a happy marriage. Della did not know a soul in Fort Worth, so her husband's lengthy absences created no shortage of stress and resentment.

"But it's my job, Della," became an oft-repeated refrain.

CHAPTER EIGHT

As it turned out, in addition to his formidable work ethic, Mr. Benedum was a capricious boss. He had more or less stolen Jimmie from his manager, Levi Smith, one dusty afternoon in an oil field out near Odessa, but he dropped Jimmie just as casually after a contentious meeting of oil men in a hangar at Love Field in Dallas.

No problem. Proving yet again that he had a great proclivity for being in the right place at the right time, James Joseph Mattern soon found fresh employment.

The very same day he was fired by Mike Benedum, Jimmie was hired by Mr. Carl Cromwell. If Benedum was the original wildcatter, Cromwell was the man who perfected the art. Cromwell was of Swedish descent, grew up in Western Pennsylvania in a large farming family, and first worked the oil fields around Titusville when just thirteen years old. By his early twenties, he was down in Texas looking to strike it rich in the fledgling oil business. With nothing but a covered wagon and some primitive drilling tools, young Cromwell had the golden touch when it came to knowing where to drill for the liquid gold. Living in a canvas tent with his wife and infant daughter outside San Angelo, west of Fort Worth, Cromwell knew there was oil beneath their feet.

Like Benedum, Cromwell could practically smell the crude oil under the ground.

Sure enough, a few days later, Cromwell struck oil for the first time.

By the time young Jimmie Mattern went to work for Mr. Cromwell some twenty years after that first strike, the Pennsylvanian was fabulously wealthy, had extravagant homes in several states, and owned a whole fleet of fancy airplanes. Cromwell lived large, and Jimmie was the man who took him where he wanted to go.

Once, they were flying from Fort Worth to Midland when Carl told Jimmie to head south so they could have a quick aerial look at a well he had recently drilled down near Kerrville. It took time to find that well, as it was a heavily wooded area without many clearings or roads nearby. But finally, they spotted it. In fact, they couldn't miss it. Oil was spewing out of the ground in great quantities and with tremendous force. The pressure was so intense, the gusher had blown the top right off the drilling derrick.

Carl and Jimmie were in a small, open cockpit, a fore-and-aft Travel Air 2000. The biplane was a quick, nimble little aircraft that Mr. Cromwell liked for short hops and oil exploration. The Travel Air provided excellent visibility, was easy to fly, and needed just a few hundred feet to take off and land.

Sitting in the forward cockpit, Cromwell turned and hollered to his pilot, "Put 'er down, Jimmie! You gotta put 'er down!"

"Pretty wooded down there, sir!"

"Goddammit, son, put 'er down and get us as close to that well as you can! We gotta cap 'er and then pay a visit to every farmer for miles around."

Jimmie could see landing would be a problem. There was plenty of flat terrain, but it was all covered with trees for as far as they could see.

"Put 'er down, goddammit!"

Well, thought Jimmie, *it's Mr. Cromwell's plane. If it were my plane I sure as heck wouldn't try to land. But here we go.*

Jimmie spotted a narrow pathway where some cutting and clearing had recently been done, maybe for the installation of electric wires. Jimmie descended, lined up the Travel Air, and shouted to the boss, "Hang on, Mr. Cromwell, it's gonna be a rough one!"

This was when Jimmie's stunt piloting came in handy. He threaded the needle with that little biplane and set her down gently. But a gentle landing did those boys and their plane no good. That strip of open land was not much wider than a Texas rancher's Stetson. The first tree they hit ripped off the wings on the starboard side of their ship and the next tree they hit ripped off the wings on the port side. The pilot and his passenger, however, escaped unscathed.

"Hell of a landing, son! Hell of a landing! Now let's go to work!"

They spent two days on the ground around Kerrville, tapping the well and signing land leases with more than forty farmers. In time, those leases would earn Cromwell millions of oil dollars.

"Easily worth sacrificing the Travel Air, son."

But, in fact, the 2000 was eventually recovered, blessed with brand new wings and a more powerful engine, and put back into service.

That was the life of a wildcatter.

In the early autumn of 1929, on a flight from Pennsylvania to Texas, Carl Cromwell told his young pilot he wanted to start an airline.

"An airline?" asked Jimmie.

"That's right, son. People want to get places fast with the greatest amount of convenience."

"Likely so, sir."

"Forget trains and cars. They're slow and old-fashioned. People want to fly."

"I think you're on to something there, Mr. Cromwell."

"Damn straight I am, son. Hell, I won't be the first or the biggest, at least not right out of the gate, but we'll see how she goes. I understand Pan Am is about to start service from Miami down to Managua, Nicaragua. I'm thinking something smaller, but more important. Jimmie, I want you to be Cromwell Airlines' first pilot."

Jimmie could hardly believe his ears.

On November 1, 1929, at the ripe old age of twenty-four, Jimmie Mattern took off from Fort Worth, Texas, in a Stinson SM-1 powered by a Pratt & Whitney R-1340 Wasp engine. On board were six passengers, all bound for San Angelo, Texas, two hundred miles to the southwest. Jimmie had them back on the ground just one hour and forty-two minutes later. Traveling by land, that same trip would have taken them in excess of six hours on bumpy, dusty roads.

The SM-1 was a sturdy, reliable airplane. For instrumentation, it had only a crude fuel gauge, a compass, and a speedometer. In those early days, blind-flying instruments like artificial horizon gauges, turn and bank indicators, altimeters, and directional gyros did not exist. This was visual flying only.

Cromwell Airlines flew Fort Worth to San Angelo to Dallas to Fort Worth twice a day, every day of the week but Sunday. Texas weather is often clear and fine, but just as often it's pure hell on small aircraft. Thunderstorms created the most havoc. They popped up at the snap of a finger with peals of thunder loud enough to wake the dead and strikes of lightning that would split the earth wide open. Often these storms appeared on the western horizon as squall lines. These tempests were moving walls of water accompanied by thunder, lightning, and sustained winds of fifty or sixty miles an hour. They moved like runaway trains across those barren flatlands. A pilot had to remain on full alert at all times.

Jimmie learned fast to turn away from those storms and hightail it in the opposite direction with all possible haste. His passengers would sometimes complain about delays, but Mr. Cromwell had told him to reply, "Better late than dead," so that's what Jimmie said. Sometimes he could outrun those wild storms and sometimes he could find calm air at a higher altitude, but on occasion he simply had to put his airplane on the ground.

During his tenure at Cromwell Air, Jimmie made emergency landings in hayfields, wildflower meadows, open prairies, backyard lawns, and even once on County Road 322 three or four miles southeast of Comanche. He had a screamer on that landing, an aggrieved woman who kept crying, "We're going to die! We're going to die!"

But no, they didn't die. They landed without a hitch, taxied to the shoulder of the highway, waited for the squall to pass, waited a little longer for the traffic to clear, and flew on.

That's what Jimmie did—he flew on. Give that man an airplane and a destination and he took to the air as effortlessly as a bald eagle. It would be easy to believe Jimmie Mattern was destined to fly.

But really, all of it—the Hollywood stunt flying, the hauling of fish out of Mexico, delivering chickens to Mexico City, carrying wildcatters in and out of Texas oil fields, transporting passengers to San Angelo and Dallas and Fort Worth—was just preparation, practice, training for Jimmie's extraordinary, record-setting flights around the world.

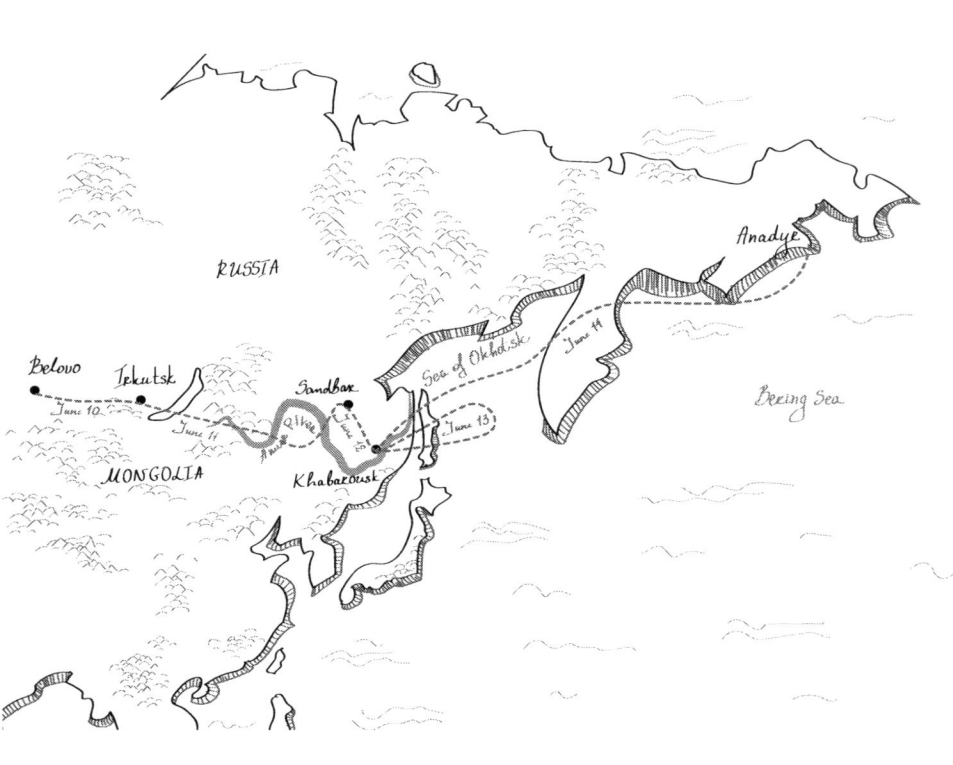

CHAPTER NINE

Belovo to Anadyr

June 10, 1933
Light rain, 46°F, moderate westerlies

Finally, in the early afternoon of June 10, under bright blue skies, Jimmie Mattern lifted off and left behind his soggy emergency airstrip on the outskirts of Belovo, USSR. One week had now passed since his departure from Floyd Bennett Field on Long Island. His dream of bettering the around-the-world flight time set by Wiley Post and Harold Gatty in July 1931 may have died on the sodden earth of Belovo, but Jimmie still intended to be the first man in history to circumnavigate the globe solo.

Back in Belovo, stuck on the ground for four days with a damaged airplane and bad weather and a bad stomach, Jimmie's will had been temporarily broken. Cold, wet, hungry, isolated, exhausted, and frustrated, he imagined returning to Moscow via the Trans-Siberian Railway and then making his way back to America, a forgotten loser.

But now, back in the air, winging his way toward Irkutsk with brisk tailwinds, the intrepid young aviator felt fully restored. A ceaseless optimist, rarely down for long, undaunted by adversity, Jimmie felt confident the flight's numerous mishaps lay in the past and nothing lay ahead but clear blue skies and smooth flying.

And, in fact, the 1,100 miles to Irkutsk proved uneventful. He covered the distance in just over eight hours. On the ground in Irkutsk, just north of the Mongolian border, Jimmie refueled and grabbed a quick bite to eat. But, anxious to make up some of the lost time, he did not rest, not even for an hour. Well after midnight, he climbed back into the cockpit of the *Century of Progress* and took off for Khabarovsk.

Irkutsk to Khabarovsk, Jimmie knew, from countless hours back in New York and Chicago studying his maps, was a solid two thousand miles and a minimum of fifteen hours flying time. Just a few hours into the flight, around 5:00 a.m., Jimmie began to realize he definitely should have gotten some sleep back in Irkutsk. At least a catnap. His eyes began to grow heavy. To keep himself awake he sang in a loud voice every song he could remember. He slapped himself repeatedly across the face and kept the small window open, despite frigid air blowing into the cabin.

Finally, dawn arrived, and after a long night of almost constant drizzle, the appearance of the sun gave Jimmie a shot of adrenaline. He flew on.

But notwithstanding clear skies and calm winds and a fully functioning airplane, Jimmie struggled all day to keep himself alert. He changed altitudes, clapped his hands, pounded the roof of the fuselage, and told himself stories of his youth back in Freeport, his bugle corps days on Oahu, his stunt flying days on the set of *Hell's Angels*. But still his eyes kept closing and his head lolled about on his shoulders.

Hour after hour he debated putting the *Century of Progress* down on the ground somewhere short of Khabarovsk, catching a little sleep, and trying to put some food in his constantly churning stomach. But instead of seeking a place to land, he kept reassuring himself he could make it. "Come on, Jim, just six more hours."

"Just five more hours."

"Just four more hours."

"Just a few more hours."

By late morning on June 11, the skies still clear and the winds calm, Jimmie felt confident he was somewhere over Northeast China. He had not sought permission from the Chinese government as he was essentially flying along the Soviet border and intended to remain over China for just a couple hundred miles.

He also knew that farther east was the Amur River that formed the boundary between the Soviet Union and China. Jimmie flew at just under a thousand feet, as he did not want to miss the Amur. The river was the essential landmark he needed to reach Khabarovsk. If he overshot the Amur, he would quickly be flying blind into the heart of Siberia.

As the first signs of dusk gathered around his airplane, Jimmie spotted the river. He breathed a long sigh of relief. An hour, two at the most, and he could put the Vega back on the ground and give his body a long, much-needed rest.

But here, really for the first time since leaving New York, Jimmie made a tactical error. His other problems had been beyond his control, mechanical and weather related. This complication could only be chalked up to poor judgment. A combination of exhaustion and lack of sustenance likely were the culprits. The young aviator who prided himself on fortitude and preparation was seriously depleted and therefore lacking good sense. He was now eight days into a journey that he had hoped would only take seven, and in those eight days he had slept a total of maybe twenty-five hours and had eaten, at most, half a dozen decent meals. Add in the constant stress, the solitude, and the need to make a relentless string of vital decisions, and it is no wonder the man was about to make a poor choice.

Jimmie turned north along the Amur when, in fact, he should have turned south. He then proceeded to fly in the entirely wrong direction for nearly two hours.

Moments after finally realizing his error, Jimmie knew he had no choice. He had to put the plane down. Immediately. Any attempt to retrace his route and make for Khabarovsk would almost certainly end in disaster.

As a precaution against a hard landing, Jimmie stuffed a couple of small pillows behind his neck to cushion the blow. He then shoved the stick forward and began his descent.

Darkness had fallen, but a waxing moon under clear skies provided some illumination for the exhausted flier. Jimmie could see the earth coming up fast under his landing gear. Seconds later, the tires touched down, bounced, touched down again, and then the *Century of Progress* rolled forward, slowed, and finally stopped in a surprisingly smooth landing.

Almost delusional with exhaustion, thinking he might actually be in the middle of a dream, Jimmie cut the switch, silencing the engine. He pushed open the hatch, stumbled out of the cockpit, and dropped nine feet to the ground, not even bothering with the step. Right there where he landed on some soft sand, the weary flier curled up on Mother Earth and fell fast asleep.

He slept without moving until the sun came up. And when his eyes opened, he saw he had landed the Vega on a narrow sandbar jutting out into the Amur River. Had his plane rolled another twenty feet, it would have wound up wet and swept away by the strong current.

Once again, Jimmie concluded he was being protected by some force greater than his own mortal being. He had been more than half asleep during that landing and possessed only a vague memory of hitting the ground and rolling to a stop.

Divine intervention?

Jimmie had no idea. Still, he felt as though an invisible hand had grabbed his airplane out of the night sky and set it down gently on the river's edge.

Refreshed by the long sleep, Jimmie stood and stretched. The early morning air felt bracing but not overly cold. The sun, low in the eastern sky, showed through thin clouds. Jimmie checked the Vega for damage and found none. The firm sand had provided an excellent landing strip. If he could swing the plane around, Jimmie felt certain the sandbar would also make an excellent place to take off.

He checked his fuel, made some calculations about the distance he had flown in the wrong direction, and determined he probably had a sufficient quantity to make Khabarovsk. Still, it would be nice to have another fifty gallons. His big problem was oil. His Pratt & Whitney Wasp engine had started to burn oil at a faster rate than during the first leg of his journey. Whether this had to do with engine wear or inferior oil, Jimmie could not be sure, but either way, he needed lubricant or engine seizure became a strong possibility.

CHAPTER NINE

Jimmie decided to take a walk and see if he might find a farmhouse or settlement nearby. No sooner had he started across that sandbar than several local peasants in flatboats appeared out of the morning gloom and pulled up to the riverbank. They had no common language with the stranger, but using gestures and visual aids, Jimmie managed to make clear his needs. Enthusiastic nods and smiles filled with rotten teeth convinced Jimmie his communications had been successful.

They poled the foreigner back across the Amur and gave him hardboiled eggs, brown bread, and hot tea. Jimmie was famished, but the second the food hit his stomach he felt nauseous. Four days after the incident, the gasoline fumes that had engulfed the cockpit of the *Century of Progress* continued to adversely affect Jimmie's health. He kept the food down but only with a determined effort.

An hour later, several of the men who had departed on foot returned to the riverbank in an old rundown cargo truck. They had smiles on their large, broad faces. Jimmie thought they looked Mongolian. Their language did not sound either Russian or Chinese.

In the back of the truck they had a fifty-five-gallon drum of gasoline and several five-gallon jugs of oil. The writing on the jugs looked Russian, but Jimmie had no way of knowing the quality or the grade of the lubricant. Not that it mattered. He needed engine oil to fly.

Jimmie attempted to discern where the supplies had come from and how they had been obtained. His inquiry proved mostly futile, though the men seemed endlessly amused. Jimmie concluded the gas and oil—and maybe even the old cargo truck—had been "borrowed" from a local Soviet collective.

It took a couple hours and some hard work, but eventually the supplies were carried by boat across the river to the *Century of Progress*. Getting the fuel out of the drum and up into the Vega's tanks proved a tedious operation, but Jimmie concluded the delay beat running out of gas or having his engine seize.

The oil he added himself. He used a funnel and ran the oil through a clean rag in the hope of filtering out any impurities. The oil was thick, like roofing tar. Jimmie knew it had been refined, but minimally. He hoped the crude would not destroy the Wasp's high-performing cams, pistons, and valves.

It was, he knew, a tight spot, and absolutely of his own doing.

Finally, by the middle of the afternoon, the plane serviced, fueled up, and turned around on that remote sandbar, Jimmie prepared for takeoff. He thanked his still-smiling hosts, warmed the engine, engaged the prop, and pushed the throttle forward.

And then, already clanking and smoking from the inferior oil, that Wasp engine roared and lifted the small Vega back into the Siberian sky.

Jimmie flew on.

By dusk, Jimmie was back on the ground, having finally reached Khabarovsk more than thirty-six hours after leaving Irkutsk. He ate, slept, and ate some more. His stomach had finally started to feel settled again. His strength returned, which was a godsend, as Jimmie knew the toughest leg of the trip lay in his immediate future. No one had ever tried to cross the North Pacific by air before and Jimmie did not intend to be the first. The distance over open water was just too great, nearly twice the distance from North America to Europe.

Jimmie's flight plan called for flying northeast out of Khabarovsk, over the remote Sea of Okhotsk, and then across the isolated Kamchatka Peninsula. At the northern edge of the peninsula, he would fly up the jagged coast along the Bering Sea to the mouth of the Anadyr River. From there, Jimmie would turn due east across the Bering Straits and finally into Nome and a return to North America.

It was a 2,500-mile haul across some of the most inhospitable terrain on Earth, in tandem with unpredictable weather and bone-crushing cold even in mid-summer. With his tanks topped off, Jimmie had plenty of fuel to make the crossing, but he knew he would need to stay on top of his game every mile of the long journey. A mistake like the one he had made back at the Amur River would likely cost him his life. His maps lacked detail. Settlements were few. High mountains, desolate Arctic terrain, and open water dominated the vast majority of the 2,500 miles he had to cover.

CHAPTER NINE

Still, Jimmie was anxious to get started. He knew the other end of this extended leg would put him back in America, just a few days out of New York City and a triumphant return to Floyd Bennett Field.

He arose at 4:00 a.m., the sun already up, ate a hearty meal, and raced into the sky. He hoped to reach Alaska by ten or eleven that night. He felt well, as strong and healthy as he had felt since leaving New York, now ten days ago.

All went smoothly for several hours. Skies remained clear and the air stable. Flying at around 3,500 feet, he had unlimited visibility. Around 8:00 a.m., he reached the Sea of Okhotsk. The weather continued to cooperate. But then, suddenly, a hundred or so miles out over the Okhotsk, Jimmie ran into a wall of clouds. Visibility dropped to near zero in less than a minute. The wall seemed to reach from horizon to horizon. Jimmie tried to fly under the mass of clouds, but even when he dropped as low as fifty feet above the sea, he could barely see the propeller spinning on the front of the *Century of Progress*. He tried to fly above the thick wall of clouds, but it proved just as impenetrable at eight thousand feet as it had been at 3,500 feet. He didn't dare fly any higher.

The temperature plummeted and ice began to form on the wings.

Jimmie's luck had run out.

He descended to three thousand feet, turned the plane southwest, and flew back to Khabarovsk. It was either that or risk winding up in the Sea of Okhotsk.

Upon landing in Khabarovsk, Jimmie calculated he had just been in the air for almost ten hours, flown 1,400 miles, and gone absolutely nowhere.

Another twenty-four-hour delay ensued. Rain, fog, and more rain. During those hours on the ground in Khabarovsk, Jimmie slept and ate and fretted. His mood swung back and forth between annoyance and elation; annoyance over all the problems and delays, elation over still being alive and still with a chance to be the first to solo.

Finally, a day after turning back, Jimmie once again took to the skies. Cold and cloudy, but the fog had lifted, the rain had stopped, and the forecast to the northeast called for sunny skies and tailwinds of ten to fifteen knots.

Jimmie would fly in a blizzard with tailwinds like that.

This time, Jimmie had no trouble crossing the Sea of Okhotsk. Far out across the sea, he could see the towering mountain peaks of the Kamchatka Peninsula. He knew the highest peaks rose over eight thousand feet above sea level and symbolically guarded the entrance to the Arctic Circle.

He also knew he was now more than a third of the way to Nome. If all went well, he would be on the ground in North America in less than twelve hours.

The Vega could fly over eight thousand feet, but in reality the small plane did not perform very well over six thousand. So instead of flying over the Kamchatka peaks, Jimmie wove his way through the passes while maintaining a northeast heading as much as possible. It appeared entirely unsettled below. No roads, settlements, or signs of civilization. But the alpine beauty stretched in every direction as far as Jimmie could see.

The splendor mesmerized him, and he flew on nearly in a state of euphoria. Flying alone in such a remote and forbidding landscape would unnerve an average person, but Jimmie experienced true happiness at times like this. He knew only a handful of courageous pilots had ever laid eyes on this spectacular terrain.

Soon he reached the Bering Sea, which meant he was now well over halfway to Nome. With tailwinds pushing the Vega's speed to almost 140 mph, Jimmie felt confident he would be back on the ground in just over seven hours.

The flight plan took the *Century of Progress* along the rugged coast, with the deep Siberian wilderness to the west and the Bering Sea to the east. After much thought and discussion back in New York, Jimmie and Fred Fetterman and a handful of other trusted confidantes had concluded that the safest way to cross the Bering Sea was to follow the coast north to the Gulf of Anadyr. From there it was just five hundred miles due east to Nome, which Jimmie felt confident he could cover in approximately four hours or less.

Unfortunately, as he approached the mouth of the Anadyr River, the *Century of Progress*, which had carried him more than eleven thousand miles across the Atlantic, Europe, and now the enormous continent of Asia, developed an extraordinarily serious problem.

Staring in disbelief at the gauges on his instrument panel, Jimmie knew he was in deep, deep trouble. He had faced problems with his compass, problems with the weather, mechanical problems, health problems, and problems with profound fatigue resulting in poor judgment. But all of those enormous problems now paled in comparison to what Jimmie saw when he peered wide-eyed at his oil gauge.

Oil pressure had dropped to zero. The engine had run dry of oil. Or would soon.

And soon after that, the engine would seize.

Jimmie knew he had no choice. He had to land, crash land if necessary, and he had to do so immediately. He had to get his airplane on the ground. If he waited, if he started across the Bering Sea and the pistons of his Pratt & Whitney Wasp engine froze inside their cylinders, the *Century of Progress* would stall, and soon thereafter the plane would fall out of the sky and plunge into the frigid waters below.

Such a fate would very rapidly bring about his death.

Landing in this remote country would present some formidable challenges, but if he could at least put his plane down safely, he had a shot at survival.

CHAPTER TEN

May–August 1931

In late May of 1931, Jimmie sat around drinking coffee in the small terminal at the San Angelo airstrip when the phone rang. Reg Robbins, on the line calling from Fort Worth, had an excellent opportunity for his old flying buddy. Jimmie and Reg had first met on the set of *Hell's Angels* a couple years earlier, and now Reg had a world record in mind—but he needed Jimmie's help to make it happen.

Jimmie heard Reg out, found the scheme both bold and enterprising, and immediately signed on to participate. "Although," he added, "first I have to make sure my boss is okay with me taking a few weeks off."

"Would that boss be Mr. Cromwell or Mrs. Mattern?"

Jimmie laughed. "Right. Make that *both* my bosses."

Mr. Cromwell, thinking it might prove excellent publicity for his fledgling airline, gave his blessing, but Mrs. Mattern was, well, less than enthusiastic about the expedition. "You'll be gone how long?"

"Hard to say with these things, hon, but I'd guess a week or two."

Della sighed and looked her husband up and down. He still looked like a boy, so cheerful and innocent. Della liked Jimmie's job as a pilot for Cromwell Airlines. He received a regular paycheck and was almost always home in time for supper. "A week or two?" she asked, and then, "And what am I supposed to do while you're gone?"

Jimmie shrugged. "Maybe you could go up to Walla Walla and have a visit with your mom and sister?"

"Maybe I could."

"So you're okay if I go?"

Della shook her head but smiled. "I can't say I'm elated, but I'd never stop you from going, Jimmie. What would be the good in that?"

Reg Robbins was a Texan born and bred, a quiet young fellow with a soft southern drawl. At first glance, he seemed an unlikely candidate for aviation heroics. But Reg had the right stuff—guts, brains, and fortitude. He also had Hank Jones as his copilot. Jones was at best an amateur aviator, but he'd made a killing in West Texas oil, so Reg welcomed him aboard.

The plan was simple: Be the first to cross the Pacific nonstop by air.

The prize: $25,000 (awarded by *The Asahi Shimbun*, a Tokyo newspaper), along with the prestige of being the first.

The game plan: Refuel in the air.

Midair refueling had been attempted and even accomplished prior to Robbins and Jones coming up with the idea, but not often and not always with great success. But these daring young aviators had the will and the gumption to try almost anything. And to make the whole business even more perilous and precarious, Reg's plan called for refueling midair over Alaska not once but twice—first over Fairbanks and then over Nome—before setting off across the Pacific.

Jimmie's role: Pilot the plane that would do the refueling.

Jimmie would pilot a Ford Trimotor, a workhorse of an aircraft with an exceptional history of reliability. This particular airplane, financed by Hank Jones, had originally been designed to carry passengers, but Robbins had turned the Trimotor into a flying gasoline can. Not only could it cover long distances without refueling, it could also carry hundreds of extra gallons of fuel that would hopefully be transferred midair into the Lockheed Vega that Robbins and Jones would be flying on to Tokyo.

CHAPTER TEN

Jimmie chose Nick Greener as his copilot. Nick loved a good adventure and was entirely unfazed when Jimmie told him about the role he would play in the midair refueling scheme.

The four pilots spent several hours on the ground discussing how the refueling operation would work. They did not, however, go aloft and practice. Essentially, the Vega would fly just ten feet below the Ford. The two planes would maintain similar speeds. Once this was established, Nick Greener would open a hatch in the belly of the Ford and lower down a two-inch lead-weighted hose, hopefully without the hose getting caught up in the Vega's propeller. Hank Jones, standing in the open cockpit of the Vega, would grab the hose and stick the end in the fuel tank. Jones would signal Greener that this task had been completed and Greener would then pull a lever and transfer the gas from the Ford to the Lockheed.

"Simple," Reg Robbins kept insisting. "Nothing to it. The key will be maintaining the proper airspeed and distance between the planes. We want to stay as close as possible so if and when we hit rocky air, both planes will move up or down in unison. If we get too far apart, any turbulence might throw us off in different directions. Or, worst case scenario, toss the planes smack into each other."

Mattern, Greener, and Jones just nodded. Damn the particulars and possible dangers. Those boys just wanted to fly.

Jimmie and Nick flew out of Fort Worth in early July 1931. Their job was to reach Fairbanks and contact Reg and Hank, who would be standing by down in Seattle. To capture the $25,000 in prize money, the nonstop flight had to originate in Seattle and end in Tokyo. Or vice versa. Due to the curvature of the earth, Reg intended to fly north to Alaska, west over the Bering Sea, then south to Japan. This would add distance to the overall trip but would allow for refueling over land rather than open water.

Jimmie and Nick flew due north to Bismarck, North Dakota, a distance of 1,100 miles. They refueled, spent the night, and in the morning took off for Edmonton, Alberta. Edmonton Municipal Airport did not have a paved runway or even a grass airstrip. It was, to Jimmie's annoyance, little more than a plowed field.

To make matters worse, the Canadian customs officer informed the two pilots that Canada had certain rules and regulations regarding uncharted wilderness air travel.

"Meaning what?" asked Jimmie.

"Meaning you'll need some additional supplies, young fellow."

"Additional supplies for what?"

"Additional supplies or you won't be permitted to proceed."

By happenstance, Hudson's Bay Company had an outfitter not a quarter of a mile down the road from the airfield. The boys needed to purchase a rifle, .30–06 ammo, sleeping bags, parkas, snowshoes, fur-lined boots, and enough rations to sustain themselves for seven days in the event of a crash.

"Some scam, hey Nick?" said Jimmie.

The shopping spree took time, as did refueling the plane. Then a thunderstorm rolled in and dumped over an inch of rain on the "runway" in less than an hour. The field turned quickly into a quagmire, making takeoff impossible.

"Maybe we could use the street," suggested Nick.

Jimmie smiled. "Damn, Nick, that's a fine idea."

Half an hour later they had a team of horses hooked up to the Ford. Those sturdy draft horses pulled the airplane out of the mud and over onto the pavement. The boys climbed aboard and taxied a couple thousand feet up the street. The Royal Canadian Mounted Police kept people, cars, and horses at bay.

Jimmie swung the big Ford around, gunned the engine, and headed west, avoiding streetcar tracks and telephone poles as he gained enough speed for takeoff. He knew if he hit a track it would swing the plane into a pole and very likely tear off a wing.

Stunt flying and oil exploration had turned Jimmie into a pilot with exceptional skills and nerves of steel. He held that airplane steady as she rolled down the street, and eventually the Ford, laden with fuel, lumbered into the air. The engine labored, however, and despite Jimmie's efforts to gain altitude,

CHAPTER TEN

they flew all the way to Hazelton, a distance of more than 750 miles, less than a hundred feet from the ground, at times just a few feet above the towering spruce trees.

Hazelton was a scheduled stop, despite the fact that the Trimotor still had over half a load of fuel. Jimmie would have flown on to their next stop—Whitehorse up in Yukon Territory—but he doubted they had enough fuel to fly that far.

To his renewed annoyance, the Hazelton "runway" looked even worse than the one back in Edmonton. Plus it was shorter, just 1,500 feet with tall trees on approach.

Jimmie brought the Ford in slow, just above stalling speed, and dropped in only inches over the treetops. The second the wheels hit the dirt, Nick Greener pulled back hard on the brake lever and the plane finally stopped at the edge of the runway less than ten feet from a steep embankment that dropped down to the swollen Skeena River.

The boys climbed out and stood at the edge of that near-vertical slope. They could only shake their heads in amazement and gratitude that their plane hadn't plunged into the swirling current below. Men and plane would have been swept away in an instant.

They again needed a team of horses to swing their plane around and pull it into a position for takeoff. What they had hoped would be a fairly routine flight from Texas to Fairbanks was fast turning into quite an adventure.

Jimmie quickly determined if he took on more fuel to make the jump from Hazelton to Whitehorse, the Ford would never get off the ground on that short, spongy runway. The airplane would plow straight into the trees before gaining enough altitude.

After talking over the situation with some locals, Jimmie and Nick decided to fly three hundred miles due north to a small airfield at Telegraph Creek. Here they could take on enough fuel to make the jump up to Whitehorse before heading west to Fairbanks. They'd learned Robbins and Jones had successfully flown from Fort Worth to Seattle and were eagerly anticipating their transpacific flight.

Even with less than half a load of fuel, Jimmie had to battle that big Ford to get her off the ground in Hazelton. Then, midway to Telegraph Creek, up in some mountain passes not far from the British Columbia–Alaska border, the boys ran into some bad weather. Jimmie had to set the plane down on a lava field, and all the way in he feared the rough terrain would knock the Ford to pieces. But the Tin Goose, as Reg Robbins had nicknamed the Trimotor back in Texas, withstood the pounding without a scratch.

The boys did not stress. They both had cool, calm demeanors. They napped, enjoyed their Hudson's Bay rations, and waited for the storm to pass. And once it did, they climbed out of the plane and surveyed the terrain. Both agreed, what with the battered lava field and the rugged surrounding mountains, takeoff would be virtually impossible. Some kind of disaster was all but inevitable. And then, undaunted, the two young fliers climbed back into the plane, swung her around, revved the engine, and put the Tin Goose back in the air.

An hour later they reached Telegraph Creek, an unmanned airfield used mostly by local bush pilots in emergencies. The boys put just enough fuel in the big Trimotor to complete the four-hundred-mile run up to Whitehorse. With clear skies and light southerly breezes, they took off immediately after refueling.

The flight north into Yukon Territory passed over flat tundra marked with rivers and lakes still uncharted.

Halfway through the flight, the winds shifted to the northeast and picked up considerably, slowing their speed to 80 mph, but nevertheless in the late afternoon they sighted the Whitehorse airfield along the Yukon River. Finally, a real airfield with both a grass and a macadam runway, the first one the boys had seen since departing Fort Worth three days earlier.

Jimmie put her down and the boys climbed out of the Tin Goose, happy to have survived their travails in the Canadian wilderness.

Town folk came out to take a gander at the big Ford. Most of them had never seen a plane that large—they were used to small, single-engine planes used by the bush pilots. They welcomed the two fliers with open arms and lots of questions. Soon Jimmie decided they would spend the night and head for Alaska in the morning.

While the plane was refueled and serviced, Jimmie and Nick took a tour of the old gold rush town, ate a hearty steak dinner at the Goldminer's Hotel, then went upstairs for some shuteye. That far north in early July, it doesn't really grow dark. It just gets dusky for a few hours before and after midnight. Dawn comes early and fast.

At 5:00 a.m., the boys awoke and soon thereafter climbed back into the Ford. They took off and headed west. They ran into good weather and light tailwinds, which they appreciated as the terrain below offered extreme beauty with mountains, lakes, and pristine rivers, but nowhere to land in the event the weather turned ugly or they encountered mechanical problems.

By late morning, they reached Fairbanks and found another first-class airfield with an extra-long paved runway. Jimmie found a telegraph office in the small terminal building. He sent a wire to Robbins in Seattle: *Nick and I arrived Fairbanks. All good. Ready to fly.*

While they waited for the Lockheed Vega to arrive from Seattle, Jimmie and Nick once again had the Ford Trimotor serviced and refueled.

Word was sent to Nome, a distance of just over five hundred miles, that the two planes would soon be on their way and the Ford would be taking on fuel upon arrival. Nome did not then have a telegraph office, so the only way to send word was by air. A bush pilot named Joe Crosson made the roundtrip in just under eight hours. Joe assured Jimmie that Nome had plenty of fuel on hand and attendants would be standing by to minimize the Ford's time on the ground.

The next day, the *Spirit of Fort Worth*, with Reg Robbins at the helm and Hank Jones in the copilot seat, arrived over Fairbanks and circled the airfield. Jimmie and Nick climbed aboard the Tin Goose, warmed the engines, and rolled down the runway. With so much fuel on board, takeoff proved a little hairy, and for a time Jimmie feared they might not get airborne. But the Ford fought its way into the sky, the landing gear ripping the tops off several towering evergreens before finally gaining altitude.

Nick shouted, "Those pines needed a haircut!"

Jimmie smiled, turned west for Nome, and leveled off at 3,500 feet.

Soon the Vega came alongside. The pilots waved. Reg gave Jimmie a thumbs up. The time had come for their first midair refueling.

Reg pulled away and took up the Vega's position directly under the Ford. Nick went aft and opened the Ford's hatch. They had discussed the whole process at great length, but nevertheless, Nick could not believe how close the Vega flew to the underbelly of the Ford. He could practically reach down and touch Hank Jones's outstretched hand as both planes roared west at close to 100 mph.

Jimmie and Reg maintained speed and course as Nick splayed out the heavy lead-weighted hose. After several minutes with the hose flailing in the wind, Hank, harnessed to the fuselage in the rear cockpit of the small Vega, finally managed to grab and control the end of the hose. He fought with it for another minute or so but eventually managed to get the end plugged into the main fuel tank. He gave Nick the signal. Nick threw the lever, opening the flow of gasoline between the two airplanes.

Reg and Jimmie, solid, dependable guys, stayed the course and flew on. It took close to half an hour to complete the operation. No end of things could have gone wrong as turbulence tossed those planes around in the Alaskan sky like seagulls on a wild sea. But each man did his job and the transfer went smoothly.

Hank uncoupled the hose and Nick pulled it back aboard the Ford.

The two airplanes flew west, following the Yukon River. Midnight approached, and with it a few hours of vague darkness. To avoid a midair collision, the pilots put some distance between their two planes. They did not want to lose sight of each other entirely, however, so Reg, flying the much faster Lockheed Vega, throttled back his speed.

Shortly thereafter, despite their precautions, the two pilots nearly collided, which would have destroyed both planes and killed the four men on board. But Reg, at the last split second, first heard and then saw the big Ford out his port window and immediately performed a vertical wing-over and just managed to slide over the Trimotor's starboard wing.

CHAPTER TEN

It was a reminder for all four of these brave young men that this was, despite their courage and devil-may-care attitude, a very dangerous business.

Where the Yukon River turned southwest and headed out toward the Bering Sea, the two airplanes flew due west. The plan was for the Trimotor to land in Nome, take on another heavy load of fuel, get back in the air, and refuel the Vega one more time before Robbins and Jones set off for Tokyo.

It was an excellent plan, and all might have gone smoothly save for one small hitch, a problem faced by aviation pioneers (and really pioneers of all kinds) since time immemorial: bad weather.

As they approached the coast and the settlement at Nome, they spotted a most unwelcome sight—fog. Thick, coastal fog. Nome was famous for the stuff. It could be as clear as just-cleaned glass one second and blanketed with dense fog the next.

Flying by the seat of his pants with just a few basic instruments, no way could Jimmie fight his way through that fog and safely land at the airport. And if he did land, take on fuel, and take off, he might never be able to find Robbins and Jones back in the air.

Reg headed northwest toward clear skies. Jimmie opened up his throttle and followed—he did not want to lose sight of the Vega. The two planes, fewer than a hundred feet between them, wound their way through some high mountain passes and eventually worked their way out over the Bering Sea, where the fog had lifted. Reg, with Jimmie on his tail, turned southeast and descended to just under three hundred feet. The Nome airfield came into view. Reg dipped a wing and then circled back to the northwest; Jimmie landed safely just minutes later.

Ground crews circled the Trimotor as soon as it rolled to a stop. They filled the fuel tanks and added a few quarts of high-grade aviation oil. Just twenty-one minutes after landing, the big Ford prepared for takeoff. As Jimmie taxied to the end of the runway, he could see the Vega out to the southeast, circling over Solomon Beach. Solomon was the rendezvous point for the second refueling, and the wide beach was an excellent place, if necessary, for an emergency landing.

Jimmie, his plane once again burdened with excessive amounts of gasoline, got the Ford in the air and headed south. The fog had lifted to around a thousand feet, but Jimmie could see the blanket was starting to fall again. He and Reg had planned to refuel at 3,000–3,500 feet, but no way would that be happening. They'd be lucky to make the transfer at five hundred.

The planes came alongside. Reg gave a thumbs up and swung the Vega away. Seconds later he took up position under the Ford. Nick opened the hatch and dropped the hose down to Hank, once again harnessed in the rear cockpit of the Vega. Their altitude was just 492 feet—an absolutely insane altitude to try this particular maneuver. But it was either try or give up.

Hank caught the hose and inserted it into the fuel tank. Nick pulled the lever. The fuel began to flow. It flowed and flowed. Back in Fort Worth, the boys had calculated that the Vega would not be able to take off with a full load of fuel, but since she was already flying, they felt confident all that extra weight would not be a problem.

And maybe they would have been correct, if the fuel transfer had taken place at three thousand feet or higher. That extra altitude might have given Reg time to gain control of his fuel-laden airplane. But 492 feet gave him virtually no time at all.

No sooner had the transfer been completed and the hose removed from the tank than the *Spirit of Fort Worth* began to fall out of the sky like a rock thrown off a high building. Reg Robbins needed every ounce of his aviation prowess to keep his little Vega aloft just long enough to make an emergency landing on Solomon Beach.

And just like that, the attempt by Robbins and Jones to fly the Pacific nonstop was over.

Although, not quite over. Those boys didn't have a whole lot of quit in them. They quickly decided to make another attempt. Reg and Hank flew back to Seattle while Jimmie and Nick waited in Fairbanks.

All this took time, but eventually a second attempt to fly nonstop from Seattle to Tokyo was set in motion.

CHAPTER TEN

Again the boys successfully refueled the Vega over Fairbanks and again they headed west for Nome. But just like the first time, the operation ran into fog as they approached the coast. This time the fog proved even more problematic, as Jimmie got lost for several hours in the mountains north of Nome. Reg, running low on fuel, had no choice but to land, again putting an end to any hopes of a Pacific flyover.

Jimmie and Nick eventually emerged from the fog and landed in Nome. The adventure was over. All agreed the hour had arrived to head for home.

By the time Jimmie made it back to Fort Worth, it was the middle of August. He had been gone almost seven weeks, a shade longer than the estimate he had initially given his bride.

Della said little beyond expressing her relief that Jimmie had made it home safely. Twice divorced, Della understood the futility of making a scene. It would do no good. She had married a man with a passion, and a man with a passion, no matter how hard-pressed, would not, and could not, be contained.

Della's deliberation could not have been more accurate.

Just days after returning from Alaska, Jimmie and Reg were busy making plans for another Seattle–Tokyo attempt. The Vega, they decided, needed a more powerful engine and additional fuel tanks, thereby creating a situation where only a single midair refueling would be necessary. They set about to make this happen.

Unfortunately, that autumn, Clyde Pangborn and Standard Oil heir, Hugh Herndon, successfully crossed the Pacific nonstop. They flew west to east, starting in Misawa, Japan, and reaching East Wenatchee, Washington, forty-one hours and thirteen minutes later, having covered a distance of 5,500 miles without landing.*

---

* Pangborn Memorial Airport in Wenatchee, built in 1941, was named in the famed aviator's honor.

But no matter—the refueling expedition to Alaska had ignited young Jimmie Mattern's taste for aviation adventure and long-distance flying records. Mere months would pass before Jimmie and Benny Griffin would concoct a plan to fly around the world in record time. And as this ambitious plan soared, Jimmie and Della's marriage, already turbulent, was looking more like a failed landing attempt with each passing day.

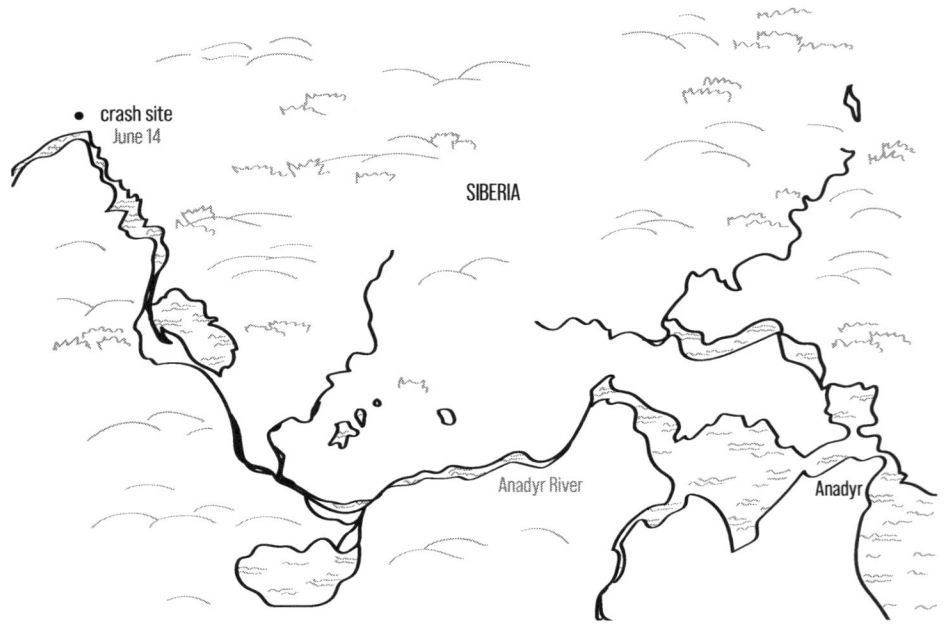

CHAPTER ELEVEN

Along the Anadyr River

June 14, 1933
Low clouds, 35°F, winds calm

Jimmie had to put the *Century of Progress* down. Now. No time to waste. To fly on, to head out over open water and try to cross the Bering Sea, would be suicidal.

Oil pressure had fallen to zero. Jimmie figured the reserve tank in back likely still contained oil, but the low-grade crude he had taken on back along the Amur River, combined with sub-freezing temperatures, had undoubtedly thickened the lubricant into tar and the lines had clogged, probably beyond repair short of replacement. Where in God's name would he get that work done out here in the middle of absolutely nowhere?

"WHY?" he demanded of himself in a loud, angry voice. "Why didn't I change the damn oil back in Khabarovsk? I had all the time in the world to do it!"

Flying the wrong way along the Amur he could write off to exhaustion and illness, but failing to change the oil when he knew the crude was low-quality was inexcusable.

Jimmie pounded the roof of the fuselage. He cursed a time or two and pounded the fuselage again. And again. But even as he unleashed his anger and frustration, he surveyed the tundra below, looking first for the Anadyr

River and then for a safe place to put down the Vega on that desolate and forbidding landscape.

Locating the Anadyr, he knew, was essential. The river would give him a point of reference as well as provide him with a potential escape route. Jimmie knew the river was the principal mode of transport in this remote area of the Siberian Arctic. If he had any chance at all of finding people and getting rescued, it would be along the Anadyr.

As he flew, his thoughts kept spinning and swirling. He reflected on the refueling trip to Alaska back in the summer of '31. That trip had definitely been the inspiration for his around-the-world excursions. He had never felt so alive as when he and Nick Greener had flown across that uncharted Canadian wilderness. But he had other, more somber thoughts as well. He thought of his mom, back home, sitting by the radio, anxiously awaiting news of his flight. He thought of Della back in Walla Walla with her mother and sister. Was *she* sitting by the radio? Worrying? Fretting? He doubted it. His obsession with flying, and his relentless desire for adventure, were the reasons for the failure of their marriage.

Not that the marriage had failed completely. Not yet. Not entirely. Sure, they had spent little time together over the past year or so, really since the trip to Alaska with Nick, but that didn't mean it was over. If he could make it home, pull himself out of this jam, maybe their marriage could be saved.

It dawned on Jimmie that in just a couple weeks, on July 27, it would be their sixth wedding anniversary. He had been such a boy. Just twenty-two years old. Still untested. Della, several years older, had seemed so mature, so . . . rooted. He wondered if she missed him, and if she would be sad if . . . if he did not return.

Jimmie tried to shake off the distracting thoughts. He knew he shouldn't be worrying about this stuff. Not right now. Not until he worked himself out of this mess. Thinking about it would drive him crazy, make him slow and weak and ineffective. Jimmie prided himself on keeping cool under pressure, on staying focused. To this end, he surveyed the terrain ahead in search of the river and a place to land.

CHAPTER ELEVEN

Still, he couldn't help but think he was just four hours or maybe less from Nome, from North America, from U.S. soil. From the land of the free and the home of the brave.

Sure, see where your bravery has taken you, Jimmie?
Four hours! Fewer than six hundred miles! Spitting distance, for the love of God! Damn crude! Damn me!

Jimmie smacked himself on the side of the head to end this disgraceful session of self-pity. He needed to stop running himself down, push aside the past, stop dwelling on his mistakes. He needed to land safely, stay positive, make one solid decision at a time if he wanted to survive, if he wanted to make it home.

He spotted the Anadyr, wide and meandering, wider even, he thought, than the Mississippi at St. Louis.

Beyond the river in all directions lay plenty of flat, frozen tundra. Jimmie prepared to land the *Century of Progress*. But as he descended to just under three hundred feet, the memory of his emergency landing in the Soviet Union the year before with Benny Griffin flashed through his brain. They had come in hard and way too hot and wound up sticking the nose of the Vega into the ground. The airplane had tipped up onto its nose and then flipped over onto its back, leaving the two pilots hanging upside down in the cockpit.

Both Jimmie and Benny had been pretty seriously injured and their plane all but destroyed. But at least he had learned something from that crash that might just spare his life—for now.

If Jimmie planted the nose of the Vega out here in the frozen boondocks, it would likely be curtains. This time, his trusty co-pilot would not be here to pull him out of the plane to safety. He also knew that what he was about to do would prevent him from ever leaving this uninhabited wasteland in the *Century of Progress*.

"Got no choice," he said out loud. "Just gotta do it."

Jimmie pulled back hard on the stick, climbed to one thousand feet, opened the throttle all the way up, topped out at almost 200 mph, and then descended again until he flew at maximum speed just a few feet off the tundra. Still at speed, he took a couple of deep breaths, eased the stick forward, braced himself, and a few seconds later—WHAM! The tires hit the frozen ground, exploded, and a split-second later, wheels and struts and shock cords shattered and splintered and flew in a thousand different directions. It sounded like the entire bottom of the aircraft had been torn off.

Landing gear intentionally destroyed, Jimmie ascended, slowed to under 100 mph, wiped the sweat from his brow, and made sure he was still breathing. It had been a very risky maneuver, and it certainly meant an absolute end to his dream of being first to fly solo around the world. But Jimmie knew he had a far better chance of landing safely without his landing gear intact. On this frozen ground, the plane might easily have nosed in and flipped over.

Engine clanking and coughing and smoking, Jimmie passed over the Anadyr one more time, slowed, descended, and as gently as possible put the fuselage of the *Century of Progress* down on the rock-hard frozen tundra of the Arctic Circle.

Jimmie's hope had been to land the Vega within a few hundred yards of the Anadyr. But by the time his ship landed on its belly, skimmed wildly across the tundra, and finally came to rest after tipping onto its port-side wing, more than a mile separated the *Century of Progress* from the wide, meandering river.

The plane had slid over the frozen ground like a hockey puck skidding across an ice-covered pond.

But Jimmie had plenty of other stuff to worry about besides the distance to the Anadyr. His leg, for starters. Upon impact, the bolts holding the Wasp engine in place up in the nose had snapped, and the big Pratt & Whitney engine had pushed back through the firewall into the cockpit, injuring Jimmie's right ankle. He could not tell yet if it was broken or just badly sprained, but the pain was formidable regardless, and getting worse.

After some amount of effort, he extricated himself, bandaged the ankle where it had been burned and bloodied, and fashioned a splint out of some tape and a piece of splintered wood. No sooner had he finished the dressing than he realized the left ankle also had been banged up, though not as severely. He dressed and splinted this one as well.

CHAPTER ELEVEN

Jimmie then took stock of his not-particularly-rosy predicament. His meager food supply was down to two chocolate bars and a few hard biscuits he had picked up in Khabarovsk. He had water, tea bags, and salt. He still had the gun, ammo, knife, fishing line, a few flies, matches, a compass, pencil and paper, and the warm fleece-lined flying suit he'd had the wisdom to include.

Jimmie felt confident if he could shoot some game or catch some fish, he could keep himself alive until help arrived. But how long would that be? Days?

Weeks?

Months?

Would they send help from Nome when he didn't show up? Likely not. To find a downed airplane in the Siberian Arctic would be a thousand times more difficult than finding the proverbial needle in a haystack. Plus, it was likely they would assume he had gone down in the Bering Sea, and any search over that remote body of water would be an act of futility.

Jimmie decided a rescue plane was a pipe dream, and even if some fool pilot volunteered to risk his neck, the chances of being found were infinitesimal. He knew if rescue was in the cards, it would have to come from local trappers or hunters on the ground.

Frozen rain began to pelt the airplane. It sounded like stones striking the fuselage. Low clouds made it difficult to see much beyond the ends of the wings.

Jimmie tidied his small cabin, struggled into his fleece-lined flying suit, and waited for the weather to clear.

Hour upon hour, precipitation fell. Sometimes it fell as rain, sometimes as sleet, sometimes as snow, which brought quiet but also worry as it quickly covered the windows and made the cabin feel even more claustrophobic.

Jimmie slept, but fitfully. He was cold and plenty worried. He did his best to stay positive. It didn't really grow dark, just dusky for a few hours. He ate, sparingly—a piece of a biscuit, a corner of a chocolate bar. He drank a few sips of water.

When he nodded off, he dreamed of hot tea with sugar, the cup warm and steaming. And when he came awake, Jimmie, always resourceful, pulled the cover off one of the Wasp's cylinder heads, cleaned it thoroughly, and fashioned a small stove for boiling water. He soon made his dream of steaming hot tea a reality. The sugar? Well, that would have to wait until he returned to civilization. If he returned.

On his second day on the tundra, the weather cleared. Jimmie, stiff and sore, climbed out of the cockpit and carefully stepped down to the ground. Both ankles hurt and were swollen, the right more than the left. But he did not think either ankle broken, just badly sprained. He could walk, but slowly and with plenty of pain.

Carrying his compass and leaning on his rifle, Jimmie made for the Anadyr. It took him close to an hour to hobble to the water's edge. He estimated the width of the river at well over a mile. No sign of civilization on either bank for as far as he could see.

Jimmie could see the current pulled hard to the east toward the Gulf of Anadyr. He believed the gulf and, more importantly, the settlement of Anadyr, lay fifty to seventy-five miles downriver. And though his maps did not show one, he assumed there was at least one other settlement between his location and Anadyr. But how far? A mile?

Ten miles?

Twenty miles?

Could he reach it by walking? Would his ankles hold up if he tried?

What about food? He'd need sustenance to do all that walking.

And what about the weather? Would he survive if bad weather rolled in? Up here above the Arctic Circle, even in June, freezing to death was a distinct possibility.

Should he go? Or sit tight?

These and a thousand other questions and concerns raced through his mind.

While contemplating his next move, Jimmie suddenly saw, on the far side of the river, one or possibly two small motorboats slowly plying their way downriver. Definitely two boats. He could see their wakes. And they were towing other boats.

CHAPTER ELEVEN

He shouted and tried to jump while waving his arms. But he couldn't jump because of his ankles so he continued to shout at the top of his lungs.

When that failed to get their attention, Jimmie raised his rifle into the air and fired off several rounds.

The boats did not change course. Jimmie could only stand by and watch as they slowly drifted out of sight.

The encounter both depressed and elated Jimmie. While he had missed an excellent opportunity for rescue, the boats proved there was traffic on the river. Where there was one, surely there would be others.

Jimmie stood on the riverbank in that vast emptiness of the Siberian tundra and made a few decisions. He assured himself he was in his right mind and then he set his plan in motion.

For the next many days, Jimmie spent approximately half his time with his airplane and half his time along the Anadyr bank. When the weather turned cold and angry, he spent more time sheltered inside the cockpit of the Vega. The cockpit provided protection from the elements and a small degree of warmth when the bitter northerlies blew and the cold rains fell. The *Century of Progress* also offered security, and even if that security was only illusory, Jimmie needed it to keep his spirits up and hold himself together.

During stretches of good weather, Jimmie made camp along the river. He constructed a low hut of grass and evergreen branches where he would spend the night. During the day, he built fires and burned damp wood that created clouds of dark smoke he felt certain could be seen for miles in every direction. He built a raft that he hoped would carry him down to the gulf.

The cockpit offered a bit of safety and security, but the river offered freedom and hope.

Jimmie hunted ducks and seagulls, but as his ammunition was limited, he fired only at close range. If he had possessed a shotgun, with, say, #7 shot, success would have been assured, but his single-shot rifle proved problematic with such small, fast game. He did eventually shoot a duck, and a valuable fowl it was, as it filled Jimmie's shrunken belly and staved off hunger, weakness, and possibly even starvation.

While at the river, Jimmie worked hard despite two bothersome ankles and a bad molar that likely needed extraction. The infected tooth pounded painfully inside his mouth morning and night.

One day he would battle bitter cold and ferocious winds; the next would bring ravenous black flies and swarms of enormous blood-thirsty mosquitoes so thick they looked like clouds moving over the tundra. He shivered in his fleece-lined flight suit one day and stood sweating in his skivvies baking the next.

Despite the miseries and hardships, Jimmie preferred battling the elements along the bank of the Anadyr to the desolate comfort of his cockpit. For although the cockpit provided safety, it was also the place where his negative thoughts ran rampant and his emotions beat and battered him even worse than the weather.

Four or five days into his ordeal—it might have been six or even seven days, as time was fast becoming surreal with twenty-two hours of daylight and little to mark time—a tremendous storm packing icy rain and harsh winds and thick fog and bitter cold struck hard and left Jimmie trapped in the cabin of the Vega for more than thirty-six hours without reprieve.

His spirit came close to breaking.

The cold.

The solitude.

The isolation.

The hunger and fear and dread.

He could feel the confidence draining out of his body.

A man of action, Jimmie found himself trapped inside that small space without options and with hope fading fast. He prayed. He asked God to give him another chance. He told God he would do better. He would take care of those who counted on him and not be so selfish and self-absorbed. He thought, again, of his mother and his wife. Typically, it was easy for Jimmie to justify his actions and decisions, to rationalize why it was perfectly okay for him to climb into a small, single-engine airplane and try to fly around the world all by himself. He had to do it. He was meant to do it. It was his destiny.

CHAPTER ELEVEN

And if he neglected his mother and abandoned his wife, well, that was okay too because some men are destined to do great things.

Yes, typically, Jimmie could slide by with this kind of thinking. But trapped in that cockpit above the Arctic Circle, a cold fog draped over his broken airplane like a dead man's cloak, Jimmie had no choice but to lay bare his soul. He asked God, and every person he had ever done wrong, especially Cleo and Della, to grant him forgiveness and to excuse his faults and foibles. He assured the audience screaming in his head that he would do better. He did not care about fame or glory or money. He just wanted to survive and do good and lead a useful, quiet life.

Jimmie slept, and his mind raced through a crazy litany of dreams. Startled awake, he found himself still trapped in the remote wilderness of Eastern Siberia. Still he had little food, and less hope. Still he had a rotten tooth throbbing inside his mouth and swollen ankles still throbbing inside his boots.

And his plane, his beautiful airplane, the *Century of Progress*, still leaned over on its side on the Arctic tundra, its engine destroyed, its landing gear demolished.

There was, Jimmie felt certain, no way out. He would die here in the cockpit of his precious Lockheed Vega, either freeze to death or starve to death, alone and forgotten.

That was rock bottom.

He fell back into a restless slumber. And when he awoke the rain had stopped, the fog had lifted, and the sun shone brightly through the windshield. Jimmie pulled back the cockpit door and climbed out. He stood on the wing and spread his arms and stretched.

"I'm gonna get the hell out of here!" he shouted into the vast emptiness. "I'm not gonna let this beat me!"

He returned to the cockpit just long enough to write a letter. He left it on the seat, packed up his few meager belongings, and trekked back to the river.

The letter explained who he was and how his plane had come to be in this remote location and where he was headed—down the Anadyr to the gulf on a raft of his own making.

Jimmie had decided to be the master of his own fate. He would not wait for someone to come save him. He would save himself.

The next morning, his raft finished, he set sail. He did not float even fifty yards downstream before the current, far more powerful than he had anticipated, swamped his raft and tossed him into the freezing cold river. Jimmie saved himself and most of his possessions, but the raft washed down the Anadyr and quickly disappeared into an eddy and out of sight.

Again discouraged, he built a fire to warm his body and dry his clothes. He slept for the next couple days in his grass-and-evergreen hut near the water's edge. When he awoke, he kept a constant vigil for passing boats and planes. He shot another duck, but it fell into the river and washed away before he could retrieve it.

Hunger.

Fear.

Loneliness.

Despair.

And relentless attacks from hordes of blood-sucking energy-sapping mosquitoes.

He started talking to himself. Out loud. Entire conversations. Convinced himself to build another raft.

The raft took three days to build. It was larger and, Jimmie thought, more seaworthy. He stowed his gear and set off. For an hour or more he made good progress. But then, suddenly, the tide must have shifted down at the gulf, and the raft began to move swiftly back upstream. Jimmie could only hang on and hope for the best.

By the time the tide slackened and the current slowed, Jimmie found himself practically back where he had started. He landed on a small island less than half a mile from the beach where he had built the raft. The island had a nice population of ducks. And duck eggs! Jimmie found over a dozen eggs. Enough food for a week! Two weeks! A *month*!

CHAPTER ELEVEN

Unfortunately, when he went to crack an egg and have a nice meal, a duckling sprang forth from the shell. A second egg proved similar. And then a third and a fourth.

Jimmie could not believe his bad luck. He felt like God was laughing at him. He started to smash the eggs open one at a time, but quickly came to his senses and set the eggs in the sun so they could hatch in due course.

Another day or two or maybe three passed. Jimmie was no longer sure about the passage of time. He did not know if he had crash-landed his airplane two weeks ago or closer to three. At times he thought he might be hallucinating. He would see boats on the river and smell steaks on the grill and hear planes in the sky and even familiar voices in his head, but there were no boats, no steaks, no planes, no voices. Just Jimmie and the river and that vast Siberian wilderness.

He saw vultures flying overhead and felt certain they had come for him. Death, he knew, was near. He felt weak from hunger and fear, from loneliness and uncertainty. But Jimmie Mattern had deep reserves, vast reservoirs of strength and courage. He might weaken. He might doubt. He might see, feel, and even taste the end. But he would not quit.

And sure enough, late one morning after nearly three weeks on the tundra, Jimmie thought he saw something out on the river. It was far off.

Was it moving? He couldn't tell.

Maybe it was moving.

Maybe it wasn't.

Maybe it wasn't there at all.

Maybe just his imagination.

He shook his head, blinked, rubbed his eyes. Took another look. Put his compass on it. Held the compass steady. Counted to sixty. Took another look.

It had definitely moved!

But what was it?

He squinted into the haze hanging over the river.

And right then the sun burst through some low clouds and lit up the sky and the river, and what had looked so murky now showed itself more clearly—

Two boats!

Definitely two boats moving slowly along the river.

Jimmie sprang into action. He needed to get their attention.

He threw wet logs on the fire to create dense smoke. He fired three and then four and then five rounds into the air. The explosions reverberated up and down the river.

But the boats did not turn. They did not even seem to move.

Jimmie stood on the beach and fired his rifle until he had no ammo and screamed until his voice grew hoarse.

CHAPTER TWELVE

August 1931–January 1932

Upon returning to Fort Worth following his midair refueling adventure to Alaska, Jimmie went back to work, flying for Cromwell Airlines. He did the Fort Worth to San Angelo to Dallas to Fort Worth run whenever he had paying passengers. Typically, this was only once or maybe twice a week. The Great Depression was in full swing and showed no signs of relenting. Millions were unemployed, and millions more earned meager wages. People were not traveling for either business or pleasure. Even when Jimmie did make the run, his airplane was usually occupied with employees of Cromwell Oil, with the company picking up the tab.

By the end of August, Carl Cromwell must've seen the bottom line. He called it quits. He shut the airline down.

"Nothing but a stinking money pit," he told Jimmie. "Maybe we'll start her up again if the economy ever comes back from the dead."

Right away he figured he'd get laid off, but Cromwell wanted him back as his personal pilot, which made Jimmie happy. But when he went home and told Della about the change, she was less than enthusiastic. "I suppose this means you'll be gone night and day again. We both know Carl Cromwell has ants in his pants."

"I think it means I'll still get a paycheck."

Della could not argue with that.

The very next day, the boss and his pilot left on an extended trip.

It seemed like the worse the economy got, the more Cromwell traveled. He had Jimmie fly him out to California, up to Montana, down to Louisiana, back to California, then all the way east to Pennsylvania. He had meetings scheduled at all these destinations, but Jimmie felt as though what Mr. Cromwell really enjoyed was the flying, being in the air, being on the move. The oil business, like just about every business across the country, teetered somewhere between atrocious and god-awful. Flying in his private airplane, whiskey and soda in hand, Mr. Carl Cromwell hovered above the fray.

But Jimmie only saw half the story. The other half was Carl Cromwell's genius, his business acumen. Sure, the economy might have been in the doldrums with the average Joe struggling to make ends meet, but Carl Cromwell exploited the financial calamity by buying up massive amounts of real estate sitting atop vast oil reserves for pennies on the dollar. Just forty-two years old at the time, Cromwell had not accumulated a personal fortune in excess of thirty million dollars by sipping whiskey and flying above the fray.

Two full weeks passed before Jimmie finally made it back to Fort Worth. When he walked into his apartment, he found it empty. No sign of Della. On the kitchen counter he found a simple note: *I've gone to Washington to visit my family.*

He called Walla Walla. It took time for the call to go through. Eventually the operator called back and connected the parties.

"Hey, Della."

"Hey, Jimmie."

"You good?"

"Yes."

"I didn't know you were going."

"I left a note."

Jimmie decided not to argue. "How's your mother?"

"She's well."

"And your sister?"

"Fine. And you?"

"I'm okay."

CHAPTER TWELVE

"Back from your trip with Mr. Cromwell?"

"Yes, though I'm sure we'll be off again before long."

"I'm sure."

"That guy doesn't know how to sit still."

"Like someone else I know."

"So, you plan to stay awhile? In Walla Walla?"

"We'll see."

"Okay."

And so it went. Tentative and strained. Arguments and big scenes had never been Della's style. Since Della had been down the marriage path twice already, she knew quarrels and reprimands and proclamations did little to improve relations or foster love. Her marriage to Jimmie, she knew, would either prevail or fade away.

After a time, they hung up, promising to talk soon.

Jimmie thought about making a trip up to Walla Walla, and likely he would have, had he not received a call from the boss the very next day. "Be ready to fly tomorrow late morning."

"Tomorrow, sir? We just landed yesterday."

"I'm needed up in the Keystone State, son. Family matter."

"Okay."

Jimmie knew all about the Keystone State. He made frequent flights up to the small Western Pennsylvania town where Mr. Cromwell's parents and siblings lived. They would fly into the single-runway airfield near Sheffield that Cromwell had built with his own money, typically stay a couple days, then fly back to Texas. Jimmie didn't have much to do during these family layovers but hang around Mrs. Wyatt's boarding house and ruminate about his dreary marriage and his desire for more aviation adventures. Still just twenty-six years old, Jimmie nevertheless felt like life was beginning to pass him by. He was neither here nor there. Married, but not really. An aviator, but not really, definitely not fully. He felt like a glorified limousine driver. Jimmie wanted more, more of everything, but he just wasn't sure how to get it.

And then on September 26, 1931, a soft knock tapped on the door of Jimmie's second-floor bedroom at the boarding house. Mrs. Wyatt, not only the owner of the boarding house but also a long-time teacher at the local school, had news for Jimmie. In her late sixties, Alice Wyatt had been a teacher for more than forty-five years and had taught all six of the Cromwell children, including Carl. Alice knew the family well, had dined often at their home, and so had tears in her eyes.

"What is it, Mrs. Wyatt?"

"Carl has been in an automobile accident, Mr. Mattern. He's presently in the hospital but the prognosis does not bode well."

Jimmie gave Mrs. Wyatt a hug and thought about the irony of Mr. Cromwell spending all those hours flying back and forth across the country in his airplanes but in the end maybe killing himself by smashing up his automobile.

Sure enough, the next day Carl Cromwell died.

Jimmie had no idea what to do. He visited the family, but they barely knew who he was. He stayed around for the funeral and waited for someone to give him direction. Several executives from Cromwell Oil flew in from Texas for the funeral. Ken Peters, a VP in charge of transportation, told Jimmie to fly back to Forth Worth.

A few days later, citing the poor economy and Mr. Cromwell's death, Peters told Jimmie his services as a pilot for Cromwell Oil would no longer be needed. Peters did, however, offer to sell Jimmie, at a very reasonable price, the company's Lockheed Vega.

Jimmie told Peters he would like to buy the airplane but would need some time to find the money.

"I'll give you a month, kid, before I put her up for sale."

Jimmie immediately put together a list of people who might lend him some cash to buy the Vega. But really, he knew there was only one decent option. The next day, having worked up the courage, he called Della.

"Hey," he said.

"Hey," she said.

CHAPTER TWELVE

"All well?"

"Yes."

"I have some bad news."

"What is it, Jimmie?"

"Mr. Cromwell died. In a car crash."

"That's awful! He was so young."

"I'm out of a job."

"You'll find something."

"I have an idea, Della."

Della did not reply.

A long silence ensued.

"It really is a great idea, Della," Jimmie finally added. "It'll be a money-maker and let me be my own boss, make my own hours, have more time at home."

Della still had money in the bank, money from her divorce. It was their nest egg, and also, in the back of Della's mind as she closed in on forty, a life preserver if her young husband ever perished flying or left her for a younger woman.

Still, she did not say no. She told Jimmie he could use a goodly portion of the bank account to buy Mr. Cromwell's Lockheed Vega.

Jimmie took possession of the Vega and boldly announced the creation of "Jimmie Mattern's Fast Plane Service." Headquartered in Fort Worth, Jimmie's company offered to fly you anywhere you desired to go in North America. He guaranteed "safe, reliable, on-time service offered at a fair and reasonable price."

It was a gutsy move.

Unfortunately, Jimmie ran into a stiff headwind before he could even pull the Vega out of its hangar at the Fort Worth Airport. The first problem was marketing and advertising. Jimmie knew all about Jimmie Mattern's Fast Plane Service, but just about no one else in the world did. And those who did know—his flying buddies and aviation mechanics and the boys down at the pool hall—barely had enough dough for car fare across town, let alone the cash to fly to New York or Miami or Los Angeles.

A month or so into his new enterprise, Jimmie found himself strapped for cash. He had just about no money to service his airplane, buy fuel, or fund an advertising campaign. So once again, he went to the source.

This time Della listened to Jimmie's pitch, but instead of remaining silent, she said, "These are all things maybe you should have considered before buying the plane, Jimmie."

"I know, but—"

"We are, after all, in the middle of an economic depression."

The insinuation being that it was quite possibly a stupid time to start a flying business.

So now Jimmie not only had an estranged wife but an aggravated and probably exasperated wife as well.

An already stormy relationship turned into a tempest.

So what did Jimmie do? He did what so many young men do when times get tough, when money runs short, when options vanish: He joined the military.

But this time when he joined, unlike when he'd enlisted a decade earlier, Jimmie had the skills and experience to hook up with the Army Air Corps. The Corps commissioned Jimmie a second lieutenant and assigned him to Hensley Field in Dallas, Texas.

Hensley was just a few miles from his apartment, but to save money, and because it didn't look like Della was coming back anytime soon, Jimmie gave up the apartment and moved into the officers' housing on base. He shared a small efficiency with another pilot, Mr. Bennett Griffin of Oklahoma City.

Jimmie and Benny hit it off right away. Jimmie was chatty and gregarious whereas Benny was more introverted and cerebral, but they shared a great love for flying. They could talk for hours on end about the history of aviation, about airplanes, about flying records, about their own memorable flights.

Back in 1927, Benny had competed in the Dole Air Race. Pineapple magnate James D. Dole, founder of the Hawaiian Pineapple Company (later renamed the Dole Food Company), offered the winner a $25,000 prize. The goal was to be the first to fly from Oakland to Hawaii. Eight planes participated in the event. Only two landed safely in Hawaii. Two crashed soon after takeoff; two vanished over the Pacific. And two returned safely to Oakland.

Benny took off successfully in his single-engine Stearman biplane with what he hoped would be enough fuel to reach Hawaii, some 2,300 miles to the southwest. Unfortunately, several hours into the flight, his engine began to overheat. Benny calculated he was not yet halfway to Hawaii, so he turned around and just barely managed to return to Oakland with his engine cooked, the valves destroyed, and less than a gallon of fuel remaining in the tank.

In fact, there was so little fuel in the tank that Benny realized the overheated engine was a godsend. Had the engine not overheated and Benny had continued on for Hawaii, the Stearman would definitely have run out of fuel a couple hundred miles northeast of Hawaii. Not too many places to land safely out there in the middle of the Pacific.

Benny had a touch of wry amusement in his voice as he recounted this stressful tale, but beyond the sarcasm he might have been telling his roommate about an uneventful walk he'd made down to the local market for bread and milk.

Jimmie knew right then and there that Benny Griffin was one cool customer, the kind of guy you wanted in the pilot's seat when the going got tough.

The boys flew all day for the Air Corps. They flew trainers, fighters, reconnaissance planes, troop carriers, transports. Over those central Texas skies, they flew simulated missions over Africa, Asia, and Europe. Unlike in the years leading up to the Great War, when apathy had reigned in the U.S. military, the generals and admirals up in Washington, D.C., had no intention of being unprepared in the event hostilities broke out around the world again.

"It's all nonsense," insisted Benny. "Nobody has the money to fight a war."

"That's exactly why someone will start one," countered Jimmie.

"How so?" asked Benny.

"Nothing like a war to get your economy revved up."

"God, I hope not," said Benny. "I had my war. I prefer a peaceful world."

"Me too," agreed Jimmie. "But history's not on our side."

On their days off, Jimmie and Benny didn't sit around and go to the movies or the local gin mill like most of the other pilots. They drove out to Fort Worth, pulled Jimmie's dusty Vega out of the hangar, fueled up, and did some flying. They flew down to Mexico or up to Oklahoma to visit with Benny's family. They flew to New Orleans. They flew to St. Louis. They flew to Denver. They flew and flew.

Those boys didn't really care where they flew so long as they were in the air.

And when not in the air, they talked about being in the air. They obsessed over flying and about other aviators—Lindbergh, of course, and Post and Earhart, Byrd and Gatty. The recently completed around-the-world flight of Wiley Post and Harold Gatty ate up hours and hours of their time. Both men agreed it had been an incredible achievement, easily one of the greatest in aviation history.

"I don't know if I'm more impressed with the flight," said Benny, "or the preparation that made it possible."

"How do you mean?" asked Jimmie.

"It took them just eight and a half days to complete the flight," explained Benny, "but it took months to plan the entire venture."

Jimmie thought about that. He thought about it for days. Weeks. Benny was right. Success was in the preparation.

And then one night in early January of 1931, Jimmie turned to Benny during dinner and said, "We could do it faster."

"We could do what faster?" asked Benny.

"Fly around the world."

"In what?"

"My Vega."

"What are you saying?"

Jimmie smiled. "It's the same plane Post and Gatty used. Same plane, same engine, but we'll plan better. Use less fuel. Stay in the air longer. On the ground less. Plan well and we can shave a day or two off their eight-and-a-half-day mark."

"Geez, Jim, you think we could?"

"Absolutely. With the right preparation we could do it much faster."

"You think?"

"Hell, Benny, we could do it in half the time."

"That would be something."

Jimmie smiled. "We could set a new world record."

CHAPTER THIRTEEN

January-July 1932

Bennett Griffin was flying airplanes before Jimmie Mattern started middle school. Born in Mississippi in 1895 and raised mostly in Oklahoma, Benny enlisted in the Army Air Corps soon after the outbreak of World War I. He received his pilot training through the Corps and shipped out to Europe where he flew sorties over France, Germany, and the Netherlands in a Curtiss JN-6H single-engine biplane.

Before the Treaty of Versailles finally brought an end to hostilities in June of 1919, Benny had flown over fifty missions, fought Fokkers in aerial combat, been shot down twice, and was rarely heard to utter a single word about any of his exploits. He possessed great courage and was a man of integrity and modesty.

After the war, he remained in the Air Corps and became one of their leading test pilots. In those heady days of rapid aeronautical development, airplanes with new engines and new designs and new technologies were being delivered to military bases almost daily. Benny Griffin flew them all and delivered detailed reports to his superiors regarding the pros and cons of every plane he took into the air.

In addition to testing planes, Benny flew for fun in his free time. Besides participating in the Dole Air Race from Oakland to Hawaii in 1927, Benny attempted to set a world record for sustained flight in 1930. Using the refueling technique later used by Jimmie Mattern and Reg Robbins over Alaska, Benny and his buddy Roy Hunt, in a modified Curtiss Robin high-wing monoplane, stayed in the air for 296 hours and 24 minutes—almost 13 days!—before a thunderstorm over the Oklahoma prairie forced them to land. Their effort, though substantial, did not come close to eclipsing the record of 17 days, 12 hours, and 21 minutes set by Dale Jackson and Forest O'Brine a year earlier.

All of this is to say when Jimmie Mattern suggested to Benny Griffin that they try to break the around-the-world record of Post and Gatty, Benny did not blink an eye before he eagerly shot up out of his chair and shouted, "Let's do it!"

Benny and Jimmie made a great team for a number of reasons. They both had tremendous amounts of flying experience. Benny had the combat experience and Jimmie had the refueling trip to Alaska under his belt, plus the hundreds, if not thousands, of hours in the air for Cromwell Oil and Cromwell Airlines.

Their personalities jelled perfectly. Jimmie, nearly a decade younger, was the far more extroverted and flamboyant personality. He was a great talker and a natural salesman. Benny, quiet and humble, had no problem taking a back seat to Jimmie. He was savvy enough to know that an around-the-world attempt needed a gregarious front man like Jimmie Mattern to create publicity and raise money.

Plus, of course, Jimmie had the plane, and, as Benny well knew, a first-class plane, easily one of the most efficient and reliable airplanes available at that time—a Lockheed Vega with a Pratt & Whitney Wasp engine. So right from the get-go Benny took the rear seat and let Jimmie call (most of) the shots. Benny was secure in his aviation abilities and knew exactly what skills and expertise he brought to the mission.

Other traits that made Griffin and Mattern a great team were their enormous respect for one another, their mutual courage, and the unspoken fact that they trusted each other implicitly. Setting off on an around-the-world flight in a single-engine airplane was not something you took lightly or did with just anyone. Both men had been flying long enough to know that trouble while in flight was inevitable. Bad weather, low fuel, oil pressure too high or too low, faulty instruments, illness, engine malfunction, lousy navigation—any or all of these scenarios, plus the entirely unexpected, could upset a flight at any time. The longer the flight, the greater the chance for mishap. Benny and Jimmie knew the best way to combat these dangerous scenarios was to take to the air with a copilot you fully and unreservedly trusted.

If any pilot in America focused more on pre-flight preparation than Jimmie Mattern, it was absolutely Bennett Griffin. Benny had quite rightly marveled at the exceptional preparation shown by Post and Gatty for their successful around-the-world flight. He convinced Jimmie early on that what they had in mind was first and foremost a business proposition. Yes, a great aviation adventure awaited them—no question about that. It would be the journey of a lifetime. And if they succeeded, they would most assuredly be hailed as heroes. All of this Benny knew and embraced. But the flying would be almost an afterthought. To succeed, they needed to prepare. And to prepare properly, they needed funding. They weren't flying anywhere without a substantial influx of money. And to raise money, Benny insisted, they needed to act like businessmen, not like a couple of fly-by-night flyboys.

Jimmie, worked up, ready to hit the skies and fly into the wild blue yonder, didn't want to hear about the boring business side of the mission. But on this matter, the older man held sway. Benny convinced Jimmie a little patience now would pay great benefits later.

"I hear you," said Jimmie, "but when do we fly?"

"Not for a while, Jim. June at the earliest."

"June?! That's six months from now, Benny! I'm ready to fly now!"

"No, you're not. And you know it. We both know there's a whole lot more to this than just fueling up and taking off."

"Okay, I know, but six months?"

"At least. There's no end of things to do, Jim. You'll see. Plus we want summer weather with plenty of daylight and warm temperatures."

Jimmie gave in to the older and wiser man's discretions, and soon thereafter he realized the extent of the preparation needed to make the trip a reality. They divided the various chores between them. Post and Gatty had taken off on their around-the-world adventure from Floyd Bennett Field on Long Island, so Jimmie and Benny decided to do the same. It made sense to fly over the Atlantic at the start of the trip, when both pilots and their aircraft were in fine fiddle, and fly across North America at the end of the trip, when pilots and plane were running on empty.

They flew the Vega from Texas to New York, leased a hangar at the airfield, and hired Fred Fetterman as their head mechanic. The three men spent several days together carefully going over the airplane and determining what needed upgrading and approximating what the upgrades would cost. Jimmie's Vega was a single-cockpit plane, so a second cockpit was a prerequisite. Instruments would be needed for the second cockpit and, if they could find the money, additional instruments added to the original cockpit. They'd need to install several additional tanks to carry the fuel necessary to cross the Atlantic and the vast distances across Siberia. The Pratt & Whitney Wasp engine needed a major overhaul. The landing gear needed beefing up to handle the extra weight. A second oil tank would be an excellent safety precaution. And finally, Fetterman believed the Vega should have a fore-and-aft communication system so Jimmie and Benny could converse during the flight.

"Trying to shout over all the wind and engine noise," Fred told the boys, "just won't get the job done."

"It all sounds pretty darn expensive," said Jimmie.

"I'd estimate twenty to twenty-five grand," said Fred Fetterman.

"Twenty to twenty-five grand?!"

"Easy. Adding a cockpit and instruments ain't exactly child's play, young fella."

"I hear you, Fred, but that's more than double the dough I paid for the whole damn airplane."

Fred Fetterman was a no-nonsense guy who was not only a first-class aviation mechanic but also an accomplished pilot. He spit a stream of tobacco juice into the spittoon in the corner and took a long look at the young aviator. "Son, you're not looking for Mr. Griffin to be your passenger. You want him to fly that airplane from the rear seat."

"That's the idea."

CHAPTER THIRTEEN

"Well, that cockpit and the necessary instruments and the fuel tanks and the overhaul of the Wasp engine, it's practically like building yourself a brand-new airplane. If you plan to fly around the world, Jimmie, you want to feel like you can rely on your equipment." And he spit another stream of juice.

Jimmie rubbed his chin and scratched his ear and looked at Benny.

Benny said, "Number sounds about right to me, Jim."

"Aw, hell."

"Plus you can likely drop ten grand or more on top of that to secure landing privileges, attain all the proper documents, purchase fuel, and just general expenses."

Jimmie shook his head. "You boys are taking all the fun out of this. And where are we gonna find thirty or forty grand with the economy mired in this depression?"

Benny shrugged. "It's all part of the preparation, Jim. No way around it. Raising money, my friend, is a big part of the pre-flight planning."

Benny stayed in New York with Fred and the airplane. He was tasked with overseeing all the mechanical work and making travel arrangements. The boys wouldn't just one day climb aboard and fly off. They had to plot their route and map out an itinerary. Airport managers across Canada, Europe, Asia, and North America needed to know the boys were coming. Their airplane, after all, would need refueling. The oil would need changing and the engine servicing. Jimmie and Benny would want to land where they knew they could count on assistance. This all took a great deal of communication and organization.

Most of this work fell to Benny. A highly organized individual, these duties fit squarely in his wheelhouse. He purchased maps and plotted the route. He wrote letters, sent cables, wrote more letters. He made calculations. He determined how far the Vega could fly when fully loaded with fuel and where the nearest airports and landing strips would be when the fuel ran low. Additionally, he had to contact embassies, apply for visas, inquire about flyover rules and regulations. Only the Soviet Union had flyover limitations. The USSR was the first country in history to claim the skies above their country as sovereign territory.

Benny patiently filled out forms and sent off all the appropriate paperwork. It took time, but permission was finally granted. It came, however, with several qualifications. The Americans would be restricted to specific Soviet airspace and they would only be allowed to land, refuel, and seek mechanical assistance at a few designated airports. Benny had to adjust their flight path because of these restrictions. He feared if he pressed for changes, the Soviet government, then in the hands of Joseph Stalin, might deny them access entirely.

Relations between the United States and the decade-old Soviet Union were not exactly stellar at that time. The Hoover administration had thus far refused to recognize the legitimacy of the communist state, which made dealings difficult for Americans doing business in the USSR.

Jimmie set up shop at the Sherman House Hotel in Chicago. The Sherman, built by the father of famed Civil War general William Tecumseh Sherman, was one of Chicago's swankier hotels, but Jimmie thought the extra cash worth it as he wanted to present a prosperous front. He entertained potential investors at the hotel, and staying at some fleabag joint would offer a second-rate impression. Benny wasn't too sure about this tactic, but he kept his trap shut. Especially after Jimmie started landing some very formidable backers like Clarence Page, the legendary World War I aviator from Oklahoma.

James Joseph "Jimmie" Mattern, good-looking with his dark-blonde wavy hair, dapper in an expensive wool and cashmere suit, and toting an aviation résumé a mile and a half long, made an excellent impression. Whether in the luxurious lobby of the Sherman, the headquarters of Standard Oil in New York, the offices of Pratt & Whitney in Ohio, or the executive dining room of the Bendix Corporation in South Bend, Indiana, Jimmie played the role of the swashbuckling aviator to the hilt. He made those CEOs and corporate execs feel like they were lucky gentlemen indeed to have the once-in-a-lifetime opportunity to participate in the around-the-world aviation adventure of Jimmie Mattern and Benny Griffin.

Ed Aldrin of Standard Oil liked Jimmie from the moment they first shook hands. He liked the young man's confidence and swagger. It fell just shy of arrogance and convinced Aldrin that Mattern might just possess the right stuff to make his flight a success. He also thought Mattern would make an excellent spokesman for Standard Oil. Ed promised Jimmie he would assist with both money and manpower. The two formed a friendship that would last a lifetime.

Executives at Pratt & Whitney and at Bendix felt the same way about young Mattern. He was a likeable guy, a solid midwesterner, and obviously one of the most accomplished pilots in the country. If anyone could beat the Post/Gatty around-the-world time, it was this kid from Texas by way of Illinois. They wanted their products associated with his ground-breaking pursuits—and okay, also with his handsome and rugged good looks.

Corporate money started to roll in and soon thereafter the Vega began its transformation into a two-man, globe-circling flying machine. By the time the winter of '32 turned to spring, the little Lockheed carried a dual cockpit and two modern instrument panels. "Modern" in 1932 was a relative term, but at least the airplane was now equipped with a fully functional compass and a turn and bank indicator, which communicated to the pilot the plane's rate, or degree, of turn. Prior to the inclusion of a turn and bank indicator, pilots relied on feel and on objects along the horizon to gauge whether their plane was flying straight or yawing to port or starboard.

The addition of the compass and the turn and bank indicator made it possible for Jimmie and Benny to "fly blind," or "fly on instruments." This was a bit of an overstatement, but it did make navigating a whole lot easier, especially at night and in thick clouds.

In early June, Jimmie and Benny flew down to Texas to take lessons in "flying blind" with pilots in the Air Corps. They spent a week with their old flying pals and quickly learned the nuances of the new instruments. They did some night flying and some foul-weather flying, and both agreed the compass and the turn and bank indicator would prove helpful, especially over open water and the Arctic tundra, where it was tough to get a bead on the horizon.

Back in New York, Jimmie, Benny, and Fred went over their flight plans one last time. It felt as though all their preparation had come together. All the mechanical and structural upgrades on the Lockheed monoplane had been completed, the engine overhauled and fuel tanks added.

The Vega even had a brand-new red-and-white paint job and a new name painted across her fuselage. They had christened her *Century of Progress*. The name was a paid promotion for the Chicago World's Fair, due to open the following spring, but it also perfectly expressed Jimmie and Benny's belief that air transportation would change the world in ways few inventions had done since man first dreamed of soaring with the eagles.

The *Century of Progress* and its two eager pilots were ready to fly.

CHAPTER FOURTEEN

July 5-6, 1932

They planned to take off on Independence Day, but bad weather and a mechanical malfunction with the wobble pump kept the boys grounded. No problem. Jimmie entertained the dozens of reporters who had gathered from all over the country to witness the departure of the *Century of Progress*. Deep into the night, Jimmie regaled them with tales of stunt flying for Howard Hughes and hauling baby chicks to Mexico and landing on lava beds in the remote wilderness of the Yukon. Young Mattern was a natural raconteur.

Finally, around midnight, he retired to his hotel room, only to be awakened a few hours later by his good friend Benny, who had gone to bed early and was now ready to fly. By 4:00 a.m. they were back at the airfield, and by 4:30, the first faint traces of an orange dawn exploding over the Atlantic, the boys had donned their flight suits and climbed up the fuselage of the *Century of Progress*.

Benny gave a friendly wave to the reporters and the hundred or so members of the public who had gathered to see them off. A wave and a smile and then he wedged his lean body into the rear cockpit.

Jimmie, of course, turned the departure into a bit more of a show.

"With a little luck," he called, "and some exceptional flyin', Benny and I'll be right back here at Floyd Bennett Field in a few days. Okay, maybe more than a few, but a whole lot less than eight days, fifteen hours, and fifty-one minutes"—a reference to the time it had taken Wiley Post and Harold Gatty to complete their around-the-world flight a year earlier. Then Jimmie gave one last wave, climbed into the forward cockpit, took a deep breath, and secured the hatch. The time had come to put his bird in the sky.

With nearly 350 pounds of men and several hundred gallons of fuel on board, the boys needed every inch of runway to get the *Century of Progress* airborne. Once aloft, Jimmie circled the airfield, dipped a wing in salutation, and headed northeast over Long Island, across Long Island Sound, and up the coast of New England.

To communicate, Jimmie and Benny spoke into Fred Fetterman's one-inch rubber tube that ran between the two cockpits. It was a basic tube with a cone on each end, but it worked pretty well as long as the boys shouted. Even then, they had to repeat themselves often; plenty of words got garbled and lost, especially with so much engine and wind noise. But they both had to admit that without the tube, it would have been virtually impossible to communicate.

The skies remained clear and the winds light out of the southeast right up over Rhode Island and into Massachusetts. As they passed over Boston, the winds shifted and pushed the Vega to the east. Jimmie momentarily lost sight of land and saw nothing out in front of him but blue sea and a deep blue sky.

A strange feeling passed over him, a kind of fluttering that spilled from his head and rippled down his spine. All that ocean soon to cross, he thought, with no land in sight.

It dawned on him at that moment—he had never really flown over open water before.

Sure, he'd flown over the Gulf of Mexico and up over the Bering Sea and a couple of times over the Great Lakes. But always land had been visible, in plain sight. And that's when he realized the feeling passing through his body, the fluttering along his spine, was trepidation. Apprehension. Maybe even a touch of good old-fashioned fear.

Jimmie thought about saying something to Benny. Benny, after all, had flown solo over the Pacific during his attempt to reach Hawaii. Surely Benny would be able to relate to what Jimmie was experiencing. But in the end

CHAPTER FOURTEEN

Jimmie kept quiet, didn't say a word. He would overcome this sudden case of nerves on his own. He would sound no alarm.

The stretch of open water from Boston to the southwest coast of Nova Scotia tested young Mattern's resilience. He definitely experienced anxiety. It not only manifested itself physically with perspiration on his brow and a racing heart, but emotionally he couldn't stop thinking about what would happen if the engine failed or the oil pump suddenly malfunctioned. Over solid ground, they would simply land. But over water . . .

These dire scenarios led Jimmie to once again consider his mother and wife.

Upon learning of his great adventure, Cleo had been brave. She had wished him well and assured him she would pray many times a day for his safe return.

Della, on the other hand, still up in Walla Walla, had barely uttered a word when Jimmie told her he intended to fly around the world. When he tried to tell her about the trip and the countries he would cross and the amazing things he would see, his wife had offered little in response. And when he asked if she would be willing to speak with the press about the trip, Della had, after a long pause, reluctantly agreed to play the part of the anxious but supportive wife.

Thinking about it now at three thousand feet over the Atlantic, land nowhere in sight, completely and utterly alone despite Benny just a few feet to the rear, Jimmie, a man possessed of great courage and solid self-confidence, felt profoundly isolated. He felt like he could just as easily be traveling through another solar system, an entirely different galaxy. It was a kind of out-of-body experience for a man typically grounded in reality. And definitely another experience he knew he would never share with Benny, or anyone else.

Jimmie decided right then and there that he would permit himself these occasional moments of doubt, fear, and rumination. To entirely deny them, after all, would be foolish. But outwardly he would project only optimism, conviction, and self-control.

They reached Nova Scotia and passed over Halifax with the skies still clear and a tailwind pushing them nicely to the northeast. Soon they passed over Cape Breton Island and once again struck out over open water.

Jimmie felt a bit more comfortable now as he knew St. John's, Newfoundland, and their first refueling stop lay just a couple hundred miles to the north. But as they approached the southwest coast of Newfoundland, a dense fog bank rose up out of the Atlantic and quickly engulfed their small plane.

For nearly three hours, the *Century of Progress* flew in circles, waiting for the fog to lift. Jimmie could again feel the anxiety rippling through his body as they flew through the fog and the minutes slowly passed.

Behind him, in the aft seat, all was calm and quiet.

Finally, with less than an hour's worth of fuel left in the tanks and flying at an altitude under five hundred feet, the ground fog began to dissipate.

"Railroad tracks at three o'clock!" Benny shouted through the rubber tube.

Jimmie glanced out the starboard window and spotted the track almost directly below. They followed that trusty iron compass right up into St. John's and soon found the Harbour Grace Airfield a mile or so northwest of town.

Rarely in his flying career had Jimmie been so happy to see a runway.

The airstrip proved little more than a dirt, rock-strewn field, but no matter. It had plenty of length, and Jimmie soon had the little Lockheed back on the ground.

A hundred or more Newfoundlanders rushed forward when the *Century of Progress* landed and taxied over to the small terminal for refueling. The boys climbed out, stretched their stiff bodies, and shook hands all around.

Jimmie beamed as the questions flew and the flashbulbs popped. Not for one second would anyone have imagined the young aviator in possession of anything but courage and confidence. He seemed not to carry an ounce of doubt or fear in his trim, lively body.

"Where are you headed?" the crowd asked.

"Around the world!" Jimmie answered.

"In that little plane?"

"Yup, in that little plane."

"How long will it take you?"

"About the same time it took God to create the world."

"A week?"

"Faster, if we can find some tailwinds."

Benny supervised the refueling and various engine checks while Jimmie went into town for a visit with the customs officer and to send a few cables back to reporters in New York. He did not tarry, however, as those lost hours in the fog needed making up if they wanted to better the mark set by Post and Gatty.

Less than two hours after landing, the boys were back in their cockpits and ready to fly. The *Century of Progress* now had its fuel tanks filled to the brim, which meant the fuel onboard weighed more than the plane itself. Back in New York, Benny and Jimmie had discussed this exact situation with Fred Fetterman for hours. They didn't need to discuss it anymore. The Vega would either get off the ground or it wouldn't.

The runway ran slightly downhill. Jimmie built up power by pushing the throttle all the way forward. Slowly, the *Century of Progress* increased its speed. A thousand feet of runway sped past, 2,000 feet, 3,000 feet, 3,500 feet—finally, the nose lifted—4,000 feet, and with literally no more runway to spare, that flying fuel tank swept up into the sky over Newfoundland. Seconds later, she vanished into another bank of fog.

The distance from Newfoundland to Ireland is about twice the distance from New York to Newfoundland. And every inch of those two thousand miles is over open water. Nothing between the coast of Newfoundland and the coast of Ireland but the ice-cold North Atlantic. And nothing between the boys at four thousand feet and those cold, dark waters but their single-engine, high-wing Lockheed monoplane. It was not a journey for the faint of heart.

As of July 5, 1932, only a handful of transatlantic flights had been attempted, and even fewer had ended successfully. Englishmen John Alcock and Arthur Brown were the first to cross by aircraft back in 1919. In 1927, Charles Lindbergh became the first to cross solo. Amelia Earhart was the first woman to solo. She had flown from St. John's, Newfoundland, to Londonderry, Ireland, back in May, just a couple months before Jimmie and Benny's flight.

The *Century of Progress* flew due east through the fog and leveled off at six thousand feet. Jimmie considered climbing higher in search of clear skies, but he knew the engine, carrying all that fuel, would lose horsepower and burn more gas at higher altitudes.

Darkness arrived. The fog persisted. The boys relied on their compass, their artificial horizon gauge, and their turn and bank indicator to maintain a reasonably steady course. Every few minutes they needed to check their coordinates, as the plane had no autopilot. This was the essence of blind flying, with thick fog and a pitch-black night.

Jimmie could hear the propeller spinning a few feet beyond his windshield, but he could not see it.

The hours passed slowly. Jimmie and Benny took turns dozing, but neither of them actually drifted off to sleep. The harsh whine of the engine, the turbulence tossing the airplane about like a cork upon a stormy sea, the endless thoughts stewing in their heads—all combined to keep the boys awake. Jimmie felt a powerful ache of loneliness, but the fear and apprehension he had experienced earlier had mostly passed. He had faith in his plane. He had faith in Benny. And maybe, most of all, Jimmie had faith in himself. But still, the loneliness was palpable. It tugged at his heart as feelings of disquiet swept over him.

None of these emotions, however, kept Jimmie from flying his airplane. He never for a moment lost sight of the mission. All through the night, despite no natural navigational aids, he tracked a true and steady course across the North Atlantic.

And eventually, a new dawn broke, the fog dissipated, and for the first time since leaving the coast of Newfoundland, the boys could see the ocean below. They descended under one thousand feet and soon Benny shouted into the tube, "Boat to port!"

Jimmie looked out the port window and spotted a small fishing skiff. The size of the boat and its apparent shallow draft made him certain land could not be far off. They had been flying, after all, for more than thirteen hours and averaging close to 150 mph.

CHAPTER FOURTEEN

Jimmie took the *Century of Progress* down to just above the surface of the sea. They flew by the skiff and shouted, "Which way to Ireland?"

The two fishermen on board shouted back, but no matter how many passes Jimmie made and no matter how loud the men shouted, the exchange of information proved impossible. After some amount of time, Jimmie dipped a wing in salute and headed east.

Within minutes they spotted land, and after consulting their maps concluded they had hit the Irish coast almost precisely where they had planned. It was a dandy piece of navigation accompanied by a bit of the Irish luck, as some of Benny's ancestors had hailed from that island country.

The boys, weary but exhilarated, briefly discussed looking for a place to land, but they soon dismissed the idea. They were now a couple hours ahead of the Post/Gatty flight time and they still had plenty of fuel.

"Fly on!" Benny shouted into the tube.

They flew on. They flew across Ireland, passed directly over Belfast, and then out over the Irish Sea. They flew by the Isle of Man, reached the coast of England, and swept over Great Britain along the border of England and Scotland.

All the fear and loneliness vanished from Jimmie's thoughts. His heart pounded inside his chest, but the pounding came now from sheer exhilaration. He could hardly believe he was suddenly flying over Great Britain!

"Berlin or bust!" he shouted into the tube.

"Verdammt recht!" Benny shouted back.

As they approached the North Sea, the weather, which had cooperated for the past few hours, once again closed in with rain and heavy fog. Visibility dropped to near zero. Jimmie flew so close to the surface of the sea that white caps splashed across the landing gear. It was the only way he could maintain any kind of visual acuity.

But then, out of the gloom, a giant ocean liner appeared dead ahead.

Jimmie pulled back on the stick, shoved the throttle forward to gain speed, and banked hard left, nearly throwing the little Vega into a rollover. Had her fuel tanks not been so close to empty, the *Century of Progress* surely would have crashed into the towering funnels of that ship.

The boys needed several minutes to recover their wits after the trauma. Jimmie climbed to six thousand feet where the fog remained thick and soupy, but at least the likelihood of smashing into something was highly diminished.

Navigating now to the southeast, they soon found themselves once again over land. The fog lifted; the Vega descended. The landscape was dotted with windmills.

"Holland!" Benny shouted into the tube.

"We've reached the mainland!"

"Absolutely. Unless we're flying in circles!"

Again they discussed landing for rest and refueling and again they dismissed the idea. They knew a world-record time between New York and Berlin was easily within their grasp. Berlin could not be more than four hundred miles, a few more hours flying at most. They definitely had sufficient fuel to make it. Plus, the weather had improved dramatically with no fog, some high cloud cover, and just a light drizzle.

They agreed to fly on.

Just over an hour later they reached the outskirts of a large city. Too soon to be Berlin, they decided, and circled in search of an airport. Soon they spotted a runway and then the terminal. Atop the terminal, in large block letters, it read: HANOVER.

Jimmie handed control of the airplane over to Benny and studied his map of Germany. He quickly ascertained Berlin was less than 150 miles due east. Another hour of flying and they could put the *Century of Progress* back on the ground and have themselves a proper meal and some much-needed rest.

But before Jimmie could put his map away, more weather swept over the airplane. A massive black cloud filled the sky and out of it exploded peals of thunder and strikes of lightning. Rain fell in great torrents. In all his years of flying, Jimmie had never, not even down in West Texas, been caught up in such a terrible storm.

Jimmie shouted into the tube. He shouted and shouted. He received no reply. Or at least he could hear no reply over the tumult.

CHAPTER FOURTEEN

The plane lurched. The plane rocked. The high winds pulled the plane higher, and moments later shoved it back down. Jimmie fought to maintain control of his airplane. But even as he battled, even as he applied all his years of experience as a pilot, he began to fear the little Lockheed could not possibly survive such a tempest.

It might all end here, he feared, almost twenty hours out of Newfoundland, with just a few miles left to reach Tempelhof airfield in Berlin.

CHAPTER FIFTEEN

July 6-7, 1932

Off to the south, Jimmie thought he saw a patch of blue sky. He pushed the throttle forward and headed in that direction. Within minutes he had piloted the *Century of Progress* clear of the monster thunderstorm. But he had also drifted off course and wasn't absolutely sure of their whereabouts. Still, better momentarily lost than dead, so for the next half hour the Vega flew in circles over the Brandenburg countryside while the storm wore itself out.

Once it did, Jimmie got his bearings and made for Berlin. And really none too soon, as the Vega's fuel tanks were rapidly running dry.

By the time they reached Tempelhof airfield southeast of the German capital, the rain had returned, but thankfully the thunder and lightning had pushed off to the north. Jimmie circled the field a couple of times to get his bearings and determine the wind direction and the condition of the runway. He spotted a large crowd outside the terminal.

"Hey, Benny," he shouted into the tube, "you see all the people down there?"

"I see 'em, Jim," Benny called back in a barely audible voice.

"You okay?" Jimmie asked.

"Looking forward to some fresh air," Benny replied.

Jimmie hoped his copilot was okay. Benny's voice sounded weak and he hadn't said much for the past couple hours. Maybe the long haul from St. John's had taken its toll.

Jimmie banked, lined up with the runway, and put the *Century of Progress* back on the ground after more than twenty hours in the air. The grass field (paved runways were nearly nonexistent in Europe at that time) was soft and spongy from all the rain, but they landed safely and taxied over to the small brick terminal building.

More than two hundred people stood in the rain to greet the two American fliers. Relations between the United States and Germany were cordial, if still strained, more than a decade after the end of the Great War. Hitler had not yet come to power. But politics notwithstanding, the two countries had a powerful emotional bond. Hundreds of thousands of Germans, after all, had immigrated to America over the past 250 years. Americans possessed more German blood than any other nationality. Plus, of course, James Joseph Mattern was half German, as his father, Philip Mattern, had been born and reared in Mannheim before moving with his parents to the United States back in 1883.

Jimmie shut down the engine and pulled open the cockpit hatch. Stiff and exhausted, he nevertheless smiled broadly to the cheering crowd as he stepped down onto the wheel and then to the ground. This was the first nonstop flight in history between North America and Berlin.

As he stood waving to the crowd, Jimmie realized Benny was taking a lot of time to exit the rear cockpit. Finally, Benny appeared. He moved sluggishly. His face looked ghostly white. Jimmie went aft to give his friend a hand.

"You all right, buddy? You look like hell."

Benny grabbed onto Jimmie's arm. "I've felt better, old boy, I can tell you that."

"What's the problem?"

"Gas fumes. Feeling a little woozy."

"Damn, Ben, you didn't say a word."

"Not much to say."

The rear cockpit of the Vega was literally surrounded by fuel tanks. For hours Benny had sat in that cramped little seat, breathing gas fumes with every inhalation. There were no sliding windows in the rear pit and Benny had feared if he opened the hatch during flight to pull in some fresh air, it might rip right off its hinges. So, stoic Irishman that he was, Benny had done his best to cope and never once had he complained.

They found a doctor in the crowd. The doctor led Benny to a private room in the terminal, gave him some deep breathing exercises to help clear the fumes, and ordered someone to fetch an oxygen cannister. For more than an hour, Benny rested on a cot while filling his lungs with pure, clean oxygen.

Slowly, he recovered.

While Benny rested, Jimmie supervised the refueling and servicing of the airplane. He also had a mechanic install a simple air vent in the rear cockpit that guaranteed Benny a steady supply of fresh air for the remainder of the trip.

The Vega again ready to fly, Jimmie took some time to eat and talk with the press. He gave a lengthy account of their transatlantic flight with a heavy emphasis on all the dangers, difficulties, and bad weather they had overcome. The endless fog over the Atlantic, the cruise ship encounter on the North Sea, and the ferocious thunderstorm over Germany made excellent storytelling fodder that needed no embellishment.

That evening and the following morning, Jimmie's account of his and Benny's flight from New York to Berlin, accompanied by a photograph of Jimmie smiling next to his airplane, appeared in newspapers all over the world. There was tremendous interest in aviation, especially in the exploits of young aviators like Lindbergh, Earhart, and Post. The fact that Jimmie Mattern was a handsome guy with a golden tongue made his story even more intriguing to both the press and the public. His smiling face on the front page sold newspapers.

Back home—in Vancouver, British Columbia, and Walla Walla, Washington—members of the press camped outside the homes of Jimmie's mother and wife. Cleo and Della endured endless inquiries from ambitious reporters. These reporters wanted to know how the women were holding up under the strain of Jimmie's around-the-world flight. But they also wanted to know all kinds of other stuff that had nothing to do with flying. They wanted to know about Jimmie's boyhood. They wanted to know if he was a good son. A good husband. They asked the women what movies they'd seen recently and what they liked to eat for breakfast. They asked about fashion and politics.

They asked the ladies if they followed baseball and if they preferred Babe Ruth or Lou Gehrig. When the women asked the reporters why they were asking so many silly questions, the reporters just laughed and said the public was interested in anything and everything the wife and mother of Jimmie Mattern had to say.

Back in Berlin, the time had come to go. Jimmie awoke from a short snooze, and Benny's head had finally cleared. The weather looked good all the way to Moscow. Sure, Jimmie had enjoyed his time with the press, but if the boys intended to break that Post/Gatty record, they needed to get back in the air and keep flying.

Minutes before takeoff, out of the blue, Jimmie was informed they would need to alter their original flight path to Moscow. They had intended to fly east to Warsaw, cross the border at Brest, then head northeast to the capital city. This flight path had been submitted to and approved by emissaries of the Soviet government weeks earlier. Now, suddenly, for reasons not explained, the boys were ordered to fly northeast out of Berlin for Gdansk, pass through Lithuanian airspace, enter the USSR east of Vilnius, then set a course for Moscow.

This change lengthened the Berlin-Moscow leg by almost 150 miles, but more importantly, for Jimmie anyway, the change made absolutely no sense. He thought maybe something was getting lost in translation, as the course change was being ordered by a Soviet military officer who spoke Russian to a German pilot who then translated into English. Jimmie asked that the order please be repeated.

The translation came back exactly the same.

Jimmie right away was ticked off. He was a clear-headed and rational thinker who preferred reason over emotion, but this last-second course change was absurd. He demanded clarification of the order.

A third time it came back the same.

Jimmie got right up in the man's face. "Listen, pal, I want to know who the hell is issuing this stupid order."

CHAPTER FIFTEEN

The Soviet officer countered with a sneer, then enunciated, slowly, in decent English, "Fly your little airplane where I tell you or you will be shot out of the sky."

Benny quickly stepped forward. He calmed Jimmie down, convinced him the change was nothing but a minor inconvenience, an extra hour at most. He then reminded his friend they were still hours ahead of Post/Gatty.

Jimmie, the younger and definitely more volatile man, seethed but submitted.

They took off and set the course dictated by the Soviet army officer. The boys knew it was just politics. America refused to diplomatically recognize the Soviet state, so in retaliation Moscow obviously had decided to give the American aviators a hard time.

"It's nothing to do with us, Jim!" Benny shouted into the tube. "No use getting all crazy and worked up over it."

"Damn politicians!" Jimmie shouted back.

"Not even worth thinking about!"

"Maybe not but it's got my dander up."

"I can see that."

"Hey, Ben?" called Jimmie.

"Yeah?"

"If we stay healthy and fly clean with no mechanical problems, we're gonna beat Post and Gatty by a mile! I calculate if all goes well, we could complete this flight in under six days. Beat their mark by forty-eight hours!"

"Let's not get ahead of ourselves, Jim. One leg at a time! Long way to go!"

They flew on through the darkness, their second night in the air. Unlike their foggy first night over the Atlantic, this one offered nothing but clear skies and light tailwinds; as a bonus, a nearly full moon hung directly over the airplane.

They had left Berlin just before 6:00 p.m. with the hope of reaching Moscow, a distance of approximately 1,200 miles, sometime around three or four in the morning. Just after midnight, by their calculations, they crossed the border where Poland, Lithuania, and the USSR intersect.

"Making good time!" Benny shouted into the tube.

"Long as we don't get shot down!" Jimmie shouted back.

The next few minutes passed uneventfully. Jimmie felt sleepy and thought about handing control over to Benny so he could take a quick catnap. But then he thought, No way, it's a beautiful night. I don't want to miss a minute of it.

The moon shone brightly and lit up the rolling landscape below. Jimmie knew he was a very lucky man to find himself in this place at this time. He needed to appreciate every single second of the journey and give thanks for his tremendous good fortune.

That's when the plane began to vibrate.

Jimmie felt the vibration and thought maybe he was just dreaming.

But no, he was wide awake.

Jimmie felt it again. The plane vibrated, and somewhere aft he heard an odd humming. Both the sensation and the sound were new to the *Century of Progress*. Jimmie had never experienced either of them before.

And then he heard a strange noise coming from directly overhead.

He glanced up at the exact second his cockpit hatch flew open and broke free.

A cold, harsh wind blew through the cramped cabin, and an instant later Jimmie heard the glass and metal hatch smash into the tail of the airplane.

The Vega shuddered and wobbled. Jimmie feared the vertical stabilizer fin had likely been damaged or maybe even knocked entirely off the aircraft.

Benny yelled into the tube. Jimmie yelled back. But they couldn't hear a word the other man shouted. There was too much turbulence, too much engine noise.

The plane started to jump all over the sky. Fuel sloshed back and forth in the tanks, causing the Vega to roll and jump even more. Jimmie knew he needed to immediately descend to a lower altitude and find a place to land.

Both men stayed cool. They didn't panic. Benny kept Jimmie apprised of their altitude while Jimmie searched for a place to put down the airplane.

That big white moon provided plenty of illumination. Jimmie spotted an open field dotted with haystacks.

"Three hundred feet!" shouted Benny.

"Coming around and putting her down!" Jimmie shouted back.

CHAPTER FIFTEEN

"Two hundred feet!"

The Vega rolled from side to side and the nose kept wanting to dive, but Jimmie held the airplane together with a steady hand on the stick and both his feet working feverishly to maintain control of the rudder pedals.

"One hundred feet!"

The ground came up fast, the tires bounced a couple of times, and then the plane settled and rolled out, slowly.

It finally came to a stop near the edge of the hay field.

They'd made it. They were down. Safely. Crisis averted. Jimmie even had time to think to himself, *We'll repair the damage and be on our way to Moscow in no time.*

But a second later the tail of the airplane began to rise.

"What the hell!" Jimmie shouted.

The tail went up and the nose of the Vega went straight down. For several seconds the plane teetered there with its nose buried in the Russian soil. And then, practically in slow motion, the fine and splendid *Century of Progress* unceremoniously flipped over onto its back.

And seconds later broke in two.

PHOTO ALBUM

Jimmie Mattern, age 3

The Mattern family in 1914 (nine-year-old Jimmie is in front).

The Matterns in the 1950s. Back row: Jimmie and Gertrude; front row: Phil, Cleo, and Roy.

In 1922, around the time Jimmie enlisted in the U.S. Army and became a private first class in the 7th Infantry Regiment. He was not yet seventeen, so he fudged a bit when the recruiter asked him his age.

Jimmie's first flight was in the rear cockpit of a JN-4 "Jenny," at the age of 22.

PHOTO ALBUM

Jimmie's first airplane, a Waco 10 with a Curtiss OX-5 engine, cost $2,625.

Jimmie and other stunt pilots perform dangerous aerial maneuvers in the Howard Hughes war movie *Hell's Angels*.

Jimmie shows off a brand-new Stinson Detroiter cargo plane in Brownsville, Texas.

Jimmie (left) and Carl Cromwell, owner of Cromwell Airlines, with a Stinson SM-1. The ship held six passengers and was powered by a Pratt & Whitney R-1340 Wasp engine.

Jimmie, far right, and fellow aviators at the National Air Races in Cleveland, Ohio, 1930. Amelia Earhart is third from left.

Jimmie (above) performs a dangerous midair refueling to *The Texan* (below), a Benedum-Trees customized Lockheed 12. *Photo Credit: C. S. Heizner*

Jimmie (center, in white flight suit) and Benny Griffin arrive at Tempelhof airfield in Berlin, July 6, 1932—the first nonstop flight between North America and Berlin. They also broke the speed record, making the trip in 17 hours and 30 minutes.

Jimmie and Benny crash-land their Vega in a peat bog near Minsk, USSR, after the vertical stabilizer was damaged.

PHOTO ALBUM

After their release from the USSR, Jimmie and Benny talk to the press.

Standing between Jimmie and Benny is aviator and SS *Leviathan* crewmember E. N. Pickerill, a fellow pilot.

PHOTO ALBUM

On August 5, 1932, the luxury steamship *Leviathan* brought Jimmie and Benny home after their ordeal in the Soviet Union. Four planes piloted by U.S. Navy airmen welcomed the heroes home with a flyover in New York Harbor.

Left to right: Jimmie, Pres. Herbert Hoover, Benny, and Secretary of War Patrick J. Hurley at the White House, after the aviators' return from the JSSR.

Jimmie's *Century of Progress* (black) and Wiley Post's *Winnie Mae* sit next to each other at Floyd Bennett Field, before the aviators' attempts to solo around the world.

Newspapers all over the world kept track of Jimmie's route and schedule.

Cockpit controls of the *Century of Progress*.

Diagram of the *Century of Progress*. Note the number and location of gas tanks and the cockpit's small size.

PHOTO ALBUM

Jimmie Mattern and his one-of-a-kind Lockheed Vega at Floyd Bennett Field on Long Island, just prior to embarking on the first attempt to circumnavigate the globe solo.

Jimmie flies over New York City on June 3, 1933,
the first day of his historic flight around the world.

Jomfruland, Norway Landing spot. AFTER- Non-
Stop- Flight from Floyd Bennet Field, Brook
N.Y. June 3-4 1933-
First- Nonstop Flight from N.Y. to Norway
1st Lap on Jimmie Mattern's Solo World Flig
(First Time it ever was Attempted.
Mr. Lystad + His Horses. Pulling Lockheed
Across Island To Pasture For Take off. (0 sc
Then immediately To Moscow. (First Solo Flight
N.Y to Moscow. June 6, 1933.

PHOTO ALBUM

The Old World and the modern era come together as horses pull the *Century of Progress* off a rocky beach in Jomfruland, Norway, June 4, 1933.

When Jimmie needed to crash-land in Siberia, he recalled his error in Minsk the year before—the wheels had hit hard, nosing the plane into the ground and flipping it over. This time, Jimmie intentionally knocked the wheels off the plane before landing the ship on its belly, so he would not be trapped in the cockpit.

Headlines from around the world chronicled Jimmie's ill-fated journey.

PHOTO ALBUM

Jimmie with the grass hut he built for shelter while stranded on the Siberian tundra.

The two photos here and the following two were taken a week after Jimmie's rescue, when a small fleet of Soviet sailors took him back to the crash site to salvage gear from the *Century of Progress*.

Jimmie shows his bathing options while living with his local rescuers. He assured his Russian friends that he most certainly had not been smiling during his isolation.

Jimmie sports the warm local garb he was offered upon his rescue.

Jimmie was all smiles when he was able to reunite with the nomadic fur traders who rescued him.

Happy to be back on North American soil, Jimmie celebrates his safe arrival in Nome, Alaska, with Sigizmund Levanevsky, the famous Soviet pilot who flew him from Anadyr, Siberia.

PHOTO ALBUM

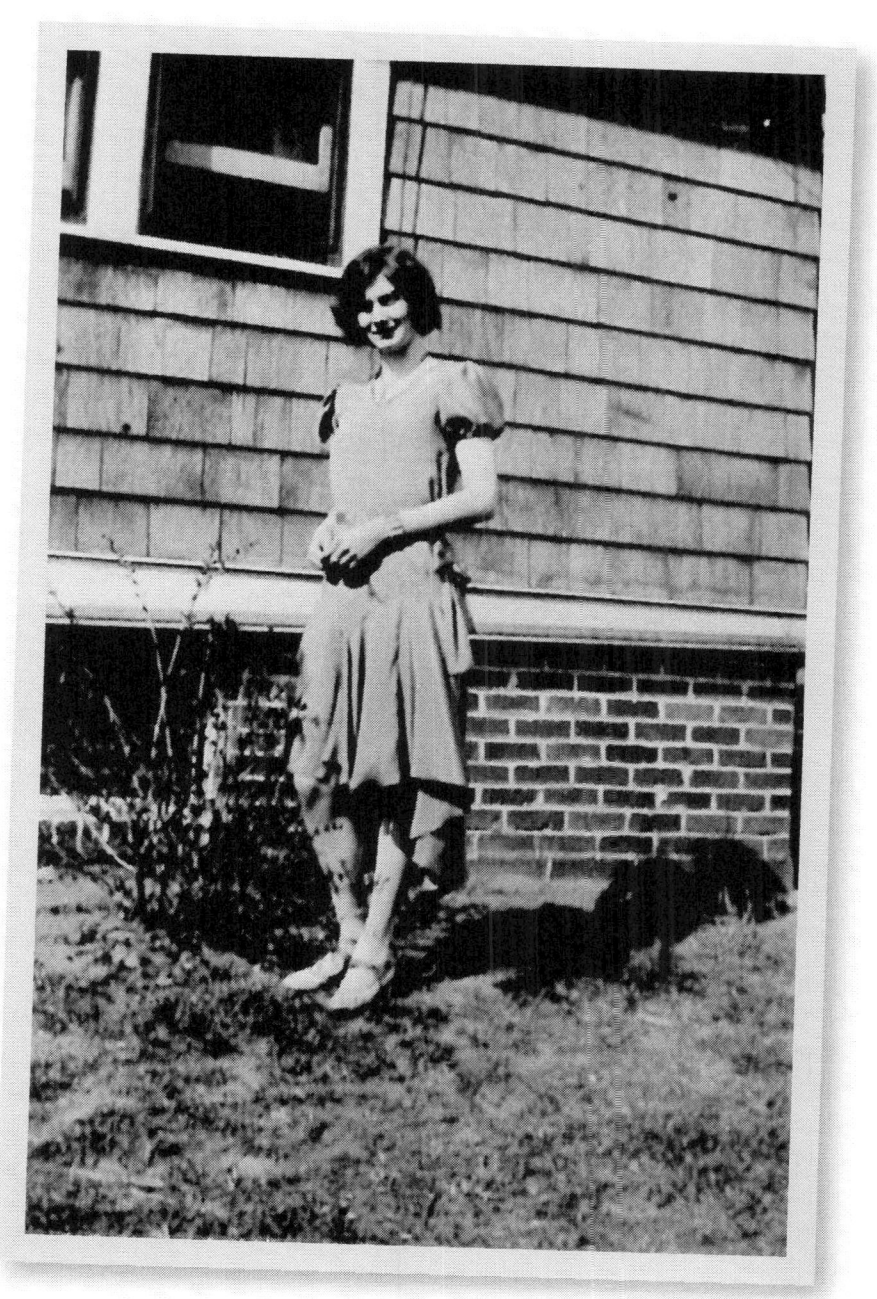

Dorothy Mattern, about 15, poses in front of her home in Des Moines, Iowa.

Jimmie gave this autographed photo to Dorothy a month after meeting her.

Dorothy's promotional photo for her dancing career.

PHOTO ALBUM

Dorothy shows off an exotic dance costume.

Jimmie and Dorothy on their wedding day, May 18, 1937, in Berwyn, Illinois. The happy couple forgot to get a marriage license and had to get one backdated at City Hall. Left to right: Billie Mills, Jimmie's best man; Jimmie; Dr. Clark, the minister; Dorothy; and Phyllis Stewart, matron of honor. Phyllis's husband, Russell Stewart, was editor of the *Chicago Sun-Times*.

Dorothy and Jimmie vacation in Miami, circa 1937.

The Matterns celebrate their 25th wedding anniversary. Dorothy's dress was made of Chinese silk brought to the United States by Pres. Abraham Lincoln's ambassador to China.

In the 1970s, Jimmie and Dorothy became franchise owners of the Ask Mr. Foster travel agency.

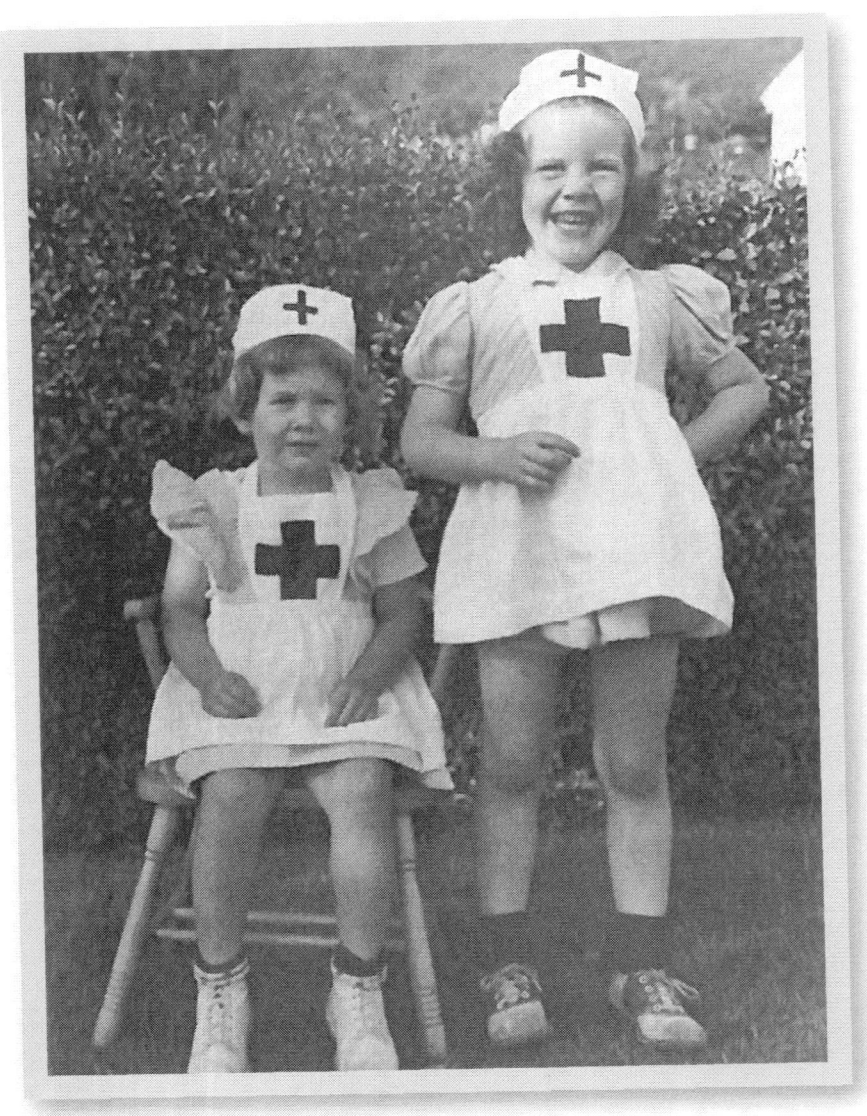

Jimmie's most important accomplishment: his daughters, Joy and Pattie. Here, the girls dress up as nurses.

Ten-month-old Joy and two-year-old Pattie.

The girls are delighted with their Christmas presents: two Corgi pups descended from Princess Elizabeth's Cardigan Welsh line, a gift to Jimmie from the Royal Air Force in London.

Jimmie, a self-taught musician, plays the organ at home for his girls. Joy is on the left, Pattie on the right.

Pattie Mattern, circa 1954, in front of Jimmie's first airplane, the Waco 10.

PHOTO ALBUM

Joy and her dad. Jimmie was always proud that Joy earned her pilot's license.

Jimmie flew all over the country in his Pure Oil Bellanca, making appearances and doing publicity for the company.
Photo credit: M. K. Aughenbaugh.

PHOTO ALBUM

Jimmie with Honey and Rusty, the Corgi puppies he received as a gift after he delivered a fighter jet to the RAF. Behind him is the Lockheed P-38 he used to train pilots via the "piggyback" method.

Jimmie Mattern (left) greets Charles Lindbergh in Brownsville, Texas, in 1928. Lindbergh was the world's most famous aviator by then, having made the first nonstop flight between New York and Paris the year before, at the age of 25.

Jimmie with Thomas Lanphier Jr., a colonel and fighter pilot during WWII who assisted in shooting down the plane carrying Admiral Yamamoto, commander in chief of the Japanese navy.

Back row, left to right: Bill Scarbrough, Dorothy, Jimmie, Steve Garrison.
Front, left to right: Pattie, Neil Armstrong, Joy.

Three of the Mercury 7 astronauts with Jimmie at the Beverly Hilton Hotel, 1963.
Left to right: John Glenn, Alan Shepard, Jimmie, Gus Grissom.

Jimmie with astronauts John Bull, Bill Anders, and Ronald Evans.

Chuck Yeager and Jimmie pal around at a gathering of aviators.

PHOTO ALBUM

SPIRIT OF '42—Gen. Jimmy Doolittle, right, and aviation pioneer Jimmie Mattern exchange stories at recent luncheon meeting of crop dusters on the Queen Mary (now a hotel) in Long Beach, Calif. Doolittle showed the spirit and charm that made him an American war hero. He led the bombing run over Tokyo in 1942.

Longtime friends Jimmie and Gen. Jimmy Doolittle chat on the *Queen Mary* in Long Beach, California. General Doolittle was an aviation pioneer who received a Medal of Honor for his daring raids on Japan in WWII.

A *Who's Who* in American aviation. Left to right: Jimmie, unnamed friend, General Doolittle, National Air Races Managing Director Cliff Henderson, and Col. William "Pete" Knight (USAF), a test pilot who in 1967 set a speed record of 4,520 mph and Mach 6.7 in an experimental NASA spaceplane.

Jimmie swaps stories with World War I flying ace and Medal of Honor recipient Eddie Rickenbacker.

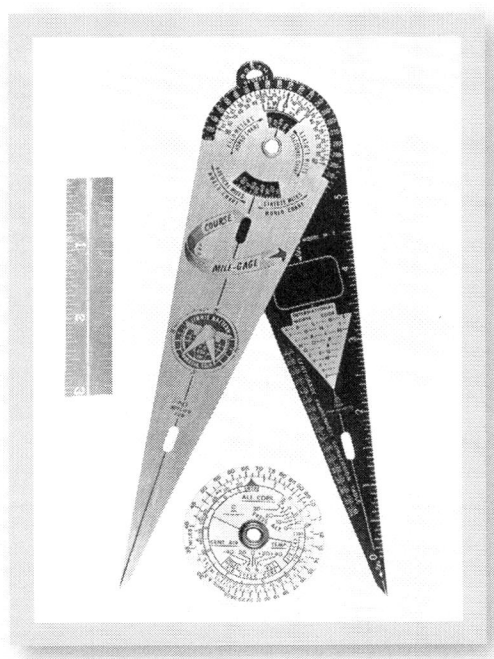

The Jimmie Mattern Course & Mileage Calculator was a pocket-size, handheld device that accurately and quickly provided valuable information to pilots. It included an altitude and speed correction dial, a Centigrade/Fahrenheit conversion table, a Morse

James J. Mattern's pilot's license. He received it August 31, 1927. Signed by Orville Wright, chairman of the National Aeronautic Association of the United States; autographed by Neil Armstrong, July 1969.

Neil Armstrong carried Jimmie's pilot's license ("aviator's certificate") to the moon with him on the Apollo 11 mission, July 1969.

PHOTO ALBUM

Top: Autographed interior of pilot's license by Buzz Aldrin.
Bottom: Photo of Jimmie Mattern and Neil Armstrong.

Promotional photos, 1932

PHOTO ALBUM

THE WHITE HOUSE
WASHINGTON

December 16, 1988

Greetings to everyone gathered in Dallas for the Texas Aviation Pioneer's Day Dinner.

Nancy and I were deeply saddened to learn that the man who was to have been your featured speaker and guest of honor, Colonel Jimmie Mattern, passed away this week. We send our deep sympathy to his wife Dorothy, his daughters Pattie and Joy, and all his family; we are keeping them in prayer.

Jimmie Mattern, whose flying certificate was signed by Orville Wright and carried by Neil Armstrong and Buzz Aldrin on Apollo 11 to the moon, was a pioneer in the truest sense of the word. From his first flight in 1924, he was a trailblazer. He was the first American to fly nonstop from New York to Berlin, the Soviet Union, and Norway, and the first to attempt a solo around-the-world flight. He held the trans-Atlantic speed record for eight years and set 15 single-engine world records. He logged 3,000 hours flight-testing P-38's and training their pilots. The list goes on.

Jimmie Mattern was a giant. As we mourn his loss, we also rejoice in his life and legacy. Surely, a special place in heaven has been reserved for this great and gentle man.

Nancy joins me in sending our good wishes to all of you during the holiday season and always. God bless you.

Ronald Reagan

Condolence letter from Ronald Reagan to the Mattern family after Jimmie passed away.

Last photo taken of Jimmie, 1988.

Bill and Pattie (Mattern) Scarbrough, married in 1960, have three girls and three grandchildren.

Steve and Joy (Mattern) Garrison, married in 1966, have three children, nine grandchildren, and three great-grandchildren.

Jimmie and Dorothy with their six grandchildren, 1974.
Left to right: Amy, Dorothy, Stephanie, Jimmie, Tricia, Mitchell, Kelly, and Shelby.

Jimmie and Dorothy's grandchildren in 2021.
Left to right: Amy Garrison Olson, Kelly June Scarbrough, Mitchell Garrison, Shelby Joy Scarbrough, Stephanie Garrison Southwick, and Tricia Scarbrough Corcoran.

CHAPTER SIXTEEN

July 7-18, 1932

Jimmie hung upside down, held in place by his flying harness and safety belt. He dangled there, eight or ten feet off the ground. The Pratt & Whitney engine had let loose upon impact, punctured the fuselage, and now rested inside the cockpit. Jimmie could see and feel the heat coming off the intake manifold. A potent smell of gasoline filled the cabin. The fuel dripped on Jimmie's back and chest, ran down his face, and saturated his hair.

He feared if some of that fuel hit the manifold, it would be curtains. Just the fumes might blow them sky-high.

For several minutes Jimmie worked to free himself, but his body weight put way too much pressure on the harness and belt. He couldn't release the buckles. He felt like a marionette dangling from unseen hands.

Fear of an explosion and the resulting fire pushed him to the edge of panic. He called out to Benny but received no response. Was his friend badly wounded? Unconscious?

Dead?

Everything had gone from heaven to hell in seconds.

What exactly had happened to the cockpit hatch? Had he failed to secure it properly back in Berlin?

Jimmie cursed and yanked on those buckles until first the harness and then the leather safety belt finally let go. A millisecond later he was on the ground, legs tangled and face half buried in the soft, boggy soil of that Russian hayfield.

But at least he was free. Or so he thought. Jimmie quickly realized he was trapped inside the cockpit. When the Vega had flipped over onto its back, the top of the fuselage had buried itself in the bog, trapping the pilot inside.

Seconds later Jimmie heard Benny's voice shouting his name. "Jim! Jimmie! You in there? You stuck?"

"Kind of, yeah!" Jimmie shouted back.

"But otherwise okay?"

"Hell no! You?"

"I'm good."

Seconds later Jimmie saw Benny's hands ripping at the ground and reaching up inside the cockpit. Soon Benny's arms were visible, then his shoulders, and then his head popped in through the hole he had just feverishly dug by hand.

Without saying a word, knowing an explosion could kill them both at any second, Benny grabbed Jimmie's legs, swung him around, and pulled his body with an extraordinary amount of vigor out through that small hole.

The two pilots, injured and undoubtedly in shock, quickly jumped up and scrambled to put some distance between themselves and the now doomed *Century of Progress*.

It was plenty depressing to stand there and stare at their ruined ship lying upside down on that Russian bog, broken in two.

The plane was dead.

Their dream of flying around the world was dead.

They felt dead.

Eventually, Jimmie, in a voice choked with emotion, said, "Thanks for saving my life, old buddy. That was some fix."

"You would've gotten out."

"I don't think so. The way I was jammed in there with my face in the dirt, I don't think I would've had the leverage to do any digging."

"Well then," said Benny in his Oklahoma drawl, "I'm glad I could be of service."

CHAPTER SIXTEEN

That's when Jimmie looked over at his friend, and with dawn just breaking over that Russian field, he saw for the first time the blood running down the side of Benny's face. "Damn, Ben, you got a pretty good gash there."

"It's nothing," Benny insisted.

"Maybe a little something."

Jimmie made Benny lie down on the ground. With the threat of an engine fire diminishing, Jimmie dashed back and grabbed the medical kit from the airplane. He swabbed away the blood on Benny's face and poured half a bottle of iodine directly onto the open wound just over the right eyebrow.

Benny's forehead had been torn open when the plane flipped over and an unsecured gas can smashed into his face.

Benny screamed bloody murder when the iodine hit that wound, but both men knew the cut needed cleansing. Then, a few seconds later, when Benny looked away, Jimmie poured the rest of the iodine on the gash. Benny screamed again, but soon thereafter Jimmie bandaged the open wound with gauze and secured the gauze with tape.

Benny felt a little light-headed but otherwise okay.

Jimmie, too, had sustained some injuries, both from the crash and from getting pulled out of the cockpit. But his wounds were mostly superficial—a bump to the head, a sore shoulder, various scrapes and abrasions. Nothing a little time wouldn't heal.

The sun exploded across the field as the two American aviators sat on the ground near the *Century of Progress* and began to discuss their next move. No sooner had this discussion started than, from several directions, a dozen or more Soviet soldiers surrounded the fliers. They had their carbines drawn and bayonets fixed. They closed in tight around the injured aviators. One of the soldiers had the gall to poke the Americans with the sharp tip of his bayonet.

Jimmie swatted the weapon away. "What the hell?"

"Take it easy, Jimmie," advised Benny. "These boys look a little edgy. Let's not provoke them."

The soldiers did not speak a word of English and the Americans did not speak a word of Russian. A standoff ensued.

It lasted well into the morning.

A Soviet general eventually arrived in a fancy automobile. Dozens of decorations plastered his uniform and he was accompanied by a large staff and several local reporters. Haughty and authoritative, the general demanded to know, in perfect if accented English, who the fliers were and why they were on Soviet soil.

Jimmie and Benny told their story. Several times they repeated the fact that they had received permission from the Soviet government to use Soviet airspace and Soviet airport facilities in Moscow, Irkutsk, and Khabarovsk. The general, who bragged about being educated in the United States, didn't buy a word of it. He demanded proof. Unfortunately, the boys did not have any paperwork substantiating their claims.

The general issued orders to his staff. Minutes later, the two Americans were loaded into the back of a truck and transported to the city of Minsk, a distance of fifty miles. There they were held in a room in a military barracks. The door was locked and guarded.

Jimmie, understandably, was upset. To say the least. The young aviator—his plane destroyed, his body beat up from the crash, his dream dead—boiled with rage. "Damn Russians!"

Benny, predictably, stayed cool. "It'll be okay, buddy. They just need to check out our story and then we'll be on our way."

"What's to check out?"

"They probably think we're spies."

"Spies! Good grief!"

"Or some such nonsense. Look, you know the military. This general's just covering his sorry behind. Once they realize who we are, they'll let us go."

They remained in Minsk for three days. They were given food and water but were not permitted to bathe, shave, or contact the outside world. A doctor, sour and stinking of alcohol, examined their injuries. He cleaned and bandaged Benny's head wound.

Jimmie continued to vehemently voice his displeasure with the situation. He demanded their immediate release every time someone showed up at the door. Benny tried to keep his friend calm by insisting the whole matter was undoubtedly nothing but a bureaucratic boondoggle.

On their third day in captivity, they were taken to a nearby railway station and loaded onto a train car. Armed guards stood at each end of the car. Jimmie demanded to know where they were going and why.

No explanations were offered.

For almost twenty-four hours they remained inside that rickety old train car as it swayed and rattled itself across the Russian countryside. The sun came up on another day, and out the dusty windows the boys could see throngs of Russian peasants toiling in the fields.

Jimmie said, "I hope they're not taking us to Siberia."

"Moscow would be my guess."

"You think?"

"This country is a communist dictatorship. Everyone's paranoid of everyone else. No one has the guts to make a decision. So yeah, I think Moscow."

Sure enough, they arrived in Moscow later that day and were transported via military vehicle to a squalid hotel and locked in a small room on the top floor. They were fed meat and potatoes and permitted to bathe and shave. Unfortunately, they were not issued clean clothes. They remained in their grimy, sweat-soaked flight suits, which they had attempted to wash by hand in the sink back in Minsk but with middling success.

The next evening, they were taken downstairs to a "reception" in a grand ballroom. There they met with several high-ranking officials in the Soviet government. Reporters captured the event on film.

Jimmie asked when they would be permitted to go home.

"Soon," the smiling politicians promised. "Very soon."

"Very soon" means different things in different cultures, they would come to learn. Another day passed. And then another. On their third day in Moscow, they were taken on a tour of the city. They visited Lenin's Tomb on Red Square and also St. Basil's Cathedral. They stood before the Kremlin and wondered aloud if they would need authorization from Joseph Stalin himself before they would be allowed to return to the United States.

The following day, at another "reception," which Jimmie now referred to as "propaganda sessions," the boys met Mr. Gregory Pope. Pope was an American doing business in the Soviet Union, likely something to do with munitions, though he would not specifically say. He did assure the boys, however, that he would contact a friend at the U.S. Department of State and make it known the two aviators were being held against their will.

This gave Jimmie and Benny hope they would soon be freed. It had been eight days since the crash and both men were eager to get home and get on with their lives. Also, they had not been allowed to make phone calls or send telegrams, so they did not know if family and friends knew of their whereabouts or circumstances. Jimmie, especially, was concerned about Cleo, and also about Della.

But still the boys had one more indignity to endure.

By this time, the upper echelons of the Soviet government surely knew Jimmie Mattern and Benny Griffin were not American spies but just a couple of young, adventurous aviators trying to set an around-the world flying record. Their names and the nature of their mission, after all, were on the front pages of newspapers all over the world.

Nevertheless, on their fifth day of captivity in Moscow, Jimmie and Benny were taken from their hotel and escorted to the Kremlin. They were marched down a long, ornate hallway and into a massive meeting room with a conference table large enough to seat thirty people. Seated around that enormous table were high-ranking officials of the Soviet government, all of them stern, serious men with scowls on their faces.

Jimmie and Benny, still in their dirt-covered flight suits, were seated next to each other in two chairs at the middle of the table.

This was not a "reception."

This was an interrogation.

The questions came fast and furiously.

"Who are you?"

"Why are you here?"

"What do you seek?"

"Are you American spies?"

CHAPTER SIXTEEN

"Who sent you?"

"To whom do you report?"

"Are you agents of the imperialist American government?"

Fortunately, the questions came through a translator, so Jimmie and Benny, perspiring now inside those grimy flight suits, had some time to think about their replies. Neither of them had expected this after all the time that had passed. They had assumed by now it was understood their mission was a peaceful one and they would be welcomed as friends.

But it quickly dawned on Jimmie that this was just a kangaroo court. These bureaucrats knew they had made a mistake holding the two Americans for so long, so now they had to make a show to justify the long and insulting detention.

Jimmie whispered his realization to Benny, who quickly nodded and whispered back, "Just play along and hopefully it'll all be over soon."

Fists pounded the enormous conference table and the Americans were ordered to remain silent and not communicate with one another. But the jig was up, even if they all played the game for another few hours.

Accusations were made; explanations given.

Threats bellowed; insincere apologies offered.

Dramatic nationalistic speeches delivered; more insincere apologies tendered by the two Americans.

And then, suddenly, several hours into all this bellicose posturing, the Soviet bureaucrats powwowed for several minutes. When they finally broke the huddle, their scowls had turned to smiles and it was announced all was well and they should all be friends.

Jimmie had a great desire to tell them all to go straight to hell, but Benny gave his buddy's arm a squeeze and young Mattern had the good sense to nip his desires in the bud. He even spent several minutes shaking hands.

Their now friendly and hospitable hosts wanted to know what they could do to make the Americans more comfortable.

Jimmie did not hold back. "You can drive us to the airport and put us on the first plane out of this dump."

The translator must've softened Jimmie's verbal blow, for the bureaucrats merely smiled and nodded.

The next day, the two American aviators, after ten days in captivity, were on their way.

CHAPTER SEVENTEEN

July 18–August 9, 1932

Within hours, Jimmie and Benny found themselves back in Berlin. They were unprepared for what followed. In New York, prior to their departure, there had been some press coverage of their upcoming flight. They had been interviewed and their names and photographs had appeared on the front pages of newspapers and magazines. Certainly, they knew many people around the world were watching their progress as they attempted to better the around-the-world mark set by Wiley Post and Harold Gatty.

But full-blown fame greeted them in Berlin. The Germans treated Jimmie and Benny like royalty. The boys were put up in fine hotels, treated to the opera, introduced to famous politicians, artists, actors, athletes, and military heroes. About the only things missing were some fresh clothes. Still wearing their crummy flights suits, they dined with Gen. Franz von Papen, who had been a general staff officer during World War I and now served as the country's chancellor under Pres. Paul von Hindenburg.

The next day, General von Papen took the two American aviators on a tour of one of Germany's flight schools. At that time, Germany was not permitted to manufacture or fly military aircraft. The Treaty of Versailles that ended World War I essentially prevented Germany from having an army, navy, or air force. But still the Germans had found the means to train their pilots. The flight school Jimmie and Benny visited outside Berlin had more than a hundred sophisticated gliders and nearly a thousand young pilots learning to fly them. The boys were told that Germany had a dozen similar flight schools across the country.

Jimmie did some quick math and calculated the Germans had more than ten thousand pilots in training. The Americans didn't have anything close to that number.

Von Papen told the boys that glider training made first-class pilots because flying a glider took exceptional skill and a complete understanding of what kept an aircraft aloft. Jimmie had the distinct feeling the German chancellor was, with a broad smile on his face, letting the Americans know the Germans were down but not out.

This attitude magnified itself the next day when Jimmie and Benny toured a high-altitude pressure chamber. These chambers prepared pilots to fly at twelve thousand and even fifteen thousand feet. This high-altitude training went on despite the fact that Germany did not at that time possess a single airplane capable of flying at those altitudes. Clearly, they were preparing for the future.

The Germans had ten of these pressure chambers across the country. The United States, the boys well knew, had one.

Jimmie and Benny agreed the Germans were preparing for a future in the sky to a far greater extent than the Americans. It also appeared as though the military applications of aviation were very much on the minds of the Germans.

"Hopefully, if there's another war," Benny said to Jimmie, "Germany and America will be on the same side."

"Yeah," agreed Jimmie. "Against those damn Russians."

Hitler was just months away from becoming chancellor.

Before leaving Germany, the boys made a few transatlantic phone calls. Such a phenomenon had only been around since 1927, but after much operator assistance Jimmie connected first with his mother in Vancouver and soon thereafter with his wife in Walla Walla. These phone calls, scratchy and prone to long delays between sending and receiving, were witnessed by members of the press, who eagerly passed along every loving word Jimmie uttered.

CHAPTER SEVENTEEN

The press could not hear the responses given by Caroline and Della Mattern, but still it was reported the women were greatly relieved Jimmie was safe and well, and, of course, they could not wait for him to return home.

The fact that Jimmie and Della had not spent a single night together in over a year was not reported.

America wanted its heroes happily wedded.

Soon the boys found themselves in Paris, where they were given an even more lavish hero's welcome. Representatives of Standard Oil of New Jersey, one of the major sponsors of their flight, greeted them at Le Bourget Field and carried them into the city in an open automobile. Large crowds cheered along the way.

At one point, Jimmie turned to Benny and said, "I don't get it. We crashed in Russia not even halfway around the world. Destroyed our plane. Why all the attention?"

Benny shrugged. "Maybe because you're such a handsome cuss."

"Come on, seriously?"

"Not a clue, Jim," Benny replied. "But we may as well enjoy it."

Jimmie definitely did that. He loved flying and would absolutely do it for its own sake, but all the attention and adulation weren't too tough to take.

A grand dinner was given in their honor, and here they met Louis Blériot, the famous French aviator. Blériot was the Charles Lindbergh of France. On July 25, 1909, he became the first flier to cross the English Channel in a powered aircraft. His fabric-and-wire monoplane, powered by a 25 hp Anzani engine, covered the twenty-two-mile crossing in just over thirty-six minutes. The short flight turned Blériot into a national hero and an instant celebrity.

For Jimmie and Benny, meeting Louis Blériot was akin to a young boy in love with baseball meeting Babe Ruth. They practically genuflected in his presence. During a meal at a famous Parisian restaurant, Blériot autographed a dinner menu for Jimmie, a treasure he would keep until the end of his life.

But without question, the highlight of the time the boys spent with the famous flier came when Louis Blériot declared, "I would say, *oui*, flying the English Channel in those early days took guts and determination in my tiny ship, but as much guts and determination as crossing the vast Atlantic Ocean? I think not. I bow to your courage and for moving aviation a step closer to the future."

Heads swollen, Jimmie and Benny departed Paris and flew across the Channel in a vintage Handley Page V/1500 that offered Pullman-car comfort. They sat in wicker bamboo chairs and were each served a steak and a glass of ale during the flight. And upon arrival at Croydon Field south of London, they encountered the largest crowds to welcome them yet.

"I still don't get it," said Jimmie, shaking his head.

"Me neither," said Benny.

"But I could get used to it," Jimmie added with a wink.

"I'm not sure it's my style," confessed Benny. "I enjoyed it at first but it's starting to get a little long in the tooth."

After parades and press conferences and banquets in London, the boys were transported to Southampton, where they boarded the SS *Leviathan*, an enormous luxury steamship, for the trip back to the United States. At this time, of course, there was no passenger air service between North America and Europe. It was set sail or stay put.

The boys did not have money to purchase tickets aboard the *Leviathan*, but the ship company made an exception due to their hero's status. They were given the bridal suite on the top deck and invited nightly to dine with the captain.

All this despite the fact they still wore the same grimy flight clothes they had worn back at Floyd Bennett Field nearly three weeks earlier. But the two young fliers were full-blooded American heroes. Everyone wanted to shake their hands and slap their backs and stand in their shadows. No one cared what they had on. In fact, the soiled leather flight suits enhanced the image of the rugged and fearless aviators.

It had taken Jimmie and Benny approximately twelve hours to fly from Newfoundland to the coast of Ireland. It took the *Leviathan* five days and four hours to sail from Southampton to New York.

CHAPTER SEVENTEEN

Upon reaching New York Harbor, the boys witnessed one of the great thrills of their long adventure. As the ship steamed past the Statue of Liberty and up the Hudson River, four biplanes piloted by U.S. Navy airmen flew just above the *Leviathan's* three towering steam funnels as a gesture of welcome to the returning aviators.

The city of New York threw the boys some party. It included a function at City Hall, where they received the keys to the city from Mayor Jimmy Walker. It featured an open-car tickertape parade up Broadway. They were fêted at a lavish reception at the posh New Yorker Hotel, with Fred Waring and the Pennsylvanians providing the entertainment.

Jimmie danced with at least half a dozen different young ladies that night. And that number would have been higher if not for the endless number of people wanting to shake his hand and pose for a photograph with the daring young flier.

Long after Benny had said good night and gone up to bed, Jimmie remained in the ballroom dancing and laughing with New York's elites. The rich and famous crowded around him as though hoping a bit of all that natural charm, good looks, and audacity might somehow rub off on them. The men especially seemed eager to crowd his space. These gentlemen could make money in the market. Some of them could sing; some of them could dance. Some could act. Some could run for office and win. Some could hit a baseball or throw a football or drive a golf ball a country mile. But did any of them have the guts, the courage, the moxie, to climb into a small single-engine airplane and try to fly it around the world?

The answer, overwhelmingly, was no, which explained why they wanted to stand next to this easy-going guy, Jimmie Mattern, put their arms around his shoulder, touch his leather flight jacket, and inhale some of the rarified air that wafted around him.

No doubt about it, Jimmie enjoyed the spotlight. He liked the nightlife. He liked the action and the tumult—and okay, he liked the girls. Sure, he was still a married man, but what was the harm in a little dancing, a little flirting?

The aviators' next stop was Washington, D.C. Just before departing New York, Jimmie called his mother in Vancouver. They had a nice chat and Cleo wanted to know when Jimmie was coming to visit. In just a few days, he told her, but not in Canada.

"Then where?" she wanted to know.

"Oklahoma City," replied Jimmie. "A family reunion. Our family and Benny's family. I'm sending a plane to fetch you."

"Oh my. Will Della be there?"

"I hope so."

Jimmie next called Della.

"I see your picture in the papers," she said.

"I can't help that."

"You look happy."

"Listen, Della, Benny and I are trying to get our families together in Oklahoma City. I'm really hoping you'll come."

"I don't know, Jimmie."

"I want you to come. My mother wants you to come."

"Why do you want me to come, Jimmie? Because you miss me? Or because you want us side by side smiling for the photographers?"

"That's not fair, Della. Us being apart was not my choice."

"You flying airplanes all over creation was not my choice."

"I know it's been hard."

"I'm glad you're back safe."

"Will you come? To Oklahoma? I miss you. I had a hard flight and missed you the entire time."

"I'll let you know."

In Washington, the boys met with senators and congressmen who all seemed eager to have their pictures taken with the dashing young aviators. Like people in Germany, France, England, and New York, these grinning, gladhanding politicians wanted to know when Jimmie and Benny planned to try to fly around the world again.

It was a question they had heard over and over.

CHAPTER SEVENTEEN

Always the boys had given the same response: "Not really thinking about the next time just yet. Just trying to recover from the first one."

But on the hot and humid afternoon of August 9, 1932, on the lawn of the White House in the District of Columbia, someone rather out of the ordinary asked Jimmie and Benny this same question.

It was supposed to be a simple ten-minute meet-and-greet. Presidents did these kinds of things all day long. Shake hands. Make a little small talk. Pose for a photograph.

But Jimmie, surely in a state of disbelief that he stood in the presence of the president of the United States, nevertheless had no qualms speaking his mind. "Mr. President, sir," he said after the small talk, "Benny and I have just returned from Russia and Germany, and I have to say, sir, I don't care much for either country. I knew animals when I was a boy back in Illinois with better manners than those Russians. And the Germans, well, if I had to venture a guess, I'd say once a warring people always a warring people."

Secretary of War Patrick Hurley joined Pres. Herbert Hoover and young Mattern at that point in the conversation, and talk turned back to the attempted flight around the world. And this was when President Hoover asked, "So, Jimmie, when do you and Bennett intend to give it another go?"

"Not exactly sure, sir."

"Well, I'll tell you, son, with this damn depression pulling our people down, making them anxious and scared, we need boys like you and Bennett out there reminding Americans that we're the roughest, toughest, bravest, most resilient people on earth. So I'll say the sooner you're back in the air, the better."

Later that same night, in their hotel room after a long day of talking endlessly about their failed flight, Jimmie broached the subject with Benny. In the morning they would be leaving for Chicago, and then down to Oklahoma where Jimmie would rendezvous with Cleo and his brother Philip and hopefully Della. The boys would be moving fast, their schedules tight, their time not their own. But the idea of another flight was now suddenly very much on Jimmie's mind, and he wanted to find out where his friend stood on the subject.

They relaxed on their beds, shoes kicked off, hands behind their heads. Back in New York they'd been treated to a shopping spree where they'd purchased new suits, ties, shirts, socks, shoes, even underwear. A couple of real fancy dudes.

"I want to try again," Jimmie offered.

"Say what?"

"The flight. I want to give it another go."

"All the way around?"

"All the way around."

Benny looked over at his friend, let a minute or so pass, and then replied, "I honestly don't know if I have it in me, Jimmie."

"Are you sure?"

Benny sighed. "That was a hell of a stressful trip, old buddy, practically from the moment we left New York, and, well, the truth is, I'm not getting any younger."

"You don't have to decide tonight."

Benny shrugged. "True. I guess I could change my mind, but my gut tells me I've used up my nine lives, and maybe it's time to go a little easier."

Jimmie nodded and, respectful of his great friend's position, did not push the matter. He remained silent for several minutes. His thoughts swirled. His imagination ran wild.

"Benny?" he said, after a time.

"Yeah Jim."

"Would you be able to keep a secret?"

"Between us? Sure, Jim."

"I'm gonna do it."

"Do what?"

"I'm gonna go it alone."

"Seriously?"

"I'm gonna be first to circumnavigate solo."

"That's crazy, Jim."

"Wiley's been making noise about it. Why him? Why not me? I learned a lot out there flying with you. I found out I have the guts."

Benny thought about it. "Okay. Sure. Why not you? And you're right, Jimmie, you definitely have what it takes."

"You think?"

"Absolutely."

They kept talking. For hours. By the time they finally fell asleep, the boys had decided to keep the flight under wraps for as long as possible. And more importantly, once news of another attempt became public, it would be billed again as a team effort:

Mattern/Griffin Round Two!

The idea that Jimmie would be attempting a solo circumnavigation, if all went according to plan, would remain a secret hopefully right up until the day of his departure.

CHAPTER EIGHTEEN

August 12, 1932–June 3, 1933

Oklahoma being Benny's home state, the enthusiastic crowd at Will Rogers Airport numbered well over a thousand when the boys flew in from Chicago on Friday, August 12, 1932. Jimmie and Benny once again received keys to the city, this time from Oklahoma City Mayor Clarence J. Blinn, who called the two fliers "modern-day Magellans with wings."

Jimmie gave a short speech wherein he called his friend Benny "the most courageous pilot I've ever known and the greatest navigator since Christopher Columbus. That man"—he pointed to Benny—"could find a grain of sand on the Mojave Desert."

Benny, of course, kept his remarks even shorter. He told the crowd Jimmie had "more guts than a bull rider." A gushing compliment in the Sooner State.

Jimmie's mother and brother Philip arrived that evening. The press took photographs of their reunion and more photographs of them sitting on the front porch of their boarding house sipping lemonade.

Della arrived quietly the following afternoon. The Mattern family had dinner together, and after the meal they attended a small party at the Griffins' house with Benny, his wife, and his parents. The conversation focused on the flight, now fading into the past. Little was said about the future.

That night, Jimmie and Della shared a bed for the first time in over a year. Even lying side by side, a wide chasm loomed between them. Conversation proved difficult. Nevertheless, in the morning, Jimmie knew his mind. He would not be deterred. He said to his wife, "Benny and I barely made it out of Germany. All this hubbub has been for naught."

"You crossed the Atlantic."

"No more exciting than crossing the street."

"That's ridiculous."

"The earth, Della. We meant to circumnavigate the earth."

"You had the courage to try."

"I can't abide failure, Della."

"In what regard, Jimmie?"

"Failure just doesn't suit me. It doesn't fit well."

"I understand, but are you referring to your failure to fly around the world or the failure of our marriage?"

"I don't want our marriage to fail, Della, but I need to finish what I started."

"You need to, or you choose to?"

"You don't understand."

"Famous last words."

"I hope not."

"No one feels they're understood."

Jimmie shrugged, and then, "Della?"

"Yes?"

"Benny and I . . . we're going to give it another go."

Jimmie wasn't sure why he had included his friend in this pronouncement. Perhaps to soften the blow or maybe to take some of the pressure off the notion of a solo flight. But either way, the words were out now. The deed was done.

"Another flight?"

"Yes."

"So then I assume you won't be coming home?"

"Well, there's all the preparation. That takes months. Then the flight . . . and then . . ."

"And then what, Jimmie?"

"Della, listen, I—"

CHAPTER EIGHTEEN

"Jimmie, please, it's not necessary. I understand. I do. You're driven. The world is changed, sometimes even for the better, by driven people. But that doesn't mean, as your wife, that I'm happy about it."

"This will be it, Della. This will be the last time. Just this flight and then—"

Della reached out and gently pressed her index finger against Jimmie's lips. "Don't. Please don't say another word. Just do what you need to do. And I will do what I need to do. And in the end, well, we'll see where we stand."

Days later, Jimmie began his quest to be the first aviator to fly solo around the world. That accomplishment alone would guarantee him a place alongside such fliers as the Wright brothers, Jimmy Doolittle, Wiley Post, and Lindbergh. But Jimmie also had his eye on a couple of records he wanted to break.

First on his list was Lindbergh's famous New York to Paris flight. Jimmie wanted to make New York/Paris the first leg of his trip and he felt certain he could easily break Lindbergh's time of just over thirty-three hours. In fact, with the right plane equipped with the right engine, he thought he could beat that time by ten hours or more.

Jimmie also felt that with precise planning, decent weather, and no mechanical problems, he could crush the Post/Gatty around-the-world time of just over eight and a half days. If everything fell properly into place, a time of six days and ten hours felt like a real possibility. Of course, Jimmie knew these were just ideas in his head and numbers jotted down on a piece of paper. The real work would be in the preparation and, of course, the flying.

Financing the operation was his first and foremost concern. The Great Depression continued to haunt the nation, although Jimmie, always an optimist, felt he could use these economic hard times to his advantage. He negotiated a deal with Nelson Kelly, the manager of Floyd Bennett Field on Long Island, to lease a private hangar for just $50 a month. Most of Kelly's hangars were empty, so fifty bucks looked better than nothing.

Jimmie once again hired Fred Fetterman to run his ground operation at the airfield. Fred had just about no work, so he signed for a fraction of what he'd been making back in the '20s, before the crash and the ensuing economic decline.

The Soviets, as promised, returned the *Century of Progress* to its rightful owner. The broken airplane arrived via cargo ship to Brooklyn and was soon thereafter shipped to Floyd Bennett Field, where Fetterman put it under lock and key in Jimmie's hangar.

"Nobody sees that airplane, Fred," Jimmie ordered. "Not until the day we fly."

"That's a tall order, Jim."

Jimmie smiled. "As few eyes as possible, Fred."

The plane, Fetterman quickly deduced, needed an entire rebuild. The crash near Minsk had pretty well totaled the Vega.

Jimmie started knocking on doors. The first he knocked on belonged to Ed Aldrin of Standard Oil of New Jersey. Ed had been a major supporter of Jimmie's first flight and he proved no less enthusiastic about this solo effort, which he agreed to keep under his hat.

"Whatever I can do, Jim, just let me know."

Standard Oil owned a number of Lockheed Vegas. Three of the planes had been retired and were primarily used for parts. Aldrin made these planes available to Jimmie and Fred.

Fred removed both wings from the Standard Oil *Eagle* and mated them to the fuselage of the original *Century of Progress*. He also purloined fuel tanks, landing gear, struts, stabilizers, and a rudder from the grounded Vegas. Fred worked his magic to make the new *Century of Progress* not only better than the original but also stronger and more rigid, and therefore more stable in the air during times of high turbulence.

The rear cockpit used by Benny was pulled out and replaced with fuel tanks. Fuel tanks were also added in the tail of the plane and in both wings.

"A flying gas can," Fred liked to call the plane.

All this went on while Jimmie knocked on more doors at the Bendix Corporation and at Pratt & Whitney. He told executives at these companies about his plans to fly solo around the world and then told them he would not even consider setting off on such a flight without their exceptional products aboard his ship.

CHAPTER EIGHTEEN

The smooth talk worked wonders.

Bendix supplied the *Century of Progress* with a brand-new instrument panel operating an array of the latest aviation instruments, including airspeed and altitude indicators, altimeter, compass, and turn coordinator.

Pratt & Whitney overhauled the entire Wasp engine in the *Century of Progress*. Using brand-new technology, the company supercharged the engine, increasing horsepower by nearly 30 percent. At the same time, due to direct injection, overall fuel consumption fell by almost 15 percent. In simple terms, this meant Jimmie would be able to fly farther and faster than he and Benny had just a few shorts months earlier.

Both Bendix and Pratt & Whitney performed their work gratis. The executives at these companies believed Jimmie Mattern was the flier who could accomplish the extraordinary feat of circumnavigating the earth solo in a small, single-engine plane. They wanted their companies, and the products they made, along for the ride.

Jimmie enjoyed the business end of flying. A year earlier, prior to his flight with Benny, this had not been the case. When he would show up looking for assistance, people would look at him the way they looked at stray cats showing up at the back door in search of food. But now that he had made his mark in aviation, doors opened wide when he stopped by to visit. People greeted him with smiles and open arms. They wanted to meet him and shake his hand. They wanted to hear all about his upcoming flight. Best of all, they wanted to help.

Jimmie set up Jimmie Mattern Inc., which he liked to call the "Jimmie Mattern Around-the-World Flight" Corporation. Headquartered at the posh Sherman House Hotel in Chicago, the company oversaw all the details of the flight. Jimmie had learned plenty from his first attempt to fly around the world and he was now able to apply that knowledge to this second attempt.

He hired a bunch of old friends to run the show. They mostly worked for nothing or very little. Sam Sackett handled legal matters. Jack Clark did public relations. Clarence Page was the business manager and tireless promoter. Harry Jameson and Billy Mills performed many of the tasks Benny had done before the first flight. They contacted foreign governments for flyover regulations, medical requirements, and visas. They contracted with various airports in Canada, France, Germany, and the Soviet Union for fuel and maintenance. Harry and Billy worked and reworked Jimmie's flight plan.

Franklin Delano Roosevelt was elected in November of 1932. Among many campaign pledges, he supported the idea of formally recognizing the Soviet Union and normalizing relations. The agreement would not be signed until November of 1933, but the mere acknowledgement from the president-elect that the two countries would cooperate made it much easier for Jimmie to deal with the Soviets this time around. He had to put up a $5,000 bond, but in return he received written permission to use Soviet airspace and the use of several designated airports and airfields for fuel, maintenance, and potential repairs.

This was an enormous load off Jimmie's mind, for he knew almost one-third of his flight would take place over the USSR.

By the spring of 1933, rumors about the flight started to pop up in news stories around the country. Always these stories mentioned both Jimmie and Benny. The press just assumed the boys would be making this second attempt together, and neither Jimmie nor Benny said or did anything to detract from this view.

Stories of Wiley Post making a solo effort around the world also flourished at this time. In fact, Post, who had already successfully circumnavigated the globe with Harold Gatty back in 1931, had set a departure date of July 4 to commemorate the country's 157th birthday. Like Jimmie, Wiley would be making his flight in a Lockheed Vega, the *Winnie Mae*.

When word of Post's departure date reached Jimmie in Chicago, he called Fred out on Long Island. "When can we be ready to go?"

"You must've heard about Wiley."

Jimmie laughed. "Let's just say I'd rather not play second fiddle to that barnstormer again, Fred."

"The plane's ready to fly, Jim. I don't mean tomorrow or even next week, but she's not far off."

CHAPTER EIGHTEEN

"How far?"

"First let me say this. It sounds to me like Post will have a Sperry gyroscope on board that'll be able to do a bit of flying while he rests, and also a radio direction finder that'll do some navigating. I'm not 100 percent convinced these gadgets are ready for real-time flying, but still, I wouldn't mind seeing them clustered on the instrument panel of the *Century of Progress*."

"Aw hell, Fred, that could set us back weeks trying to get Bendix to supply us with that new stuff. Maybe months."

"Just trying to keep you safe, Jim."

"Safe's for second place."

"Then like I said, we're close. Today's Tuesday. I think you could take it up for a test spin by the end of next week."

"I want to do it on the q.t."

"So we roll her out early one morning. Just the two of us. No fanfare."

"And if all goes well?"

"If all goes well, we bolt in the rest of the fuel tanks, run and secure the fuel lines, fine-tune the Wasp one last time, and bust loose."

Jimmie ran some calculations in his head. "With a little luck, the paper trail should come to an end in a couple weeks. Maybe sooner. All visas secured and contracts signed. Not that I'm going to let paper stop me anyway. When the plane's ready to fly, we fly. I'm thinking that might be as soon as early June."

Fred glanced at the calendar over his desk. "Barring unforeseen problems, I think that first week of June hits the mark."

"That puts us a month ahead of WP."

"You'll be back home in your easy chair before he ever takes off."

The call ended. Jimmie pulled on his sweatpants, sneakers, and T-shirt. He left his room at the Sherman House Hotel. He passed through the lobby and went out onto Madison Street. He ran east, passed over the Chicago River, and kept going at a good clip all the way out across Grant Park to the outer harbor on Lake Michigan. Sprinting south along the water, he stopped every hundred yards or so to do a dozen or more pushups. This had been Jimmie's routine for months. Every day he ran and did pushups and pullups and situps. Every day he ate well, drank little or no alcohol, and slept at least eight or nine hours every night.

The guy had himself in fine fiddle, maybe the best shape of his life. He had recently turned twenty-eight and so was in his prime. He felt great, mentally and physically.

And now, come hell or high water, Jimmie Mattern intended to fly his Lockheed Vega, the *Century of Progress,* solo around the world.

CHAPTER NINETEEN

The Anadyr River

June 25, 1933
Clear skies, 52°F, winds calm

Jimmie squinted and studied the river. He thought about all those long runs along Lake Michigan to get himself physically and mentally prepared for this flight around the world. He thought about the months of work and the tens of thousands of dollars spent and the endless stress and the sacrifices so many people had made to make the trip a reality—Cleo and Della in particular—and for what?

So he could stand here on this sandy riverbank in the middle of nowhere, sick and broken and slowly starving to death?

Jimmie could not help but juxtapose his present predicament with the one he had enjoyed just a few weeks earlier back in New York. What was that line from the Dickens novel? "It was the best of times, it was the worst of times."

And those times separated by just a few days, a few weeks. He had been on top of the world and now . . . the abyss.

But he squinted again into that intense Arctic sunlight and studied the river and felt the pull of hope. You must have hope, he told himself a hundred times a day.

Lose hope and all is lost.

And then, a moment later, he was sure, absolutely sure.

It was a boat!

And it was unquestionably moving in his direction, directly toward him.

It was a large rowboat and now he could see the oars dipping in and out of the water and glistening in the bright sunlight.

And behind the first boat, a second boat.

The boats progressed slowly across the river, but clearly the men in the boats had seen the smoky fire or heard his rifle's roar and had changed course to see if someone needed help. In these parts you did not move on if someone was in distress.

Jimmie waved wildly and hoarsely shouted at the top of his lungs. He could hardly believe his rescue was suddenly at hand. After so much time, it seemed impossible.

He wondered if maybe he was asleep and merely dreaming. Hope, after all, if he was honest, had faded. Great despair had overwhelmed him for the past several days. He had fought against this despair, but each small battle had weakened his resolve.

But now this!

The boats drew closer. Slowly closer.

Jimmie could see their faces now: wide and dark and flat with eyes set far apart. He thought they looked Mongolian but assumed they were, like the natives of Alaska, Eskimos, though he was not sure "Eskimo" was anything more than a generic term for people who lived above the Arctic Circle.

Not that who they were or what they were called mattered one whit. They were his rescuers, his saviors.

The men in the front boat wore smiles. Deep furrows lined their round faces, ravaged and weathered by life in this harsh Arctic environment. But nevertheless, their eyes looked soft and their smiles genuine.

Jimmie waved.

They waved back.

Hallelujah!

CHAPTER NINETEEN

The two large, flat-bottomed rowboats pulled up onto the sandy beach. Two men in the front boat stepped over the bow onto dry land. They were short and squat with ragged haircuts and teeth missing and in bad repair.

Jimmie reached out his hand in greeting. The men did not take it. It was not their custom to shake hands.

Jimmie tried to explain. All at once he wanted them to know who he was, why he was here, how he had come to be here, where he had come from, what had happened.

Of course, also, he had not spoken to a soul for days, weeks, and so his desire to speak, to communicate, was very close to overwhelming. Jimmie wanted them to know about the plane, about the crash, about his rafts, his grass hut, the ducks, the duck eggs, the mosquitoes, and maybe, most of all, about the suffering.

He wanted them, also, to know how grateful he was for their kindness, for their willingness to come to his assistance.

But all his words and actions spilled in vain. These indigenous people, these nomadic fur traders, who lived their whole lives along the Anadyr, with only sporadic contact with the outside world, did not understand a word Jimmie said. Nor did they comprehend his flailing arms or his pointing in various directions or his attempts to mimic a plane in flight. The *Century of Progress* was a mile away, entirely out of sight, so these people didn't have a clue that Jimmie was a pilot or that he had arrived in this remote, desolate place aboard an airplane. This tall, skinny, bearded, emotional man just as easily could have dropped out of the sky from some distant planet.

But one thing was perfectly obvious to these native Siberians, these trappers and hunters and fishermen, these simple family men who lived life close to the earth: This man standing all alone on the distant shore of the Anadyr, far from any settlement and without a boat or tools or proper gear, needed help.

And help was most assuredly one thing they were happy to give.

After a few minutes, they had Jimmie and his two leather satchels aboard the lead boat. They spread a bear hide on the deck and made room for their visitor to stretch out his long legs and lean back against the bulkhead.

Soon after, the boats headed upriver, away from the Bering Sea, away from "civilization," but Jimmie didn't care. A garrulous and extroverted fellow, Jimmie had been alone long enough. He had been hungry long enough. He had been filled with trepidation long enough. Just to find himself in the company of these Arctic nomads, despite the near impossibility of any but the most rudimentary communication, provided Jimmie with enormous relief and a sense of joy unlike anything he had ever experienced in his life.

He sat back against his gear in the belly of that boat and thanked God and these people for his liberation. He didn't care if it took six months to get back home, back to the States, back to his life, back to—if she would have him—his wife.

Time no longer had any measurable relevance. The fact that he would survive the crash, and its subsequent trial, was all that mattered.

For the first time in recent memory, Jimmie took a series of long, deep, relaxing breaths. He felt the pressure in his chest diminish with each exhalation.

A flock of long-tailed ducks flew overhead. One of the men put his hands to his mouth and perfectly imitated their call. Several of the ducks immediately broke formation and flew in low to investigate. When they came in over the boats, another man raised a rifle and shot two ducks out of the sky with two shots.

Without the issuance of a command, a skinny sled dog in the second boat jumped over the gunwale, retrieved the two ducks from the river, and brought them back. A woman's hand reached over the side, took the ducks, then grabbed the dog by the scruff of the neck and pulled the beast back into the boat.

My God, thought Jimmie, *all this time trying in vain to kill a duck and all I needed to do was sound like a duck and it would've practically flown onto my plate.* Then he understood he was in the hands of people who knew how to survive in this harsh environment.

The long Arctic afternoon wore on, and as it did, Jimmie relaxed more and more and began to take stock of his surroundings. He counted fourteen individuals between the two boats. Jimmie could not be certain, but he

CHAPTER NINETEEN

believed the hunting party was made up of three distinct families. He thought it was a hunting party because both boats were filled with pelts, hides, and furs. They had rifles and plenty of ammunition on board, and also fishing tackle, a supply of food, and cooking utensils.

Clearly, they were not just out for a leisurely day on the river.

Behind the boats they towed a variety of steel traps, some, he thought, for land animals like bear and fox, and others for water animals like beaver and otter. Jimmie knew nothing for certain, but he had plenty of time to sit back and try to deduce who these saviors were and how they stayed alive.

He counted three adult women, four adult men, and an assortment of children ranging in age, he supposed, from infancy through the teenage years. The youngest child was still breastfeeding and spent all its time cradled in his mother's arms. Two other young children hovered close to this same mother.

The two oldest children, both boys, did much of the rowing. They did not row fast, but they rowed with great deliberation and they held a steady course. Slowly, the two boats plied their way up the Anadyr.

All members of the party, Jimmie noticed, were dressed in furs, despite the fact that the high summer sun had warmed the temperature considerably. He decided this was likely what they wore all year around, just as wild animals wore the same coat throughout the seasons.

Some had the furs turned inside out with the fur against their bodies and the raw skin of the animal exposed to the air. Others, more traditionally, had the fur on the outside. The men, primarily, turned the fur to the inside.

Jimmie wondered if this was custom or simply personal preference.

He would have enjoyed asking these men about their customs and their way of life. Jimmie was a curious man. All his life he had asked a lot of questions. How else can you find out what you want to know? And conversation was one of his favorite pastimes, right up there with flying and planning trips around the world.

After all the weeks of solitude, with only himself to talk to, it drove him half crazy to sit in this boat among men and not be able to converse. Sitting alone in the cockpit of his ruined airplane during those storms of snow and ice and wind, Jimmie had done enough thinking and ruminating for two lifetimes.

He wanted to spend the rest of this lifetime sitting back and chewing the fat, laughing and taking it slow and easy.

Despite his gnawing hunger, Jimmie had no way of asking for food other than rubbing his belly and mimicking putting food in his mouth, chewing and swallowing. These gestures must have meant something else to these Arctic wanderers, however, for they merely nodded and smiled when he made them.

Jimmie did not think they took pleasure in his hunger, and so concluded they interpreted his gesturing as a sign his belly was full.

Nothing could have been further from the truth. His belly was empty and had been for days. He had all but lost his desire for food, though he knew when food was eventually offered, he needed to eat, as he desperately needed sustenance to regain his strength.

He felt weak and lethargic, as though it would take a tremendous effort to even stand up and take a step.

His muscles ached and his joints creaked.

His teeth hurt. And a few days ago he had noticed they had actually started to loosen inside his mouth. At first, Jimmie had thought this was just his imagination, but when he reached in and wiggled his upper incisors, sure enough—they moved considerably, causing him no small amount of consternation. And that damn infected molar.

But despite all this angst and uncertainty, Jimmie assured himself all would be well. He had, after all, been saved.

He looked out over the river. All was calm. The hour grew late but the sun still hung high in the Arctic sky here near the top of the world. Twenty-two hours of daylight this time of year with a couple hours of dusk before the sun rose on a new day.

All this daylight had caused Jimmie to lose track of the days. He was no longer certain of the date, the day of the week, or how many days had passed since the crash. He thought a week to ten days but decided it had probably been longer.

CHAPTER NINETEEN

He wondered if these nomads bothered to keep track of the days and weeks and months. Or did they just abide the seasons and daily changes and forego all the stress and strain associated with the constant counting of minutes and hours?

Open tundra reached as far as Jimmie could see on both sides of the river. It was at once a beautiful and terrifying landscape. There were no trees at all, only patches of grass and ground cover and small wind-blown shrubs. In the distance loomed low, rolling hills, some spotted with remnants of stark white snow.

There were no signs of life, though Jimmie knew the tundra teemed with both plant life and animal life. Tough, resilient species of plants and animals had adapted to the long, frigid winters and short, intense summers.

Like his saviors. These small, rugged nomadic trappers would look entirely out of place in Chicago or New York or Los Angeles, but here along the Anadyr, skimming quietly over the placid surface of the river, they existed as the wolves and bears and elk existed.

They mostly passed the time with the men cleaning weapons and repairing tools, while the women doted on the children and cleaned hides. A soft, continuous banter drifted between them, punctuated by hearty laughs and occasional knee slapping. Jimmie wondered if they were talking about him, though in reality they paid him little mind and almost seemed to have forgotten he sat among them.

None of it mattered.

He felt safe.

He had been saved.

He would not starve or freeze to death in his pathetic cockpit or along the lonely banks of the Anadyr River.

Around the world, people had no idea Jimmie Mattern had been saved. By this time many assumed he was long dead. Weeks, after all, had passed since he had last been seen in the city of Khabarovsk along the border with China.

Mattern had left Khabarovsk and set off on a long and dangerous flight across the Sea of Okhotsk and the Bering Sea for the Alaskan village of Nome and a return to North America. But hours, then days had passed without a word from the flier.

He was now weeks overdue.

The consensus was Mattern had run out of fuel. Either that or mechanical problems had sent Mattern's Lockheed Vega crashing into the sea.

Hope was still alive among family and friends and fellow aviators, but with each passing day this hope diminished.

Newspaper headlines told the story:

NO WORD FROM INTREPID AVIATOR

LONE FLYER LONG OVERDUE IN ALASKA

SOLO AVIATOR FEARED DEAD

MATTERN REMAINS UNREPORTED

HUNT FOR MATTERN APPEARS HOPELESS

The Soviets were out looking for Jimmie.

The Japanese sent ships and planes into and over the Sea of Okhotsk.

And, of course, the Americans were searching and praying.

But all in vain.

Some called the searches a fool's errand. The *Century of Progress* had gone down. It had either crashed into the ground or fallen into the sea. Mattern, like so many adventurous and courageous fliers before him, was dead.

Although, when reporters pressed his bride, Della Mattern disagreed. "I do not doubt for one second that Jimmie is still alive. He is a great flier and he knows how to survive. He may be in some distress, but I can assure you, we have not heard the last of Jimmie Mattern."

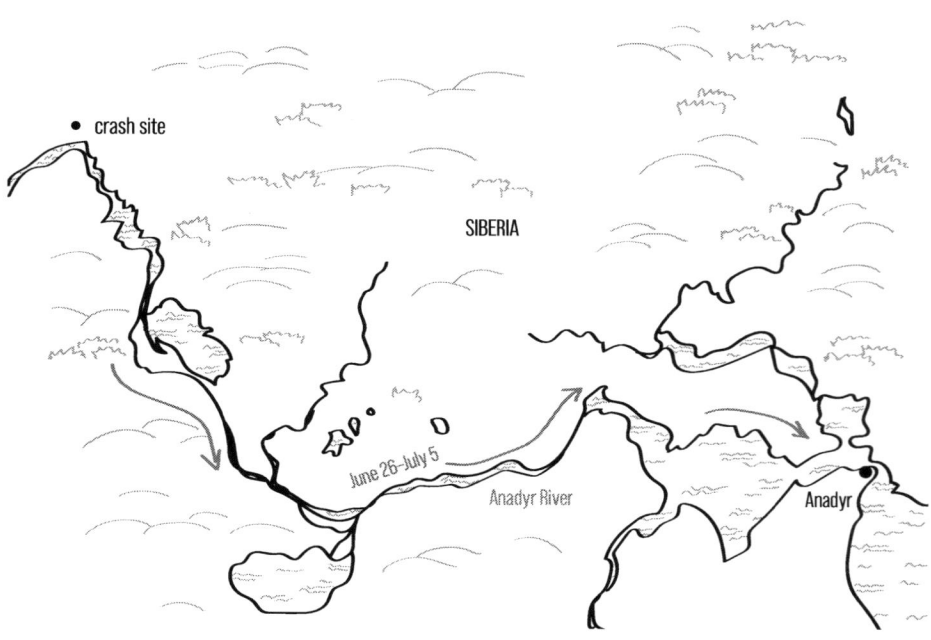

CHAPTER TWENTY

Along the Anadyr River

June 26–July 5, 1933
Cloudy skies, 34°F, winds calm

Late in the evening of that first day on the boat, it started to grow cool. By eleven o'clock, the sun hung low on the western horizon as a purple dusk swept over the tundra. Jimmie unsnapped one of his leather satchels and pulled out his heavy leather flight suit.

His hosts eyed him closely.

Jimmie removed his boots, pulled the suit on over his legs, and squirmed his arms into the jacket. It was a snug fit, especially over his clothes. He had to work to pull the long zipper up and around his neck.

His boatmates were fascinated by that zipper—they had never seen one before. It was something altogether miraculous. Their clothes and furs were held together occasionally by buttons but more frequently by simply wrapping a piece of cord or strap of leather around the garment and pulling tight.

The women and children in the boat leaned forward and tugged the zipper up and down several times with great delight. Jimmie made no effort to stop them. He enjoyed the close contact and the carefree smiles on their faces, especially the children.

Soon thereafter the two boats pulled up onto a wide, sandy beach. Everyone disembarked and went immediately to work without a word. The children collected wood and started a fire. The women unpacked the gear, cleaned the ducks, and prepared a meal. The men set up camp, including several tents and a pair of low tables.

Jimmie tried to help but realized he was mostly getting in the way, so he stepped aside and watched the Arctic nomads work with practiced precision. Everyone had a variety of jobs and only the smallest children remained idle.

Before long, right around midnight, a vague darkness covering the sky, they sat down to eat their meal. They did not use chairs but either sat on the ground covered with a square of leather or squatted on their haunches and consumed, with vigor, the oily duck meat, brown bread with honey, and a variety of roots, herbs, and grasses.

Jimmie quickly realized these same roots, herbs, and grasses had been available to him right under his nose, but his ignorance of the local flora and fauna had very nearly done him in. Survival in the wild, he had to admit, was a lost art in Western civilization.

The meal was served in an enormous iron pot, easily the largest Jimmie had ever seen. His hosts enthusiastically reached into the pot with dirty hands and pulled out fistfuls of food. The food went directly into their mouths and was chewed and consumed with audible delight.

Jimmie experienced an immediate revulsion. But no, he quickly realized, this was simply their custom, their culture. And something about the sheer joy they took in each and every bite soon had him smiling. Rarely in his life had he seen food devoured with such unadulterated pleasure.

After some hesitation, he reached his hand into the pot. He pulled out a piece of duck meat. He placed it in his mouth, chewed, and swallowed. Almost immediately the bit of duck meat made him feel unwell. He tried a piece of brown bread in the hope it might settle his stomach. That was all he could manage. Seconds later, he slipped off into the shadows and for the next several minutes retched until long after his stomach was empty.

The problem was not all those dirty hands in the pot. The problem was not the duck meat or the brown bread. The problem was Jimmie's weakened condition and his lack of food over his long period on the tundra.

CHAPTER TWENTY

Once the retching had stopped, Jimmie crept into one of the tents and crawled into a corner. The adrenaline that had sustained him the past few weeks drained from his body. He spent the night shivering and sweating and drifting in and out of a light delirium.

Jimmie was saved, but he was also sick. He had used up his stores of energy to stay alive, but those stores were now depleted.

The nomadic Arctic trappers did not hurry in the morning. The women arose first, fed the children and dogs, brewed herbal tea, and then sat around the fire fixing breakfast, mending clothes, and repairing traps.

Jimmie stumbled out of the tent, but feeling dizzy and disoriented, he quickly sat down not far from the fire. For several minutes, the women glanced repeatedly at him and spoke rapidly in hushed voices. Eventually, one of the women stood, walked over to Jimmie, leaned close, and, using both hands and no little force, pried open his mouth.

He was too weak to resist.

She reached into his mouth with unclean fingers and gave his teeth a gentle tug. Several of the molars rocked back and forth.

The stocky, squat woman turned to the other women, nodded, and then walked off across the tundra ripe with foliage. She returned several minutes later holding a plant that had been torn out of the ground by its roots. The entire plant was thrown into a pot of boiling water and left there to brew while the men rose, relieved themselves in the river, and ate breakfast. Immediately after breakfast, the men set about removing the pelts and furs from the boats. They carried their loads to a shelter on a high plain several hundred yards off the river.

While the men worked, the woman who had gathered the plant removed it from the boiling water and poured the dark brew into a tin cup. She handed the cup to Jimmie and mimed for him to drink.

Jimmie drank two cups of the strong herbal tea, and not long after he began to feel markedly better.

The women likely did not know the medical term for their guest's condition, but they easily recognized the symptoms—lethargy, pale skin, dry hair, bleeding gums, and the most telltale sign of all, loose teeth.

Scurvy was a common enough problem for those living above the Arctic Circle. They well knew its signs and how to treat it.

Jimmie didn't know the signs associated with scurvy, but he felt pretty sure he was depleted in Vitamin C and probably several other essential nutrients. The tea tasted of mint, so he thought it might have been thyme, an excellent source of Vitamin C. Just minutes after drinking the brew, he felt well enough to stand and move around and even eat a bit of brown bread and honey without feeling nauseous.

So now, he realized, these simple nomads had saved his life not once but twice.

He lavished the women with thanks.

They giggled and averted their eyes.

By midafternoon, the party had packed up their camp and returned to the river. To Jimmie's enormous relief, they now headed downstream, toward the settlement of Anadyr and the Bering Sea, rather than upstream and farther from civilization. He had feared the trappers might be setting off on a summer-long expedition, and he would have little choice but to remain with them, perhaps for several weeks or even months.

For four days and nights they rowed and floated down the Anadyr. Late on the first day, they passed the spot where Jimmie had been rescued, and that night they camped not far from where he had travelled by raft before the tide turned and the current pushed him back upstream.

All of that suddenly felt so long ago. Just as his flight over the Atlantic and Great Britain and Europe and Asia now felt like a lifetime ago.

That night in camp, feeling still stronger and more himself, Jimmie opened his satchels and set out his few belongings for his saviors to peruse. The teenage boys spent an hour playing with his pearl-handled hunting knife. They had never seen anything quite like it. Also of great interest was his Pratt & Whitney tool kit, especially the simple pair of pliers. The children spent hours opening and closing those pliers and using the tool to pick things up and put them down.

The men spent the night bent over Jimmie's large array of maps.

Before retiring to their tents, Jimmie gave most of his possessions away as gifts. He felt it was the least he could do for what they had given him.

The only possessions he retained were his compass and watch. He still hoped to one day complete his journey around the world, and to do so he would need his compass so that he might navigate his way home. The watch was one of a kind, made just for Jimmie by the A. Wittnauer Company, the famed Swiss watchmakers.

On the afternoon of the fourth day, they came upon a small settlement comprised of a few wood shacks and several tents. Jimmie did not think it was Anadyr, which he believed was a village of several hundred inhabitants. This looked more like a temporary encampment, maybe set up for the summer trapping season. Still, he hoped he would find someone who could speak English and get word of his safety to the outside world. Jimmie worried constantly now about his mother and wife and friends suffering over the uncertainty of his fate.

But to his dismay, his hosts did not land at the settlement. Instead, they merely waved and then rowed across the river, half a mile wide at that point, and made camp on the other bank.

For five days they stayed put without moving. Jimmie tried to make them understand he wished to visit the settlement, but his efforts proved in vain. The nomadic trappers had pivoted into rest mode, rarely rising except to eat, relieve themselves, and fetch firewood.

Jimmie kept himself busy, and reasonably calm, by writing in his journal. His hosts, especially the children, took great interest in his scribbling. They had never seen anyone use pencil and paper before. The entire lot would stand behind Jimmie and look over his shoulder as he scratched out his thoughts and observations.

Late in the afternoon of the third day, a boat arrived at camp from the settlement across the river. Three men stepped out of the boat and came ashore. They had heard news of a stranger and wanted to see with their own eyes.

Jimmie chattered at them a mile a minute, but, like the others, these men did not understand a word he uttered. They did, however, invite the stranger to return with them to the settlement.

Somewhat reluctant to leave his saviors, Jimmie nevertheless gathered his gear and stepped into the boat. He did not know if he was crossing for a quick visit or if he was going for good. All he knew for sure was that he needed to reach Anadyr, and his best chance might be to cross the river and hope he could communicate his desire to someone who would understand.

The settlement sprawled across the riverbank for half a mile or so. It was populated by the same indigenous people who had rescued Jimmie eight days earlier. No one in the settlement spoke a word of English or any other language Jimmie could understand. They were friendly and curious and welcoming, but the inability to communicate left Jimmie frustrated and irritable. Every day he felt better and stronger, but with his improved health came a greater desire to escape these confines and return to civilization. One day after another passed with little to do and nothing to make him think the next day would be any different.

Wooden crates were strewn around the settlement with MADE IN AMERICA stamped on the sides and top. Jimmie pointed over and over to the crates and to the word AMERICA, and over and over the villagers smiled and nodded. They managed to communicate that the crates had delivered flour and sugar, guns and ammunition, ropes and traps—all the basic staples that made their lives here above the Arctic Circle bearable. They seemed to understand that this stranger in their midst had come from AMERICA.

Coming from AMERICA made Jimmie a welcome guest, even a luminary.

Jimmie ate well. He ate fish, fowl, bread, vegetables, and honey. He slept well also, either in the tent of the local chief or, when the weather was pleasant, outside under a large overturned sled covered with bear and caribou hides. He walked for exercise and each day his ankles felt better and stronger. In the evening he played a game with the other men that resembled checkers, only the board was larger, and instead of checkers they used small bits of bone or hide. The games never really seemed to end and winning did not appear to be the ultimate goal. Still, Jimmie was happy to sit in the company of others, even if he could not communicate with words.

He longed to converse. It had been weeks by this time. The last conversation he had held in English was back in Khabarovsk with a member of the Soviet Air Force, who basically knew how to say "hello," "goodbye," and "thank you." His last conversation of any substance had been back in Moscow in early June.

Jimmie felt strong and well fed and well rested, but the time had come to regain control of his life. He was thankful for everything these people had done for him, but he needed, desperately, to start moving again. And short of that, dammit, he at least needed someone to talk to! Anyone! About anything!

Keeping his desires in check proved a difficult chore. A man who typically held the reins with some determination, Jimmie had no choice but to relinquish control and allow providence to take its own course. A thousand times a day he belittled himself mentally and emotionally for not changing the oil in the *Century of Progress* back in Khabarovsk. And another thousand times a day he ordered himself to stop dwelling on the past.

His anxiety reached its peak on the afternoon of the fourth day at the settlement when he and several other men rowed across the river to the encampment of his rescuers. They had gone! There was no one left and no sign they intended to return anytime soon.

Jimmie lost his cool. He began to rant and stomp the ground. Whatever he had been doing to hold himself together snapped. For several minutes he hyperventilated. The other men ignored his behavior, as it was out of their realm of experience. They simply turned away and chatted amiably about the weather or perhaps their wives.

But then out of his pocket, Jimmie pulled a thick wad of American dollars. Greenbacks. He had a grand total of $163. He thrust the crumpled-up money at the men.

They did not take it.

Jimmie pointed at the boat. He mimed the act of rowing. "Anadyr!" He shouted. "I need to reach Anadyr!" And he again thrust the roll of bank notes at them.

Incredibly, they seemed to understand. For a minute or so they spoke among themselves. A mere minute after that they climbed back into the boat and returned to the settlement where Jimmie collected his gear.

And then off they went.

Three men took turns at the oars. They rowed all afternoon and well into the evening. They camped on the riverbank and in the morning they reached a broad lake. A simple sail was raised and a steady breeze out of the west made the crossing brisk and easy.

Beyond the lake, the river was wide and the current ran fast. In short order they reached Anadyr.

All those long, agonizing days and nights, and in the end, Jimmie had been just a two days' row from civilization.

Anadyr was an established village of several hundred people. There was a wooden dock with gas pumps. There was a general store with food and supplies for sale. There was a dirt road leading away from the river and wires strung on poles carrying electricity.

Walking up the dusty dirt road away from the river, heading for the small town, Jimmie felt certain he heard Russian being spoken.

Word spread quickly that a stranger, an American, had arrived from upriver, and folks turned out by the dozens to see for themselves.

Before long, a young man stepped up to Jimmie and said, "I am Nicholas."

Jimmie heard these three simple words and broke into a broad smile. He embraced Nicholas and rejoiced, "Good God, man, am I ever glad to see you!"

The two men conversed in English for several minutes.

Jimmie told his story.

CHAPTER TWENTY

Nicholas told Jimmie that word had arrived weeks ago to keep an eye out for an American flier who may have crashed in the area.

Jimmie could hardly accept this new reality. He had to choke back tears.

"I have been missing for quite some time," he told Nicholas. "Since around the middle of June. More than two weeks."

"Closer to three weeks," corrected Nicholas.

"Three weeks?" asked Jimmie. "Are you sure? What is the date?" Jimmie had been keeping track of the days and the date both in his head and in his journal.

"Five July," said Nicholas.

"July fifth? Seriously?"

Nicholas nodded. "Five July 1933."

Jimmie could only shake his head. He had obviously lost all track of time. Probably back in the cockpit of his airplane. Or maybe alone along the Anadyr. A week or more, lost. It was all that relentless daylight. Twenty-two hours of daylight and a couple hours of dusk. Nothing close to the dark of night.

But what did it matter?

It didn't matter.

Nothing mattered now but that he was here. In Anadyr. With Nicholas. Speaking English.

He gave the young man another hug.

Nicholas accepted it graciously and then led Jimmie into the dining room of a nearby house, where Jimmie sat down and ate a hearty meal of roasted caribou and potatoes with gravy, vegetables, and pie.

The food just kept coming.

Jimmie ate until he could eat no more.

Eventually he asked Nicholas if Anadyr had a telegraph office.

Nicholas nodded and led the way.

The telegraph office occupied a back corner of the post office. It took some time to find the telegraph operator. Once the man was at his machine, Jimmie dictated a short message. He sent the same message to two different recipients.

He sent one to his pals and business partners at Sam Sackett's law office in Chicago, Illinois, and one to Thomas Kinkaid, Moscow correspondent for *The New York Times*.

The cable read, simply:

SAFE AT ANADYR, SIBERIA. JIMMIE MATTERN.

CHAPTER TWENTY-ONE

Anadyr, Siberia

July 5–July 18, 1933

Almost from the moment of his arrival in Anadyr, Jimmie's life, and his accompanying emotional state, unfolded like a Coney Island roller-coaster ride—which, by the way, Jimmie had ridden back in late May prior to his departure. It was called the "Switchback Railway," and the bumpy, noisy, wooden contraption had scared the undaunted aviator half to death.

Initially, Jimmie believed the Russians wanted to do everything in their power to assist the American flier in his desire to continue his around-the-world journey. Nicholas and others, both in and out of the Soviet military, were cooperative and friendly.

But behind the scenes, over the next many days and even weeks, young Mattern would be used by both sides, especially the Soviets, as a political football. Negotiations between the United States and the USSR over formal diplomatic relations had stalled, and Joseph Stalin, unbeknownst to Jimmie, would use the aviator as a pawn in an effort to gain an advantage over the newly elected American president, Franklin D. Roosevelt.

The first few days, however, went well.

Nicholas made sure the American had access to the telegraph office. Jimmie sent telegrams to friends and loved ones assuring them all was well.

He sent a second cable to Kinkaid of *The New York Times*, informing the correspondent he had a wild and adventurous tale to tell.

And when Jimmie sought news from America, Nicholas provided whatever information he had at his disposal. Jimmie was particularly interested in a pilot by the name of Wiley Post. Jimmie knew his old friend and flying competitor had set a date of July 4, 1933, to commence his around-the-world flight, and he desperately wanted to know if Post had departed. At that point Jimmie still held out hope that his American sponsors could fly another plane into Anadyr, thereby allowing him to continue his mission that had started over a month earlier back at Floyd Bennett Field on Long Island.

It turned out Post was still on the ground in New York. His plane, the *Winnie Mae*, another customized Lockheed Vega, had experienced mechanical problems, but it sounded as though Post was waiting to learn the fate of his friend Jimmie Mattern before setting off on his globe-trotting jaunt.

This news heartened Jimmie, but of course he knew Wiley was a very competitive guy and would likely hit the skies as soon as he heard Mattern was alive and well. It was a fine and gracious gesture for Wiley to remain grounded while Jimmie's fate remained a mystery, especially considering the pilot of the *Century of Progress* had pulled a fast one by feigning another Mattern/Griffin duet. But first around-the-world solo was an aviation record of singular distinction, so Jimmie knew Wiley and the *Winnie Mae* would soon be airborne.

The two fliers, after all, were competitors as well as friends.

While he awaited word from America, Jimmie asked the Soviets if it would be possible to retrieve his airplane, or at least any parts of the *Century of Progress* that might be salvageable. To his astonishment, his hosts not only agreed to Jimmie's request, they also provided him with free labor and a motorized barge complete with crew.

Before heading back up the Anadyr the following morning, Jimmie rounded up a couple of cameras. He thought for the sake of posterity it might be a good idea to make a photographic record of his time in Siberia.

And beyond posterity, Jimmie also believed his story and any accompanying photographs might just be worth a few dollars.

The flotilla consisted of two motorized vessels. The first was a large and powerful launch with a crew of eight Soviet sailors, all of whom had volunteered to assist the American.

Behind the launch chugged an enormous, flat-bottomed barge carrying all the equipment needed to dismantle the *Century of Progress*. Self-powered, it could not move quite as fast as the launch, but on board rode a dozen local trappers and hunters eager to put some paper money in their pockets. They had signed on to haul airplane parts from the crash site to the river and load those parts onto the barge.

The launch had a well-stocked mess, where Jimmie ate a couple of delicious meals and partook of a sip or two of icy Russian vodka. The launch also provided Jimmie with a comfy bunk, where he enjoyed several lengthy naps.

He could hardly believe how drastically his life had changed. Just days ago, he was starving on the riverbank with his hopes of survival at a low ebb. Now he sat amongst a cast of friendly Soviet sailors encouraging him to eat and drink and enjoy life.

It took a mere five hours for the small fleet to reach the temporary camp where Jimmie had lived for several days with his rescuers. Five hours! At the time, Jimmie had felt like civilization was a million miles away, a place he might never again reach, but in fact he had been just five hours from a telegraph station.

The crew stopped and went ashore. To Jimmie's great delight, the families that had rescued him were in residence. They greeted Jimmie like some long-lost brother. Pictures were snapped and food consumed before the flotilla continued its upstream journey.

Another hour and they reached the small island where Jimmie had discovered duck eggs but had quickly found they were too close to hatching to eat. Here they took more photographs, but mosquitoes as large as hummingbirds and more ravenous than locusts quickly drove the sailors back onto the river, where the breeze kept the blood-sucking pests at bay.

Soon thereafter they reached the place on the Anadyr River where Jimmie had waited day after endless day for a passing boat.

"There!" he pointed.

"Where?" the sailors asked. "There is nothing."

"Yes! This is it! Definitely! Land here!"

The sailors swung the launch toward shore and inquired about the whereabouts of their passenger's airplane.

Jimmie pointed again. "Up and over that rise."

The launch was anchored in the channel and all went ashore on the barge. In total, they were twenty-two men, including Jimmie, Nicholas, eight Soviet sailors, and a dozen local laborers. They hiked to the top of the low rise and from the summit they could see the airplane in the distance lying on its belly on the open tundra. It looked small and insignificant amidst the melting snow and Arctic grass and bushy shrubs in summer bloom.

To the men, especially the indigenous nomads who traveled by self-powered boats and dog-powered sleds, it seemed impossible such a machine could have carried a man through the air more than halfway around the world.

Pulling and lugging tools and heavy equipment, the salvage party slowly made its way across the tundra. Once they reached the plane, they marveled again at its diminutive size and then voiced their amazement that the American had survived first the crash and then all those long days on nothing more than a few biscuits and some chocolate.

Additional photographs were taken, including photos of Jimmie inside the cockpit of the *Century of Progress*, standing beside his airplane, and kneeling in the grass with rifle in hand. Jimmie smiled broadly as Nicholas snapped these pictures, but he told his fellow travelers over and over that he most certainly had not been smiling during his isolation.

The time came to see what could be salvaged from the *Century of Progress*. They first removed the instruments and any maps Jimmie had left behind. In a cupboard behind his seat, Jimmie found the motion picture camera and half a dozen rolls of film he had shot while flying up the coast of the United States and Canada. The Atlantic crossing had been too socked in to shoot, but he had taken some additional footage over Great Britain and Europe.

CHAPTER TWENTY-ONE

Jimmie had hoped to remove and transport the wings of his ship, but it quickly became apparent this would prove impossible. He settled on the propeller and the Pratt & Whitney Wasp engine. To free the engine from the fuselage Jimmie used an axe, as the Lockheed Vega's body was made mostly of laminated plywood.

An overwhelming fatigue bore down on Jimmie at almost the same instant the engine split away from the ruined fuselage and fell to the ground. The exhaustion was clearly a combination of the physical exertion and the emotional trauma of seeing the *Century of Progress* ruined and smashed to smithereens. Long buried in his thoughts had been a whimsical chimera that his airplane might somehow be made to fly again.

The axe once and for all destroyed his fantasy.

Jimmie, with some reluctance, said goodbye to his *Century of Progress* for undoubtedly the last time. Then he, along with several of the sailors, trudged back to the barge and returned to the launch. Immediately he stretched out on his bunk and fell asleep.

He awoke a few hours later when the rest of the party arrived at the Anadyr, their makeshift sled carrying his airplane engine and its Hamilton propeller. The task had been an arduous one and Jimmie gave them all great thanks.

Nicholas took more photographs. He snapped photos of Jimmie standing along the riverbank and sitting outside his simple shelter of evergreen boughs and tundra grass where he had spent so many long, restless nights. Jimmie did his best to smile in these photos, but his expression could not hide a deep weariness.

The men ate a hearty meal and drank several toasts to their successful mission. The Soviet sailors especially knew how to toast. They toasted long after any and all reasonable and applicable toasts had been offered.

Jimmie hung in with the shots of vodka for as long as he could, but before long, exhausted and a little depressed, he took his leave. He retired to his bunk, put his head down, and fell back to sleep until the following morning.

Due to rain and fog and a strong upstream current, it took most of the following day to make the return trip to Anadyr. Once the party arrived, the salvaged parts of the *Century of Progress* were stored in a weather-proof shed until arrangements could be made to have the gear shipped back to the States.

Jimmie was given a private room in the local barracks, and in that room was a bed with a box spring and mattress. He could not believe his great good fortune. He slept and slept and slept. And when not sleeping, he ate and ate and ate.

Slowly his strength, stamina, and good health returned, although he did continue to suffer from fatigue, along with digestion issues resulting from the local diet, which consisted of much oily fish and heavy bread.

During this time, Jimmie still believed his departure from Anadyr, from Siberia, from the Soviet Union was imminent and without a doubt he would be back in America within days. Unfortunately, he was sorely mistaken.

The days began to pass and Jimmie's frustration began to mount. At first he thought it was nothing more than poor communications. The telegraph lines would work perfectly one day and not work at all the next. One morning he was able to raise an American cargo ship out on the Bering Sea, but minutes after making contact the signal suddenly and inexplicably died. A day or so later he managed to contact a radio operator in Nome, but again, after exchanging a few bits of information, the signal ceased.

"We are a very remote outpost, Jimmie," explained Nicholas. "I am sorry, but these failures happen all the time."

"It's frustrating."

Nicholas nodded. "For all of us."

"I just want to be on my way."

"I understand, but you must be patient."

Jimmie did his best. Three days passed. Five days. A week. He slept as much as possible and carefully controlled his diet. He walked for exercise. He grew stronger. He played card games with the sailors. He learned to play a three-string guitar called a *balalaika*, an instrument with a large triangular body and a long thin neck. Jimmie practiced and practiced, as he had little else to do and it kept both his hands and his mind occupied. He took Russian lessons from Nicholas and some of the sailors, but they were far more interested in learning English than in teaching Jimmie Russian. In public they all spoke very highly of General Secretary Stalin and the Soviet system, but in private they all wanted to go to America.

Little by little, Jimmie began to realize more than poor communications had him grounded here in Anadyr. All the international political intrigue would not become clear to Jimmie until after he was back in the United States, but evidence began to mount that the Soviet government, likely from as far away as Moscow, was dictating the terms of his circumstances.

An Alaskan bush pilot, Bob Ellis, stood by over in Nome, ready and willing to fly across the Bering Sea and pick up Jimmie, but the Soviets refused to let Ellis into their country. The cargo ship *Northland* roamed the Northern Pacific awaiting orders to dock at Anadyr and retrieve the American flier, but Moscow would not give the ship permission to enter Soviet waters.

Jimmie demanded explanations for all the delays and excuses and miscommunications, but Nicholas and the small military contingent stationed in Anadyr merely threw up their collective arms, shook their heads, and insisted, "This is the way of life in the Soviet Union."

"Damn the way of life in the Soviet Union!" Jimmie bellowed.

The officers just smiled and shrugged. "In the Soviet Union, nothing gets done. You hurry up and wait. It drives us all crazy. You are not the only one."

Jimmie argued, but in vain.

And then, on the afternoon of July 15, ten days after his arrival in Anadyr, Jimmie received word—Wiley Post had lifted off from Floyd Bennett Field on Long Island in his airplane, the *Winnie Mae*, and was at that time flying up the east coast of North America.

Jimmie's heart sank. Here he sat on his duff on the eastern edge of Siberia, just hours from Alaska, just days from New York City, but . . . stuck.

Trapped.

All jammed up.

Entirely powerless to control his fate.

And all while Wiley, free as a bird, flew up the coast and prepared to cross the Atlantic and circumnavigate the globe. Jimmie did not wish ill of his old friend. Just the opposite. He wished his fellow flier godspeed, tailwinds, and clear weather. But Jimmie also wished Joseph Stalin and his pathetic bureaucrats would give him the green light so he could get back in the air and beat Wiley's butt back to New York.

Instead, early one morning, a cadre of those Soviet bureaucrats showed up at the barracks to interrogate the American aviator. Of course, they didn't call it an interrogation; they simply said they wanted to chat, to set the record straight.

Jimmie, they inferred, had been making noise that the reason his plane had crashed on the tundra was due to inferior Russian oil ruining his engine. He had purportedly been overheard to say that this inferior Russian lubricant had clogged his oil lines and caused his engine to seize, thereby leading to his crash.

At first, Jimmie did not deny or confirm that he had made these accusations. He simply sat and listened and then demanded to know when he would be permitted to leave.

The bureaucrats informed Jimmie that he had arrived in the USSR without the proper visa and therefore would not be permitted to leave until a proper visa was issued. Jimmie insisted this was pure baloney. He said he had applied for and received all the proper documentation before leaving America. They said the visa in his possession restricted him to travel in and around Moscow. It did not give him permission to travel to other parts of the country.

Jimmie was still a young man at this time, but he was old enough and savvy enough to see the writing on the wall.

These goons didn't give a damn about his visa. They just wanted him to knock off railing about inferior Russian oil being the cause of his crash. That was publicity they did not want.

Additionally, they wanted the American flier to play up how well he had been treated since being rescued by "Soviet citizens" in the Siberian outback.

Dammit, thought Jimmie. *It's all about politics.*

"The oil was crap," he finally told them, "but the truth is, I should've drained the sludge out of my engine when I had the chance. So that's on me. As for being well treated, with the exception of you fine and upstanding gentlemen, it's been absolutely aces. The finest, most hospitable people I've ever met in my life."

A few days later, on July 18, 1933, the Soviet Union's most famous aviator, Sigizmund Levanevsky, arrived in Anadyr with orders from Joseph Stalin himself to transport the American flier, James Joseph Mattern, back to the United States.

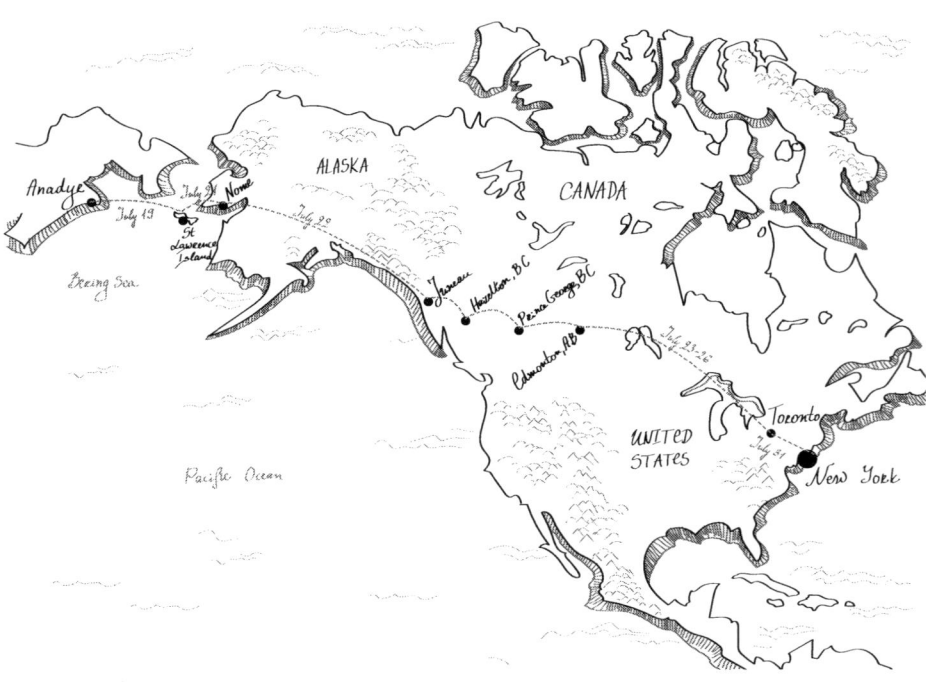

CHAPTER TWENTY-TWO

Anadyr to New York

July 19-31, 1933

Another couple days passed before Levanevsky and his crew finally arrived in Anadyr. But still Jimmie was made to wait while the Soviets had their pontoon-equipped seaplane, a German-built Dornier Do J Wal, serviced and refueled. The Dornier Wal was a massive, twin-engine flying boat capable of covering enormous distances with a full load of fuel. But even after the servicing and refueling was completed, Jimmie remained in Siberia.

Levanevsky was little help. Aloof and perhaps a bit shy, he was cordial but otherwise kept his distance. He had obviously been ordered by his superiors to perform this mission, but befriending the chatty, overly friendly, gregarious American had definitely not been part of those orders.

When Jimmie asked when they might expect to depart for Alaska, Levanevsky, through an interpreter, replied, "Only one man knows the answer to that question."

Jimmie assumed this nebulous remark referred to the General Secretary, but when he asked if this was so, Levanevsky merely shrugged and offered only the slightest hint of a smile.

Jimmie knew then that he and the famous Soviet aviator were just a couple of very small fish in a great big ocean.

The order must've finally been given, for early one morning Jimmie was rousted out of bed and told to pack his gear and be at the dock in five minutes. Sure enough, upon rising, he heard the two powerful engines of the Dornier warming up along the river.

The time to leave the Soviet Union had finally arrived!

Jimmie pulled on his Russian pants and Russian boots, zipped up his flight jacket, shoved his few personal items into a leather satchel, grabbed the two boxes of gear salvaged from the *Century of Progress* (the Wasp engine and propeller would eventually be shipped via cargo ship), and raced down to the Dornier.

No sooner had Jimmie climbed aboard than Levanevsky, at the helm, put the powerful seaplane in motion.

At this time, even as the Dornier taxied across the bay and turned into the wind for takeoff, Jimmie had plans to reach Nome, take whatever steps necessary to procure an airplane, and return to Anadyr, where he would take a deep breath and then resume his solo flight around the world. The Soviets had granted him permission to do this.

But not five minutes after getting airborne and heading out over the Bering Sea, Levanevsky received a radio message: Wiley Post, flying the *Winnie Mae*, had reached Alaska and was expected momentarily in Fairbanks.

The news soon reached Jimmie in the back of the plane. Fairbanks, he knew, was deep into Alaska, hundreds of miles east of Nome, almost to Canada. Barring misfortune, Post would soon be back in New York City, whereas Jimmie, if all went well—which it probably wouldn't, if recent history was a harbinger—would still be days behind his rival.

Right then and there, Jimmie's dream of being first to fly solo around the world, which had occupied virtually all his thoughts and actions over the past year, finally and forever died. He felt the air, and some part of his life, leave his body. For an hour or more he sat on that jump seat in the rear of the Dornier in an emotional stupor.

CHAPTER TWENTY-TWO

Truth be told, he could not help but feel just a little sorry for himself. All the preparation and all the energy spent—only to be waylaid by bad weather and bad luck and bad oil.

To hell with flying back to Anadyr, he thought. *To hell with flying around the world. To hell with records and glory. To hell with all of it. I just wanna get home.*

A few hours later, adding insult to the emotional injury, the big German seaplane ran into a wall of dense fog over the Bering Sea a couple hundred miles west of Nome. Levanevsky, lacking the necessary equipment to fly blind, put the seaplane down on Powooiliak Bay just off the coast of St. Lawrence Island. There the Soviets and their American guest, now in American waters, spent a long night bobbing on a gentle sea.

Jimmie did not sleep a wink and spent the better part of eight hours considering what could have been.

In the morning, under clear skies, they took off again for the final leg into Nome. But again they ran into trouble when the Dornier began to cough and sputter. The airplane, Jimmie realized, was rapidly running out of gas. It turned out a miscommunication back in Anadyr had resulted in the fuel tanks only being half filled.

Levanevsky flew on until the gas ran out, then he glided for as long as his seaplane would stay airborne before splashing down in Norton Sound with land in sight and Nome just a few miles to the northeast.

And there they floated and drifted for several anxious hours until a tug arrived and towed the Dornier up the coast and into Nome Harbor.

It was a humbling and embarrassing return for the intrepid American aviator.

But still, Jimmie was back on American soil. He was free again. Liberated. And despite a vast whirlwind of emotions cycling through his thoughts, Jimmie knew without question that this deliverance, this liberation—both from his crash and his captivity—signified more than all the other sentiments and sensations put together. If he had learned one undeniable fact during his long, harsh trial in Siberia, it surely was the profound purity of freedom—freedom to come and go as one pleases, freedom from fear and hunger, freedom from cold and isolation, freedom from despair and petty despotism.

By the time Jimmie stepped off that seaplane onto North American soil, nearly seven weeks after departing Floyd Bennett Field, five weeks after crashing on the remote Arctic tundra, he had come to terms with his recent past and now wanted only to look to the future.

James Joseph Mattern did not know it at the time, but the story of his survival in the remote wilderness of the Siberian tundra had captured the imagination of people around the world. Across Asia, Europe, and North America, newspapers put out extra editions simply to print the latest news about the American flier. Radio programming was regularly interrupted to provide listeners with updates on Jimmie's whereabouts.

The president of the United States even mentioned the stranded aviator during one of his weekly fireside chats from the White House. FDR wished young Mattern well and said he prayed for his safe return.

Yes, Wiley Post was big news also. More than fifty thousand people were on hand when he arrived back at Floyd Bennett Field on July 22, 1933, after completing his solo flight around the world in a mere seven and a half days. Post was given a ticker-tape parade down Broadway. His photograph adorned the front pages of newspapers and covers of magazines. He had an audience with President Roosevelt. Will Rogers interviewed him on the radio.

But even during the height of Wiley Post mania, Jimmie Mattern remained in the news. His around-the-world odyssey held the public's attention during those intoxicating summer days in a way that Wiley Post's relatively stress-free journey never could. Wiley took off from Floyd Bennett Field on a Saturday morning and returned one week later, about the same length of time as a typical family's summer vacation to the beach or the mountains. He had some bad weather here and a mechanical problem there, but for the most part Wiley flew and refueled and flew and refueled and flew some more until he got back to New York. It was without question a tremendous achievement and the young flier was celebrated for his courage and his success.

But as a story, as a narrative, as a human drama that easily could have turned into a terrible tragedy, the Post flight could not hold a candle to the Mattern flight. Jimmie's flight had it all: a handsome and dashing pilot, a disappearance over the Atlantic, endless weather, mechanical and fuel problems, and finally, over one of the most forbidding and remote places on the planet, the CRASH!

For days and then weeks, any trace of the daring aviator and his *Century of Progress* vanished from the face of the earth. As time passed and hope faded, more and more people assumed Jimmie Mattern was dead, either from a fiery crash on land or a plane torn asunder when it smacked into the Bering Sea. And all this while back home in Walla Walla, his devoted and loving bride— or so reported the newspapers—assured the nation her husband was alive and well and would most certainly survive his deprivations.

And how right Della Mattern was!

When news began to filter out of Siberia that Jimmie Mattern had indeed survived a crash landing and then weeks alone on the Arctic tundra, the narrative was complete.

A legend was born.

Back up in Nome, finally unshackled from his Siberian confinement, Jimmie had no notion of any of this. He had not read the papers and he did not have access to a radio. He was just happy to see some American faces, hear some plain-spoken English, and eat some good old-fashioned American chow.

He passed just one night in Nome and then beat it south for Juneau in a bush plane piloted by Alaskan native and aviation legend Bob Ellis. After impatiently waiting for the fog to lift in the Alaskan capital, Ellis flew his passenger southeast to British Columbia, where Jimmie rendezvoused with members of his rescue team.

This team was made up of Fred Fetterman, pilot Bill Alexander, a couple of old friends, and Irving Friedman, a Brooklyn brewer and president of King's Brewery, which stood just a few miles from Floyd Bennett Field on Long Island. Friedman had followed Jimmie's around-the-world flight with great interest, and he had been heartbroken when the flier disappeared in

Siberia. When word reached Brooklyn that Mattern was alive and well, the wealthy brewer offered to fund a rescue mission to Alaska.

The team had flown out of New York in a spacious Bellanca Pacemaker and had made good time until they experienced engine troubles west of Edmonton, Alberta. Alexander had been forced to land at the small grass strip in Hazelton, British Columbia, where Fred Fetterman had been busy for the past few days making repairs.

Jimmie flew in with Bob Ellis just as Fred finished repairing the Bellanca's 220 hp Wright Whirlwind J-5 engine.

After an exuberant reunion wherein Jimmie detailed his trials and tribulations in Siberia and with the Soviet government, the team decided to start back east. Alexander relinquished control, and for the first time in more than six weeks, Jimmie slipped into the pilot's seat, put his hands on the stick, and fired up the engine. Takeoff proved problematic as the Bellanca was underpowered and overloaded with both fuel and passengers, and that grass runway, designed for small single-engine bush planes, was, at most, 2,500 feet long.

Jimmie just barely cleared the tall conifers at the eastern edge of the strip.

"Living dangerously, hey Jimmie?" Fred shouted from the navigator's seat.

Jimmie smiled and shrugged.

Their destination was Edmonton, where another plane awaited Jimmie, but they flew only as far as Prince George, British Columbia, when the engine began to misfire. Fred insisted they land so he could take a look at the valves and correct the problem.

"If you want to guarantee yourself plenty of delays," Jimmie joked, "make sure to bring your mechanic along for the ride. They hear bad stuff coming from the engine, propeller, and wings that nobody else in the world can hear."

The team spent the night in Prince George, Fred did his thing, and bright and early the next morning they prepared to fly on. But it had rained overnight, leaving the grass field a water-logged quagmire.

Jimmie had barely cleared the trees at the far end of the field when the Wright Whirlwind engine momentarily stalled due to the nose of the

Bellanca pointing almost straight up at the heavens. But Jimmie leveled off, the cylinders fired, and the Pacemaker flew on.

Jimmie began to wonder if some strange extraterrestrial being wanted to keep him out of the sky.

The Bellanca landed in Edmonton where Jimmie, after thanking Friedman and his crew and slapping Fetterman on the back, transferred into a Curtiss O-40 Raven and took off by himself for the first time since his disastrous flight out of Khabarovsk back on June 14.

For a dozen hours over the next three days, Jimmie flew without incident under deep blue skies with favorable westerlies on his tail. He had plenty of time to sit back and relax and ponder all the crazy stuff that had happened since he'd flown out of New York nearly two months earlier. He knew he had stories to tell and he felt confident people would want to hear those stories, and maybe, if he was lucky, they might even pay to hear those stories.

When all this was finally over, Jimmie knew he would need to find a way to make some money.

But, par for the course, Jimmie's around-the-world flight would not be complete without one more mishap. This one occurred over Lake Huron, when the O-40 Raven suddenly blew a cylinder, black smoke poured out of the engine, and compression began to fall. Jimmie knew he would never make it to New York City, but he did manage to clear the lake, skirt just south of Toronto, and land at Buffalo Municipal Airport.

Safely on the ground, Jimmie again had to wonder if maybe his around-the-world flight had been cursed from the beginning.

Ed Aldrin of Standard Oil came to the rescue. Ed had a Lockheed Vega very similar to the *Century of Progress* ready to fly. He had the plane delivered to Buffalo so that Jimmie could have the distinction of flying solo back to New York. The around-the-world record belonged to Wiley Post, but Aldrin believed, and many agreed, that Jimmie Mattern deserved special recognition for his heroics.

James Joseph Mattern was, without question, an aviation pioneer.

On the final leg of his solo flight around the world, Jimmie took off out of Buffalo at 12:57 on the steamy afternoon of Monday, July 31, 1933. All went well over the Finger Lakes and Catskill Mountains. He soon reached the Hudson River and headed south.

This Lockheed Vega, unlike his *Century of Progress*, was equipped with a new air-to-ground radio. As Jimmie flew low over the newly built George Washington Bridge just before 4:30 p.m., he radioed the tower. He kept his message brief, announcing only that he would soon land at Floyd Bennett Field on Long Island.

He flew south across Manhattan and into Brooklyn. Minutes later, the bisecting runways at Floyd Bennett came into view. Jimmie could not believe he was finally back—he had been gone for almost two months. He had assumed the flight would take a week. Or less.

Eight weeks and two days. Most of it on the ground. Lost and hungry and often without hope.

But here he was—home again!

At precisely 4:33 p.m. on the final day of July 1933, James Joseph Mattern, after surviving one calamity and disaster after another, landed safely on the same runway from which he had departed all those weeks ago.

Thousands stood by to welcome the courageous and undaunted flier home.

CHAPTER TWENTY-THREE

July 31, 1933–February 14, 1934

The crowd at Floyd Bennett Field on that hot, humid summer afternoon was small but boisterous. Word had not spread of Jimmie Mattern's imminent arrival back where he had started in early June. And maybe that was a good thing, for the lone figure who emerged from the cockpit of the Vega looked quite different from the wide-eyed and cocky young aviator who had boldly told the crowd all those weeks ago not to blink or they might miss his return.

Jimmie looked tired. He looked beyond tired; he looked exhausted, worn out, whipped to the proverbial bone. If the crowd hadn't been a good distance away, they might have thought the typically cheerful flier looked defeated.

His ordeal had stripped him of almost twenty pounds, a lot of weight for a man who did not carry much excess baggage. His broad shoulders drooped. His face looked haggard. For one of the very few times in his life, Jimmie had to force himself to smile. He was exceedingly happy to be home, back in America, back on familiar soil, but his days alone on the tundra—coupled with his frustrating weeks trying to get out of the Soviet Union and then the long, grueling trip from Alaska—had all taken their toll on the young man from the Midwest.

Plus, Jimmie had on cheap Russian boots and even cheaper Russian pants, and his stomach churned from the humid, unsettled air over upstate New York that had tossed and jostled his plane all the way from Buffalo to

Poughkeepsie. And, as a bonus, when he attempted a casual carefree leap off the cockpit step of the Vega, Jimmie tweaked his ankle that had been injured in the crash. He nearly collapsed.

After a brief pause, he straightened and strode forward to meet the crowd, a painful limp that left a look of agony on his already tired and tortured face.

But Jimmie Mattern possessed more moxie and far more determination than most men, and maybe at that moment he also heard the famous words of P. T. Barnum ringing in his ears: *The show must go on!*

These people, Jimmie knew, had not come out today to see the long-lost aviator cranky and beaten and tired and limping like some old broken-down codger. They had come out in the heat to see a strong, vibrant flier who had braved the elements, who had dared to fly solo around the world, who had overcome tremendous adversity and endless calamities. They had come out to see a hero, an authentic and bona fide American hero!

And by God they would get what they had come to see.

Jimmie did not disappoint. In a matter of seconds, his limp disappeared and his gait grew long and bold. All the pain and loss and defeat vanished from his face, replaced by that famous Mattern smile.

Jimmie was the battered prizefighter who answered the bell for the fifteenth round.

He was the anguished poet who had lost all hope but scribbled on.

He was the wounded soldier who rose from the trenches for one more assault.

Floyd Bennett Field was just the beginning.

The very next day, New York City Mayor John Patrick O'Brien gave the returning hero a ticker-tape parade and a ceremony at City Hall attended by thousands who welcomed Jimmie home with thunderous applause. And what Mayor O'Brien had to say during his remarks set the tone for the weeks of celebration ahead: "One cannot but marvel at the youthful pluck and determination that enabled Jimmie Mattern to survive his memorable flight. The consummation of a well-designed plan for an around-the-world dash is a subject of great glory and acclaim, but more glorious still, in my humble opinion, is the surmounting and conquest of so many unforeseen setbacks, troubles, and difficulties. The fact, Jimmie, that you stand before us today alive and well is an obvious testament to your bravado and to mankind's ability to overcome adversity."

The mayor's words, along with Jimmie's photograph, hit the front pages of newspapers from Maine to California and from Florida to Washington.

In what felt like a matter of hours, young Mattern had requests pouring in from all over the country. Just about every major metropolis in the nation wanted to give Jimmie Mattern the key to their city.

Flattered and flummoxed, Jimmie, despite his exhaustion and fragile state of mind, accepted virtually every offer.

For the next several weeks Jimmie kept moving, hardly pausing long enough to take a deep breath. From New York he went to Philadelphia, then to Baltimore, then to Washington, D.C., where for the second time he shook hands with a U.S. president. With the press snapping photos, a beaming FDR slapped Jimmie on the back and repeated more than once, "Good show, Mattern. Well done. America's mighty proud of you, son. A hero for our troubled times."

A bit later, in a brief private conversation, President Roosevelt asked the young aviator about his time in the Soviet Union.

"They saved my life, sir," Jimmie replied. "But I wouldn't give you a wooden nickel for their government or that bum Stalin."

"The man cannot be trusted," the president responded, nodding.

And then it was off to Pittsburgh and Cleveland and Chicago, where the World's Fair known as "A Century of Progress" was in full swing. "Jimmie Mattern Day" at the World's Fair brought forth tens of thousands of people to see the famous aviator and hear him talk about how he survived all alone out on the cold, barren Siberian tundra.

Jimmie told the same stories in Milwaukee, Kansas City, St. Louis, Oklahoma City, Dallas, and Salt Lake City. The crowds grew larger and larger. Jimmie loved the crowds, and he loved the limelight, the energy, the attention. But he also struggled daily with fatigue and pain and nagging feelings of anger and what he thought might be mild depression. His anger he aimed squarely at the Soviets, at Stalin, for holding him without cause in Anadyr for two weeks, for keeping him from accomplishing his goal of first to fly solo around the world.

But his anger was mostly whitewashed by melancholy, for Jimmie knew deep in his heart the reality was this: He owned the crash of the *Century of Progress*, owned it lock, stock, and barrel. He had no one to blame but himself and his own foolishness for not changing the oil in his airplane. Had he drained that sludge out of the engine and replaced it with proper aviation lubricant, all would have been well.

Wasn't it pretty to think so?

Fifty to a hundred times a day he held this conversation with himself. Back and forth. Up and down. Inside and out. It was getting damn boring. He was plenty sick of it.

Besides, he kept reminding himself, *what does any of it matter?*

I'm here, for crying out loud. I survived. I have my life to live and so what if Post beat me home by a few days?

And so, he kept his chin up and a smile on his face, for Jimmie believed the nation, now in the depths of what the newspapers called "the Great Depression," needed heroes more than ever, heroes with inspiring stories. If he could play some small role in lifting up peoples' lives, if he could offer them a brief reprieve from the hardships of hopelessness and unemployment, from the humility of no work and no paycheck, from the stress and strain of unpaid bills and hungry children—if his story of survival could accomplish any of these goals, then clearly his fatigue, pain, frustration, and gloom would have been well earned and worth the misery.

Following an appearance in Salt Lake City, Jimmie made his way north to Walla Walla. The time had come. It could no longer be put off.

They had spoken by phone since Jimmie's return, but they had not yet seen one another in person.

CHAPTER TWENTY-THREE

It was a bittersweet reunion.

After a reluctant hug that turned tender, Jimmie told Della he had read some of the things she had told reporters during the weeks when he had been missing.

"I never for a second thought you were dead."

"Thanks for standing by me."

"I don't know that I was standing by you, Jimmie. I just told them what I thought."

"Still."

"I know you're a fighter."

"I thought about you all the time out there. It was hell, Della. I missed you so bad. I just wanted to—"

"I don't think we should go there, Jimmie. I really don't. I understand it must've been very rough for you. All alone. Isolated. Afraid. Not sure if you would survive. But I don't think we can use that terrible experience as a means of judging the strength of our relationship."

"But Della, I just wanted to hold you and pull you close."

"I understand, Jimmie, but how do you feel now?"

"Now?"

"Yes. Now that you're safe and well, no longer dealing with the possibility of death, how do you feel? About us? About—"

"Della, I—"

"About our relationship? Our marriage?"

Jimmie could not immediately answer. He knew his wife was a straight shooter and a stickler for the truth. And she always knew, in a heartbeat, when he was anything less than perfectly honest with her.

"It's okay, Jimmie," she said after some time passed. "I've made a life for myself here. I have family around me. I'm comfortable and reasonably content. If you wanted to be part of my life, I'd love to see if it would work. But I think this stage is too small for you. I think you need a bigger stage. After all you've just been through, you might think a quiet life looks appealing, but I think before long . . ." Della smiled faintly. "I think before long you would be bored silly in this small town."

Jimmie had not arrived in Walla Walla with any grand expectations. He had simply come to see his wife. In the back of his mind he had likely known she would set the tone, make sense of the situation, and set them on the proper path.

"I'm kind of lost," he confessed.

"Who wouldn't be," she replied, "after all the craziness you've been through these past two years?"

"I don't know. I just—"

"Believe me, Jimmie, these feelings of being adrift will pass."

"You think?"

"I think by nature you are an optimistic man."

"I believe I am."

"And an idealist. You just need to relax and let some time pass."

"It's been tough. Adjusting. Readjusting. The demands. And the crowds. People wanting a piece of me."

Della smiled. "You're a natural, Jimmie. Just be yourself. Enjoy it."

It sounded like good advice.

And so, they agreed, for the time being, to do nothing. Their lives would go on. They would neither live together nor divorce. Time, Della insisted, would sort things out.

Jimmie stayed a day or two and then went on with his tour. While in Seattle, he received an offer from the owner of the Paramount Theatre in New York. The offer sounded so outrageous, Jimmie made the gentleman repeat it a second and then a third time. And then he asked, "You're serious?"

"One hundred percent serious, kid. You'll pack 'em in."

"Pack who in?"

"Everyone and their grandmother."

"You're crazy."

"When can you start?"

One week later, Jimmie began a two-week stint at the Paramount. The gig paid him $17,000 a week, $34,000 total for standing up on stage for an hour or so a couple of times a day and talking about his flight around the world, especially those details pertaining to his time trapped alone out on the Arctic tundra.

Immediately following his Paramount performances, he headed to Chicago, where the State-Lake Theater hired him for another two-week stint. The State-Lake shelled out less cash than the Paramount, but in the Windy City Jimmie only had to do one performance a day, except on Saturdays, when he did two.

Every performance, both in New York and Chicago, was standing room only.

On the last night of the State-Lake gig, Ernie Byfield, the owner of the Sherman Hotel in downtown Chicago, where Jimmie had stayed prior to his around-the-world flight, sat out in the audience and watched the show. After the show, Ernie slipped backstage and made Jimmie a very generous offer.

"I'll give you a classy suite, free booze as long as you don't abuse the privilege, all the food you can eat at half price, and a thousand bucks a day."

"What?" Jimmie reamed his ear out.

"A thousand bucks a day. And on top of that I'll guarantee you a two-month stand. Longer, if things work out."

"And what do I give you in return, Mr. Byfield?"

"Just that million-dollar smile, kid."

Byfield was exaggerating, but not much. The Sherman Hotel had a nightclub attached called the College Inn. Jimmie's job was two-fold: hobnob with the crowd and change the nature of the joint. The hobnobbing included getting up on stage between musical sets and entertaining the folks with stories of his exploits. Jimmie had been doing this for so long, he could practically do it with his eyes closed.

The College Inn had become a hangout for lowlife hoods like Al Capone and the Purple Gang from Detroit. Mr. Byfield wanted to put an end to the riffraff. Jimmie attracted the aviation set, including designers, engineers, and famous pilots like Jimmie's friends Wiley Post, Jimmy Doolittle, and Eddie Rickenbacker. And because it was the Golden Age of Aviation, this crowd brought in entertainment celebrities such as Jack Benny, Milton Berle, Red Grange, Jack Dempsey, and Will Rogers, who soon became a fast friend of Jimmie's and wrote a series of popular articles about the young flier's courageous aviation feats.

The College Inn soon became the hot ticket in Chicago nightlife and Jimmie played a large role in making that happen.

His wife had been right. Jimmie needed a big stage.

And then there were the girls.

It seemed like every night it was a different girl.

Jimmie was once again fit and strong, both physically and emotionally. His fighting weight had returned and the various pains in his ankles, knees, and back had pretty well vanished. All the anger and frustration and melancholy had also vanished, replaced with confidence and plenty of good cheer, along with an ample supply of money in his pocket.

The girls could not resist. They wanted to be near him. They wanted to be at his table, on his arm, at his side when the photographers pointed their cameras and flashed their bulbs. Jimmie loved every minute of it—the excitement, the adulation. But he was still a married man, and as a married man he held true to his vows. Flirting, dancing, having a drink, joking around, maybe even a kiss or two were all acceptable in Jimmie's mind, but anything more, any additional advancements, were out of the question.

Jimmie more and more doubted his marriage to Della could be resurrected, but until their union was formally dissolved, he felt he owed her his loyalty.

This chivalry remained in place until one evening in the winter of 1934, when he spotted a new dancer among the female ensemble that entertained the audience while the big bands played their swing and jazz. She was an extraordinary dancer, so graceful and nimble.

The way she moved her long, slender body across the stage caught Jimmie's eye, but once the stage lights lit up her face, young Mattern could

CHAPTER TWENTY-THREE

not take his eyes away. Instantly he knew she possessed the most beautiful face he had ever seen.

She looked all at once sweet, innocent, and alluring. She looked—glamorous.

Jimmie felt quite certain she danced just for him.

CHAPTER TWENTY-FOUR

February 14, 1934–April 26, 1936

Her name was Dorothy Joan Harvey. Born on Valentine's Day in 1913, she was just twenty years old when Jimmie first set eyes on her.

Like Jimmie, Dorothy was a midwesterner, born in Chicago and raised in Des Moines, Iowa, by her mother and father, Sarah and Clarence Harvey. At the tender age of four, she was stricken with polio. Her condition grew so severe, doctors feared she might lose her life. But Dorothy, showing early on a strong, steely resolve, slowly recovered and eventually beat the often-crippling disease.

Her right leg, however, did not grow at the same rate as her left. It would wind up almost two inches shorter.

This handicap did not prevent Dorothy from pursuing her dream. From an early age she loved dancing, and by the age of eight, her body again strong and now sinewy, she began to take formal dancing lessons. Her instructor was twenty-one-year-old Rose Lorenz, who immediately loved the young girl for her energy and tenacity. Rose recognized from their very first lesson that young Miss Harvey was not about to let a little thing like a shorter leg from a bout of polio stand between her and her dream.

For twelve years, Dorothy and Rose worked and studied and danced together. She grew into a tall, lean, powerful dancer through her own forceful will and Rose's relentless tutoring. All her life, Dorothy insisted Rose Lorenz had been heaven-sent. The two women would remain steadfast friends for the next sixty years.

After high school in Des Moines and two years at Drake College—where she enjoyed being a Delta Gamma sorority girl more than studying—Dorothy, with her father's reluctant blessing, moved to New York City to pursue a career as a dancer. Her exceptional skills clearly evident at her first audition, she was hired by Florenz Ziegfeld to perform in his theatrical productions widely known as the *Ziegfeld Follies*. But not long after hiring Miss Harvey, Ziegfeld died of a heart attack and J. J. Schubert of the Schubert Organization picked up her contract.

Dorothy performed in Schubert Brothers shows in New York and Chicago. She then had a two-month hiatus before the shows were to start up again at the famous Municipal Opera House in St. Louis. Dorothy was packed up and ready to move back to New York for two months when she received an offer from Ernie Byfield to dance at the College Inn.

This was the girl Jimmie spotted on stage that winter night in 1934.

At the end of the show, he stood at the edge of the stage and said hello. She said hello back but barely met his eyes.

Jimmie spent the next week or so watching his new favorite dancer. He thought she seemed shy, so decided it might be best to keep his distance. But closer to the truth was the fact that Jimmie had developed an instant crush on the girl and felt his tongue grow thick every time she passed by. This was an unfamiliar feeling for the dashing aviator, as he was typically easy and confident, and successful, with the ladies.

Finally, on Valentine's Day 1934, Dorothy's twenty-first birthday, Jimmie, in a moment of inspiration, made his move.

Every night the band broke into the moody Kern and Harbach show tune "Smoke Gets in Your Eyes." During the performance, several of the dancers, including Dorothy, would move through the audience smoking cigarettes in long, elegant cigarette holders. They would stop at random tables, blow a smooth smoke ring, usually over a gentleman's head, and then place the cigarette in the table's ashtray before gliding off across the floor to the slow rhythm of the music. As the tune wound down, they would return to the table to collect their cigarette, blow another smoke ring, and then return to the stage.

On this night, Valentine's Day, Dorothy stopped by Jimmie's front row table, where Jimmie sat with several VIPs. Dorothy blew a smoke ring in his direction, left the cigarette burning in the ashtray, turned, and swung away.

When she returned a minute or so later, the ashtray was empty. No cigarette! Jimmie had tamped out the ash and flame and stowed the cigarette and holder under his chair. Dorothy looked momentarily puzzled, then noticed everyone at the table smiling from ear to ear.

Jimmie Mattern had the biggest smile of all.

He bent down, retrieved the cigarette from under his chair, presented it to Dorothy, and offered her a light.

She fixed her sky-blue eyes on the famous flier, shook her head, smiled, and graciously accepted.

Jimmie looked into those beautiful eyes and was struck speechless. After the show, when finally his ability to speak returned, he asked the young beauty if she would like to come up to his suite and see his etchings.

Miss Harvey was indeed quite young and, at least off stage, rather shy, but she was not naïve. Boys had been making passes at her for years. And so, she put her hand on her hip, looked at the tall, handsome stranger (although, like all the dancers at the College Inn, Dorothy knew exactly who this tall, handsome stranger was), and replied, "That's quite a line, Mr. Mattern. Has it ever actually worked?"

Jimmie laughed and finally relaxed. He went on to explain that the German government had just that day sent him eight original etchings commemorating his record-setting flight from New York to Berlin with Benny Griffin back in the summer of 1932. Each etching, he told Dorothy, depicted a famous building in the German capital.

Dorothy had heard plenty of stories about Jimmie but decided he sounded so sincere she agreed to go up and have a look after the show.

They spent the next few hours up in Jimmie's room talking quietly and politely and sharing their life stories. Jimmie, usually full of bravado and spewing forth with far-flung stories about his aviation exploits when in the company of a young lady, found himself listening more than talking and feeling unexpectedly calm and content.

After Dorothy stood, shook Jimmie's hand, and departed, Jimmie sat on the edge of his bed for a long time, thinking hard and not moving. He was a few weeks shy of his twenty-ninth birthday. He had flown a small plane around the world all by himself. He was famous. He had money in the bank and money in his pocket. He was happy. He was also, of course, married. But he nevertheless thought he might just be, rather suddenly and inexplicably, for the first time in his life, in love.

He had thought he loved Della. But he had been so young when they met, so naïve and inexperienced, that as youth will do, Jimmie had confused infatuation and adoration with love.

Dorothy moved something else entirely inside young Mattern. He could not pinpoint exactly what it was—her beauty, yes, those eyes and lips, but also her serene demeanor, her inner strength and quiet confidence, so glamorous up on stage, dancing, and yet so incredibly down to earth. All of this and more had Jimmie practically cross-eyed. But maybe most of all, after just a few hours in her company, he felt so at ease with Dorothy, so comfortable, like he could just be himself, like he didn't have to put on a show.

The very next day, without having a clue if Dorothy reciprocated any of his feelings, Jimmie sat down and wrote a letter to Della. He told her he thought the time had come to make their break complete. He accepted his share of the blame, but insisted their marriage was no longer viable and the only right and proper thing to do was divorce and move on with their lives.

Jimmie did not mail the letter that day, or the next, or even the next. He let it rest for a week, penned a slightly edited version, and then, still uncertain of Dorothy's feelings, he mailed the letter off to Walla Walla.

Jimmie felt reassured about Dorothy's feelings when one evening in the spring she told him her parents were in town and she wondered if he would like to meet them. Jimmie jumped at the chance. And at that meeting, as a way to impress the parents of the girl he loved, Jimmie asked Sarah and

Clarence Harvey if they would like to go for an airplane ride. They certainly would. Neither had ever been aloft before.

They flew from Chicago to Milwaukee, a short flight of less than a hundred miles, but one Jimmie made unusually exhilarating by performing a variety of loops, rolls, and spins that left Mr. and Mrs. Harvey feeling just a little queasy. He then flew very low over a friend's house, so low the Harveys could see the gentleman barbecuing in his back yard with his shirt off.

At the airfield in Milwaukee, Clarence Harvey remarked, "Well, young man, that made quite an impression."

Sarah Harvey laughed and added, "But maybe we make the return flight just a little less exciting."

Later that evening, alone with Dorothy, Jimmie asked, "Do you think they liked me?"

Before Jimmie received a reply to the letter he'd sent Della, the time came for Dorothy to leave Chicago and head for St. Louis, where she would perform at the Municipal Opera House, more casually known as the Muny, with the Schubert Organization. Over the next several months, she performed in such shows as *Naughty Marietta*, *Show Boat*, *Student Prince*, and *Bittersweet*.

Right around this same time, Jimmie's contract with the Sherman Hotel ran out and he took a job with the Pure Oil Company out of Pittsburgh, Pennsylvania. Originally, Pure Oil hired Jimmie as a spokesman. He flew around the country and made appearances similar to what he'd done at the Paramount and the State-Lake Theater and the College Inn—he talked about his flight around the world, focusing primarily on his troubles in Siberia. The only difference was now he wore a Pure Oil hat and shirt, stood in front of his Pure Oil Bellanca airplane, and made appearances at Pure Oil service stations and lunch counters.

For several months in the second half of 1934 and into 1935, Jimmie visited over half the states in the Union doing publicity for Pure Oil. He set his own schedule and came and went as he pleased. A look at his flight log shows far more flights in and out of one particular city than any other: St. Louis. Rarely did a week go by without Jimmie putting his Pure Oil Bellanca down at the Lambert-St. Louis Municipal Airport. He saw all of Dorothy's performances several times and always took his favorite dancer out to eat after the show.

Dorothy very much enjoyed Jimmie's attention and his company, but the fact was this: He was a married man. And because he was a married man, she refused to permit their liaison to develop beyond a friendship.

Jimmie assured Dorothy he was married on paper only and that he had been estranged from his wife for years. He also insisted a divorce was in the works.

She believed Jimmie, but nevertheless, their relationship remained platonic.

Della eventually replied to Jimmie's letter, but it was not exactly the reply Jimmie had hoped for. Clearly, Della felt jilted. She insinuated another woman must be involved. Further, she said she had married Jimmie when he was young and broke, financed his first airplane (actually his second), and now that he was rich and famous, he wanted a divorce.

Jimmie, after calming himself, had written back insisting there was not another woman (he had not even so much as held Dorothy's hand at this point), shrugged off the notion that he was rich, and said fame, at best, was fleeting.

The letters flew back and forth. Jimmie could not decide if Della wanted money or if she, like many jilted spouses, was simply angry and hurt that her husband wanted to end their marriage.

He thought about simply telling her the truth—he was in love with another woman—but he didn't want to hurt Della, nor did he want to give her ammunition if she decided to turn their ruined marriage into a public spectacle.

The executives at Pure Oil found their association with Jimmie exceptionally profitable and decided to give him his own radio show. They called it *The Diary of Jimmie Mattern*. It starred, of course, James Joseph Mattern, and ran five nights a week for twenty-three weeks on seventy-two radio stations that reached from coast to coast.

CHAPTER TWENTY-FOUR

It seemed the country simply could not get enough of Jimmie Mattern.

Pure Oil poured one million dollars into the show's advertising and production, an extraordinary sum during those difficult years of the Great Depression.

The early shows covered Jimmie's youth. From there the diary took the listener to Canada and the Presidio, to Hawaii and those voyages across the Pacific. Following his stint as a bandleader, Jimmie learned to fly and soon went to work as a stunt pilot for Howard Hughes on his World War I epic, *Hell's Angels*. After his Hollywood gig, Jimmie cut his teeth as a wildcat pilot down in Mexico and Texas.

Jimmie exaggerated and embellished some of his adventures—"hangar flying," they called it—but mostly he just stuck to the script. The simple truth was that young Mattern had lived quite an adventurous life with plenty of real drama and excitement.

The show grew more and more popular as time went on, especially after Jimmie began to recount his around-the-world flights. Countless American families gathered around their radios after supper to hear about Jimmie Mattern's aviation escapades.

Jimmie did much of the narrating, but numerous guests appeared on the show to add color and broaden the appeal. Wiley Post made an appearance. So did Will Rogers. Benny Griffin came on to discuss the 1932 flight that ended near Minsk, when the *Century of Progress* crashed and flipped over onto its back, injuring both pilots.

Over those twenty-three weeks, Jimmie essentially told his life story. And he was paid handsomely to do so.

When the show concluded, Jimmie met with executives of Pure Oil. They wanted Jimmie to stay on in some capacity, but he declined. Nearly two and a half years had suddenly slipped by since his return from Siberia, and Jimmie had spent a good deal of that time talking and talking and talking some more about his flight and about those difficult days out on the Arctic tundra. He was sick and tired of talking about those days. He was ready to turn the page and look to the future, hopefully a future that involved aviation.

To this end Jimmie called on his old employer, Mike Benedum, president and CEO of the Benedum-Trees Oil Company of Pittsburgh, Pennsylvania. Benedum had canned Jimmie on a whim one day in Dallas after a particularly contentious meeting with other oilmen, but Jimmie, never a man to hold a grudge, had remained on good terms with his former boss. When raising money for his second around-the-world flight, Jimmie had called on the wealthy wildcatter and Mike Benedum had written a generous check.

At the Benedum-Trees Building in downtown Pittsburgh, Jimmie learned that Mr. Benedum had gone to Miami until spring, so he made the decision right then and there to head south. He invited Dorothy to accompany him. She balked, but when he told her his mother was coming also, as a kind of chaperone, she happily agreed to go.

The threesome drove to Miami Beach and checked into the Roney Plaza Hotel at 22nd Street and Collins. Their suite overlooked the beach. Jimmie quickly made his presence known, and within a day or two he and Dorothy and Cleo were having drinks with Mike Benedum in the art deco bar of the Raleigh Hotel. No question about it, Jimmie Mattern knew how to schmooze. Mike Benedum didn't offer Jimmie a job that day, but it wouldn't be long.

They stayed at the Roney Plaza for two months. Jimmie had plenty of cash from his windfalls at the Paramount, the College Inn, and Pure Oil. They hobnobbed with a very diverse crowd. One night they dined with Ed Sullivan, a prominent social columnist who would later go on to star in radio and television. Another night they dined with Dick Merrill, chief pilot for Eastern Air Lines. And on yet another night they dined with J. Edgar Hoover, head of the Federal Bureau of Investigation.

Jimmie got along with everyone. And, of course, everyone wanted to hear about his crash in Siberia and get all the details of how he managed to survive.

They had a fine time in Miami Beach, and it culminated when a letter arrived from Walla Walla wherein Della finally agreed to grant Jimmie his wish. And although several months would pass before the divorce became finalized, Della's letter meant Jimmie and Dorothy could officially start dating. Which, of course, made them extremely happy, but it made Caroline Mattern positively ecstatic, as she loved Dorothy Harvey like she loved her own children.

Cleo spoke openly and at great length about Dorothy one day becoming her daughter-in-law and, God willing, the mother of her grandchildren.

Back up north, Jimmie met more formally with Mike Benedum at his headquarters in Pittsburgh. Benedum offered Jimmie a position as the company's aeronautical director. Essentially, the job meant Jimmie would oversee the company's small fleet of planes and pilots. He would make sure the planes were properly serviced and equipped with all the latest safety equipment. Also, he would be responsible for making sure the company's pilots had all the proper qualifications and the best training.

But the best part of the job description came last. Mr. Benedum wanted a corporate plane, the latest and greatest flying machine available. And he wanted Jimmie to get that airplane custom built. And once it was ready to fly, Benedum wanted Jimmie to be his personal pilot.

"Are you going to fire me," Jimmie joked, "like you did last time?"

Benedum laughed, the two men shook hands, and Jimmie had a new job.

And now that he had a real job with a weekly paycheck from a reputable company, Jimmie did what he had been wanting to do for a very long time. On bended knee, he took Dorothy's hand in his and asked the girl he loved if she would be his wife.

CHAPTER TWENTY-FIVE

May 18, 1937–January 15, 1938

Due to circumstances beyond their control—work commitments, the death of Dorothy's father, a delay in Jimmie's divorce—a full year passed before Dorothy and Jimmie finally exchanged vows on May 18, 1937, in Berwyn, Illinois, just outside Chicago.

In attendance were family and friends who cheered and applauded when the groom kissed the bride. The mothers of the bride and groom might have been the happiest guests of all; Cleo Mattern and Sarah Harvey had started to fear this day might never come. So many obstacles had stood in the way. But finally their children had wed and so great was their joy that at the reception, no doubt after several toasts, Cleo started calling Sarah "Susie," and forevermore Sarah Mabelle Brim Harvey would be known by that nickname.

Most present knew the story of Jimmie and Dorothy and how long they had waited to become man and wife. But what no one knew—not even the happy couple—was that the union was sealed without a marriage license, a comical glitch that was rectified some hours later at the city hall.

Jimmie might've been hitched, but he was not a man to stand or sit still for long (unless he was at the helm of an airplane), and sure enough, immediately after the reception, Jimmie flew off to New York City. A New York to Paris air race had been announced and Jimmie had a strong desire to take part, hopefully in the new long-distance Lockheed twin-engine aircraft being built for Benedum-Trees Oil Company. Jimmie had convinced Mr. Benedum the race would be excellent publicity for the company.

But no sooner had Jimmie arrived in New York than he learned the government had cancelled the race. No specific reason was given, but Jimmie and some of the other pilots believed it had to do with casualties. More and more fliers were getting killed while participating in events like the New York to Paris air race.

Just a couple months earlier, Amelia Earhart, easily the most famous female aviator in the world, had nearly crashed over the Pacific during her attempt to fly around the world along the equator. Commercial aviation was still in its infancy during the mid-1930s, and every time one of these risk-taking fliers crashed and burned, the public's trust in flying as a safe mode of transportation plummeted.

In response, the government had started to crack down on these attention-getting races and record-setting flights.

Disappointed about the race but eager to return to his bride, Jimmie flew back to Chicago, where he and Dorothy packed up and set off for their honeymoon in Hollywood. They flew first class aboard a Douglas DC-3, lounged on comfy sofas, and celebrated their union with a pair of chilled mimosas.

The newlyweds checked into the luxurious bridal suite of the swanky 200-room Hollywood Plaza Hotel on North Vine Street, not far from the corner of Hollywood and Vine. The suite had all the latest amenities, including a balcony off the bedroom overlooking the pool, a radio and a Victrola with a large selection of 78s in the sitting room, and an enormous bathroom with a tub easily large enough to accommodate the newlyweds.

Hollywood was the absolute center of the motion picture business, but in the mid-1930s it still had a small-town vibe. Downtown stretched just a few blocks north to south from Hollywood Boulevard to Sunset Boulevard and west to east from Wilcox to Vine. All the best restaurants and nightclubs in town were located within this small radius. The newlyweds could walk to The Brown Derby, Grauman's, and Chasen's in just a few minutes.

Jimmie, who excelled at keeping friendships alive, still had plenty of contacts in L.A. from his time there serving as a stunt pilot on Howard Hughes's epic picture *Hell's Angels*. On just their third night in town, the newlyweds were invited to a party in their honor. The party was given by Jimmie's old pal Woody Van Dyke, a successful director at MGM, and his wife, Ruth. Present at the festivities were such stars as Jean Harlow, Spencer Tracy, Barbara Stanwyck, and Robert Taylor, along with producer/director Hal Roach and the incomparable movie mogul and MGM founder Louis B. Mayer. Mayer was by a landslide the most powerful person in Hollywood, and here he stood kissing Dorothy's hand and cheek while telling her she possessed an exquisite beauty and should consider a career in the moving-picture business.

Dorothy blushed and found it difficult to speak.

A bit later, film director and choreographer Busby Berkeley asked Dorothy to dance. By this time in his career, Berkeley had choregraphed some of the most famous and elaborate dance routines ever put on film. And here was young Mrs. Mattern being swept around the dance floor by the man responsible for *Flying High*, *42nd Street*, *Wonder Bar*, and *Gold Diggers of 1935*. Dorothy, however, was not intimidated. Dancing was what she did best, and soon the entire party stopped to watch the duo swirl and spin around the room.

Dorothy spent the next three days walking three feet off the ground.

The honeymoon lasted several weeks, but it was not all play and no work, at least not for Jimmie. The Lockheed airplane factory was located just a few miles from the Plaza Hotel over in Burbank on the north side of Griffith Park. At least twice a week during their honeymoon, Jimmie drove over to the factory to check on the progress of the plane Lockheed was building for Benedum-Trees.

The full name of the model under construction was the Lockheed Model 12 Electra Junior. It was an all-metal twin-engine aircraft with room for eight passengers and two pilots. The standard Lockheed 12 had retractable landing gear, full instrumentation (including air-to-ground radio and autopilot), and a pair of Pratt & Whitney R-985 Wasp Junior engines producing 450 hp.

These SB radial engines had a top speed of around 225 mph at five thousand feet. Designed and built originally for the airline feeder market (carrying passengers from small cities to larger cities with larger airports), the Lockheed 12 also found popularity among corporations and wealthy individuals. Most 12s rolling off the assembly line came with a lot of customization. This was certainly the case with the Benedum-Trees 12, and why Jimmie, as director of the aviation division, spent so much time in Burbank during his honeymoon.

After cancellation of the New York to Paris air race, Jimmie came up with a new plan and a new way to promote Benedum-Trees Oil Company. And being a first-class salesman, he sold his plan to Mr. Benedum. The plan was simple: first to fly around the world without stopping or landing.

"Yup," he told his boss, "New York to New York nonstop."

"Have you gone loopy, Jimmie?" Benedum asked. "How in blazes do you intend to do such a thing?"

"Midair refueling, sir. I've got it all figured out."

Jimmie did, too. The company's customized Lockheed 12 would have an extended range due to the addition of two extra fuel tanks that could, under optimal conditions, keep the plane aloft for up to six thousand miles when fully fueled. L.A. to New York and back without refueling was possible. New York to Paris was a cinch. Jimmie envisioned crossing the Atlantic and refueling somewhere over France or Germany. A second refueling would occur on the eastern side of the Ural Mountains and a third somewhere over Western Siberia, perhaps near where he had crash-landed. The fourth and final refueling would take place over British Columbia. From there, the fast-flying Lockheed could easily make it back to New York.

"That's an ambitious plan, Jim," said Mike Benedum. "If all goes well, how long will it take?"

"Couple days," answered Jimmie. "Three max."

"A successful flight could make Benedum-Trees a household name."

"That's the idea, sir."

"We'll give it a whirl."

Green light from the boss in hand, Jimmie set his plan in motion.

CHAPTER TWENTY-FIVE

Unfortunately, just as Jimmie and Dorothy were wrapping up their honeymoon and heading east to start their life in Pittsburgh, tragedy struck the aviation community. On July 2, 1937, Amelia Earhart and her navigator, Fred Noonan, disappeared near Howland Island out in the middle of the Pacific Ocean, a thousand miles or so southwest of Hawaii. A desperate search ensued for Earhart and her Lockheed Electra 10E over the next few weeks, but neither the plane nor its famous pilot was ever recovered.

Earhart's Lockheed Electra was a very similar aircraft to the Electra 12 under construction out in Burbank for Benedum-Trees. The disappearance of the plane gave Mike Benedum pause about the circumnavigation flight Jimmie Mattern had proposed. Jimmie explained that Earhart had planned to land at Howland Island and refuel. Trying to find a tiny island barely one square mile out in the middle of the vast Pacific Ocean, he said, was akin to trying to find a needle in a hay *field*, let alone a haystack.

Privately, Jimmie and other ocean fliers had told Earhart that her plan to refuel at Howland Island was foolish and far too risky. Such a small target would be difficult to hit. But always headstrong, Amelia had gone forward anyway, and the result quickly spiraled into one of the great tragedies in aviation history.

Jimmie reminded Mr. Benedum that their plane would only be landing once—at the end of the flight, back in New York.

"All refueling," he explained, "will be done five thousand feet or more above the earth."

Benedum nodded, sighed, and said he would continue to consider the plan.

But in the end, it made no difference. The government, out of hand, rejected Jimmie's midair-refueling, around-the-world proposal.

"No way," the official from the Bureau of Air Commerce down in D.C. told Jimmie. "Not a chance. You'll never get approval after Post and Earhart."

Wiley Post and Will Rogers had died when their airplane crashed near Point Barrow, Alaska, in the summer of 1935. Jimmie and Will had been good buddies, and for nearly a year Rogers had bugged Jimmie about flying him to Alaska and Siberia on a "reconnaissance trip."

"What do you mean, 'reconnaissance trip'?" Jimmie had asked.

"You know, just to check things out. Get the lay of the land. Hell, Jim, just for the adventure of it. Because we can. I can't think of any better reason than that. I've crossed the barren wasteland of Siberia by train, but land that big needs to be seen from the air!"

Jimmie had liked the idea, but he'd been so busy at the time making appearances and then going to work for Pure Oil and doing the radio show. The opportunity to fly to Alaska and then on to Russia with Will just never panned out. And now for the past two years, rarely did a day go by that Jimmie did not think about how differently things might have turned out if he and Will had made that trip. Jimmie didn't consider himself a better pilot than Wiley, not by a long shot. But he did believe he was a safer pilot. And he further believed that, considering the weather report Post and Rogers received on the morning of their doomed flight, he never would have taken off out of Fairbanks for the trip north to Point Barrow.

Sure, he'd made some crazy flights in his day, but Jimmie did not consider himself a risk taker. Before climbing into the cockpit, he eliminated all the risk he possibly could. Wiley—well, Wiley was a different breed of cat. He flew first and thought about the consequences later. Like up there in Alaska. The weather had been atrocious in Fairbanks, and even worse at their destination of Point Barrow—intense cold, thick ground fog, visibility near zero. Jimmie felt confident he never would've taken off in those weather conditions. He would've waited it out, gone back to bed, stayed patient. Not Wiley. And likely not Will.

A couple of very ornery, impatient guys.

They took off. And paid the price.

The ultimate price.

Jimmie liked to think if he and Will had made that trip to Alaska back in the summer of '35, they would all still be alive. That regret stayed with him his entire life.

No sooner had the newlyweds settled into their new home in Pittsburgh than yet another opportunity to head north to Alaska suddenly presented itself. The Soviet flier who had flown Jimmie from Anadyr to Nome was in distress.

CHAPTER TWENTY-FIVE

Sigizmund Levanevsky, with a crew of six on board a Soviet Bolkhovitinov DB-A, was attempting to fly from Moscow to Fairbanks directly over the North Pole. The crew had departed Moscow August 12, 1937, and by early the following morning, all radio contact had ceased and the plane had gone missing.

Dorothy was home in Pittsburgh and Jimmie was in Burbank preparing to take a test flight in the Lockheed 12. Suddenly Jimmie was told he had an emergency phone call. It was the Soviet ambassador to the United States, Konstantin Umansky. The ambassador informed Jimmie of Levanevsky's plight, then asked the American flier to lead a rescue mission. Ambassador Umansky did not need to mention what Levanevsky had done for Jimmie back in '33.

Jimmie did not hesitate. Within hours of the call he had Benedum's permission to use the new airplane, and soon thereafter the Lockheed 12 was ready to fly. But before he could take off, Jimmie had to call his bride back in Pittsburgh. Before he had a chance to explain, Dorothy said, "Jimmie, I just heard the strangest thing on the radio. The announcer said you were going to fly to Alaska to look for some missing Russian pilot. I thought to myself, maybe they should speak with Jimmie before they announce such things."

Well, Jimmie was, in fact, heading for Alaska to look for some missing Russian pilot, and his new bride, for the first time, was about to find out what it was like to be the wife of the daring flier James Joseph Mattern. Della had suffered through many long, stressful flights over the years; now it was Dorothy's turn.

The long-distance Lockheed 12 performed flawlessly. Jimmie and his navigator, Hank Jones, flew from Oakland to Fairbanks in just under twelve hours. From Fairbanks they flew north to Point Barrow, the same flight path that had so recently spelled doom for Wiley Post and Will Rogers.

But this time the weather was fine. The boys arrived safely and spent the next few days participating in search-and-rescue operations with several other pilots. But in the end, the search proved futile. The team concluded that Levanevsky and his crew had likely gone down somewhere in the Arctic Ocean or East Siberian Sea.

Jimmie spent another day visiting with the "King of the Arctic," Charlie Brower, who had been the first American at the scene of the Post/Rogers crash site two years earlier. For several hours the two men discussed the details of what had caused Wiley's plane to stall and crash into shallow Walakpa Lagoon. It was a tough conversation for Jimmie.

The following morning, Jimmie and Hank headed home. On board they had several small items from Wiley's wrecked plane—"mementos," Charlie Brower called them—including the throttle handle and cable, the metal Lockheed insignia from the fuselage, a seat belt, and a seat. Years later, Jimmie and Dorothy's daughters would play in the attic among these precious relics.

All the way back to Burbank, the Lockheed 12 once more performed impeccably. It was an absolute pleasure to pilot the 12, and Jimmie announced to the press upon arrival that it was the finest plane he had ever flown.

But he stayed in Burbank for less than an hour, as word arrived that Dorothy had been hospitalized.

The following morning Jimmie was at his wife's bedside. An unspecified stomach ailment had landed Dorothy at Mercy Hospital in downtown Pittsburgh, but the local paper reported that she rallied miraculously upon her husband's arrival. No one uttered a word, but it had most probably been a case of nerves that had sent young Mrs. Mattern's stomach into convulsions. It was not easy for a brand-new bride to have her husband five thousand miles away in an untested airplane on the edge of the Arctic Ocean.

His wife again healthy, Jimmie set about putting the finishing touches on the Benedum-Trees customized Lockheed 12. She wore whitewall tires. The nose of the shiny metal fuselage was adorned with a rodeo rider on a bucking bronco. The Stars and Stripes and a large, colorful map of Texas decorated the rear of the fuselage. And above the side windows, the ship's name was displayed in large, fire-engine-red capital letters: *THE TEXAN*.

Texas was, after all, where the young wildcatter M. L. Benedum had first struck oil and made his fortune.

The interior of *The Texan* was both elegant and plush. Thick maroon carpeting covered the floor. Davenports and lounge chairs filled the cabin. A

CHAPTER TWENTY-FIVE

well-stocked galley provided first-class food and beverages, including a fine selection of whiskeys and bourbons. The airplane even had a pair of telephones hooked into the air-to-ground radio, allowing passengers to connect with people from Maine to California.

Once he deemed it complete, and proud as a peacock, Jimmie flew *The Texan* to Austin, where she was properly christened and given a grand party attended by several hundred people, including employees of Benedum-Trees and aviation enthusiasts from around the country. It was a splendid event. Upon its conclusion, Jimmie, his boss, and several company execs flew off on a whirlwind trip around the country, partly to check out various business ventures but mostly just to show off their fancy new airplane.

Everywhere she landed, *The Texan* dazzled.

That all took place in the late fall of 1937.

Just before Christmas of that year, Jimmie flew Mr. and Mrs. Benedum down to Miami for the winter season. Dorothy came along also, as Jimmie would be flying in and out of Miami for as long as the boss was there.

Jimmie and Dorothy settled into a nice little cottage in Miami Beach a few blocks from the ocean and just a dozen miles from the airport where *The Texan* was hangered.

The couple spent time with old pals like Ed Sullivan, Dick Merrill, and the Ritz Brothers, a comedy trio who performed at many Miami Beach nightclubs. It was a fine and relaxing time, and Jimmie and Dorothy spent much of it talking about starting a family.

But then, early one morning around four o'clock, the phone started ringing. At first, Jimmie, sound asleep, thought it was a dream. But the phone kept ringing and ringing.

Finally, he reached over and picked up the receiver.

"Yes, hello, this is Jimmie Mattern. What is it?"

"It's Tom Henderson over at the airfield, Mr. Mattern."

"Yes, Tom?"

"It's the hangar, sir. The hangar housing *The Texan*."

"What's the problem with the hangar, Tom?"

"It's on fire."

In less than two minutes Jimmie was out the door, Dorothy on his heels. They climbed into their automobile and raced off.

Fifteen minutes later, engine roaring, they pulled into the airfield parking lot and jumped out of their car. They could see flames shooting out of the hangar and black smoke billowing high into the early morning sky.

Jimmie rushed forward. Two firemen had to physically restrain him or he would have run headlong into the burning hangar.

The Lockheed 12 was no more. When the flames from the fire had reached the fuel tanks, *The Texan* exploded.

Later that day, in an interview with a reporter from the Miami Herald, Jimmie remarked, "I have to say it's the worst day of my life. The saddest and worst day. Maybe even worse than the day I lost my Vega on the Siberian tundra."

CHAPTER TWENTY-SIX

September 5, 1938–April 29, 1942

If January 15, 1938, was the worst day of Jimmie Mattern's life, perhaps September 5, 1938, was the best—or certainly one of the best—of his life. To be sure, Jimmie had celebrated some stellar days. Like the day he married Dorothy. And the day he spotted those two rowboats on the Anadyr River in Siberia.

And, of course, the day he first piloted an airplane.

But few men experience anything comparable, emotionally, to the birth of a child, especially their first child. On September 5, 1938, less than eight months after the loss of *The Texan*, Patricia Glee Mattern arrived in the world to the great delight of her parents, Dorothy and Jimmie.

Patricia "Pattie" Glee was born at West Penn Hospital in Pittsburgh, Pennsylvania, at seven o'clock in the morning, weighing six pounds thirteen ounces. Her father took one look at his infant daughter and deemed her "absolutely stunning—a perfect specimen."

Dorothy's mother was also on hand to witness the arrival of her first grandchild. Susie took one look at the baby girl resting in her mama's arms and announced that Pattie looked "exactly like her daddy."

The family did not remain long in Pittsburgh. Ever since the loss of *The Texan*, Jimmie had felt like a third wheel at Benedum-Trees Oil Company. Mike Benedum had hemmed and hawed about replacing the ship, and in the end had decided not to bother—which meant Jimmie did not have a lot to do or a plane to fly. Benedum kept him on the payroll but Jimmie felt unnecessary and unhappy. He needed a change.

So the small family packed up their belongings and headed south for Texas, for Jimmie's adopted hometown of San Angelo, right smack in the heart of the Lone Star State. Ten years earlier, while flying for wildcatter Carl Cromwell, Jimmie had single-handedly put San Angelo on the aviation map when, in need of a place to land his plane, he started using a farmer's soybean field on the outskirts of town as a runway.

Out of that necessity grew a small airport. And there, in the winter of 1939, Jimmie found work flying men and supplies in and out of the surrounding oil fields.

But the work was sporadic and the wife quietly unhappy. Dorothy, after all, was a city girl, and San Angelo had little to offer beyond pretty sunsets, a diner, and a drive-in movie theater. The year 1939 produced some of the greatest films of all time—*Gone with the Wind*, *The Wizard of Oz*, *Mr. Smith Goes to Washington*, *Stagecoach*—but even these excellent features could not keep Dorothy down on the farm.

The family stayed in Texas through the winter, spring, and dry, hot summer of 1939 before calling it quits. Both Jimmie and Dorothy knew where they could find happiness. San Angelo had just been a way station.

In late August, Jimmie headed west to California to follow up on a possible job at his old haunts in Burbank. Dorothy, in the early stages of a second pregnancy, stayed behind in San Angelo with little Pattie and Grandma Cleo to await word.

While Jimmie was en route to California, Germany invaded Poland. The next day, France and Great Britain declared war on Germany, and World War II, so long in coming, commenced. The war would adversely affect the lives of millions of people over the next six years, but its arrival proved providential for a young pilot with a growing family looking for work.

Jimmie was headed for Lockheed headquarters in Burbank, hoping to find work as a delivery pilot, or, more hopefully, a test pilot. His reputation as an aviator preceding him, and war in Europe now a reality, Jimmie was hired on the spot.

War meant two things to the executives at Lockheed: expansion and revenue. Already a sizeable company and, with thousands of workers, one of Southern California's largest employers, Lockheed was about to explode as orders for bombers and fighters and cargo planes poured into the corporate offices. These orders came from the U.S. Department of War, as well as war departments in France and Great Britain.

When Jimmie arrived at Lockheed, the company had eleven test pilots on staff testing a wide variety of airplanes from single-engine pleasure craft to the enormous B-17 Flying Fortress. Lockheed produced airplanes for both the civilian market and the military. But following the Nazi invasion of Poland in the late summer of 1939, the company's factories turned out almost nothing but military aircraft for the next six years.

Jimmie was hired immediately as the company's twelfth test pilot. By the middle of 1940, the company would have more than fifty test pilots. Many of them would perish doing their jobs. By the war's end, of those original twelve, only three would still be alive. During the Second World War, tragedy and loss did not only occur on the battlefield.

Employment assured and a nice little house in Burbank secured, Jimmie called his wife with the good news. A few days later, the three generations of Mattern ladies hit the road in San Angelo and headed west to start anew. Dorothy did most of the driving while Cleo entertained one-year-old Pattie in the back.

The trip took several days due to lousy roads, old maps, a flat tire, wrong turns, a leaky car radiator, Pattie's rambunctious nature, and Dorothy's all-day, all-consuming morning sickness. Stops were frequent and often lengthy, as neither Dorothy nor Cleo had a hurried nature. By late in the afternoon, the ladies typically stopped for the night at some roadside motel, and they rarely got back on the road before midmorning.

At night they would call Jimmie and he would ask after their progress.

"Carlsbad!" he'd shout. "How can you only be in Carlsbad? You spent last night in Midland. It can't be a hundred and fifty miles to Carlsbad! How in blazes can you drive all day and only cover a hundred and fifty miles?"

Jimmie most certainly possessed a hurried nature. The man was always in a rush. From his first airplane flight, the young flier had measured success by the number of air miles he could fly in a day.

"Jimmie," Dorothy would reprimand her husband, "you mind your business and we'll mind ours."

Jimmie knew—by his wife's tone as much as her words—to back off. Dorothy was as sweet as clover honey and as calm as a Bing Crosby ballad. Until pushed.

"Sorry," he countered. "I just miss you is all."

"Well we miss you too, but traveling across the desert with a temperamental car, a pregnant lady, and a one-year-old is not exactly a picnic."

"Sorry, honey," conceded the fearless test pilot. "I didn't mean to suggest it was."

But the next night, when the ladies reported in from Las Cruces, the conversation unfolded in much the same way.

"Las Cruces? That can't be a hundred miles from Carlsbad! Did you sleep till noon and stop for the night after lunch?"

"Don't start, Jimmie Mattern."

"Just anxious to see you is all."

And so it went.

Eventually the ladies did arrive in Burbank late one sunny afternoon and a joyous reunion of Matterns ensued.

In the days and weeks ahead, Dorothy and Cleo turned the house on Harvard Road in the Wildwood Canyon a few miles east of town into a warm and cozy home. Dorothy blossomed with her pregnancy, and all the lonesomeness of San Angelo faded with trips to Hollywood and the sight of old friends.

Cleo delighted in caring for her granddaughter, and every day she and Pattie took long walks through the rolling hills under the beautiful Southern California sunshine.

CHAPTER TWENTY-SIX

Jimmie was a happy man having everyone back together again.

Christmas came and went, and a new year arrived with nothing but war news in the papers and on the radio. Roosevelt, despite covertly supplying the Allies with weapons, including Lockheed bombers and fighters, insisted America was and would remain a neutral nation. Just about everyone knew his stance was political poppycock, but the façade held for nearly two years, until the Japanese attacked Pearl Harbor and the U.S. had no choice but to enter the conflict.

But even as war fever rose, peace and joy reigned at home.

On a spectacular spring day, May 11, 1940, the Mattern family welcomed Joy Joan Mattern into the world, instantly doubling her parents' happiness.

Grandma Cleo was at the hospital for the birth, as was Grandma Susie, who was spending the summer with the Matterns. Cleo and Susie had become fast friends and they had no greater pleasure in life than their two beautiful granddaughters.

"Joy Joan," her father declared, was another "perfect specimen."

All who came to visit and ogle the newborn agreed—including Jimmie's old pal from his stunt-flying days, Jimmy Stewart. By this time, Stewart had starred in *Mr. Smith Goes to Washington* and become a famous Hollywood actor. But Jimmie and Jimmy were old flying buddies who occasionally did a bit of imbibing together. The actor complimented Dorothy on the beauty of her two daughters and was then introduced to Cleo and Susie, who stood off to the side, somewhat dazzled by the presence of the film star. Jimmy complimented the two grandmothers on their beauty as well, and then he turned to his old buddy and said, "Two mothers-in-law in the same house! Good heavens, man, how do you manage such a thing?"

A good laugh was had by all, and the famous actor's words never forgotten.

Jimmie spent a couple weeks at home following Joy's birth. He helped out around the house, played with Pattie, and just enjoyed being in the bosom of his family. But soon the time came to go back to work. The Nazis had overwhelmed Europe and were on the verge of crossing the English Channel and invading Great Britain. Lockheed could not develop, test, build, and deliver airplanes to the island nation fast enough. The factories were operating twenty-four hours a day seven days a week to keep up with orders.

If the world were to be saved from Hitler and the Nazis, companies like Lockheed needed to manufacture the necessary weapons of war to combat the threat. There were no alternatives.

Jimmie and his fellow test pilots at Lockheed understood this and so spent hours in the air every single day testing the latest planes developed by Clarence "Kelly" Johnson and his crack team of aeronautical engineers.

The main Lockheed factory and assembly plant was located on the grounds of the Lockheed Air Terminal, just off San Fernando Boulevard. At its height of activity from late 1940 through the end of the war in the summer of 1945, the plant employed nearly one hundred thousand workers. The assembly lines never stopped moving, not even on Christmas Day or New Year's. It produced more than 20,000 airplanes during the war, including 2,600 Ventura medium bombers, 2,700 B-17 Flying Fortress heavy bombers, 2,900 Hudson light bombers, and more than 10,000 P-38 Lightning interceptors.

So important to the war effort was the Lockheed plant that the entire facility, spread over nearly a hundred acres, was camouflaged to fool possible enemy reconnaissance. The factory buildings, assembly lines, and airplane hangars were hidden beneath enormous burlap tarpaulins painted to depict peaceful, semi-rural neighborhoods. Strewn across the grounds were automobiles made of rubber, houses made of plastic, and thousands of trees and shrubs made from chicken wire and covered with feathers to make them look real, at least from the air.

That one facility churned out over 6 percent of the entire wartime production throughout the United States. To say the Lockheed plant in Burbank was vital to the Allied war effort would be an understatement. That assembly plant, together with other American aircraft factories, ranked in importance right up there with Douglas MacArthur, Dwight Eisenhower, and Franklin Roosevelt.

Jimmie, now in his late thirties, reported to work here each day. Just as he had been in the middle of the action during the Golden Days of Aviation in the late 1920s and early 1930s, here again he found himself in the middle of

CHAPTER TWENTY-SIX

the colossal effort to bring defeat upon the Axis powers of Germany, Italy, and Japan.

In addition to testing aircraft, Jimmie, like many of the test pilots, spent a good deal of time delivering finished airplanes, often to distant destinations. He flew dozens of B-17s and Hudson bombers from Burbank to New York for shipment to Great Britain. At times he made two or even three roundtrips in a single week. He would fly a bomber or fighter cross-country, land at midnight, catch some shut-eye, grab a morning flight back to L.A. on American Airlines, report to work, climb into the cockpit of another finished bomber or fighter, fly it across the country, catch some sleep, board another American Airlines ...

Over and over.

Rest and repeat.

It was a lot of time away from his wife and girls, but with the world at war it was no time to complain or shirk one's duty. And just as in the old days, Jimmie enjoyed being part of something bigger and grander than himself.

In addition to cross-country runs, Jimmie delivered a variety of aircraft to other parts of the United States as well as to Canada, Central America, and even as far south as Venezuela, where he flew a custom-built Model 18 Lodestar. Normally an eighteen-passenger aircraft built for small regional airlines, this Lodestar had been customized and outfitted as a surveillance plane for the Venezuelan military. Paid for by the U.S. Army Air Corps, the Lodestar was to be flown by Venezuelan military pilots. Their job was to search for German U-boats along the coast of South America and in the Caribbean Sea.

Despite the long haul from Burbank to Caracas, a distance of nearly four thousand miles, Jimmie arrived on time and made the delivery without a hitch. However, upon arrival he learned he was contracted to provide some basic instruction on how to fly the new airplane, a small detail his boss had neglected to mention back in Burbank.

For the next several days, he found himself in the co-pilot seat speaking English to Venezuelan pilots who only spoke Spanish. It proved quite a fiasco, as even simple words like *left* and *right* and *up* and *down* proved difficult for the Venezuelan pilots to understand.

More than once, this inability to communicate nearly led to disaster.

Jimmie was plenty glad to get out of Venezuela in one piece.

Getting back to Burbank proved another adventure and entailed several flights and numerous stops, including Port au Prince, San Juan, Havana, Miami, Chicago, Salt Lake City, and finally Los Angeles. Upon landing, Jimmie made a beeline for home, where he spent the next few days relaxing with his wife and playing with their girls.

A few months later, Jimmie received a very special assignment. It involved the delivery of a Lockheed Hudson bomber to Montreal, Quebec. The bomber was to be a Christmas gift to the United Kingdom's Royal Air Force from the employees at Lockheed. More than fifty thousand employees had donated two hours of their time free of charge to build the bomber.

Once the Hudson was completed, Jimmie was asked if he would deliver the bomber to Montreal on Christmas Day. This meant being away from his family over the holiday, which he feared might upset Dorothy, even though the task seemed like a worthy cause in support of the war.

But when he broached the subject with Dorothy, she immediately gave her full support. "I think you should do it, Jimmie. It's an honor to be asked."

"What about Christmas?"

"Joy is too young to know it's Christmas," Dorothy replied, "and we'll just have to keep Pattie distracted. Just promise me you'll be home by New Year's Eve, and we'll pretend New Year's Day is Christmas."

Jimmie gave his promise, then he hugged and kissed his bride and told her she was easily the greatest wife and mother who had ever lived. Dorothy just smiled and shook her head. She knew well the man she had married.

Jimmie took off from Burbank on December 22 to be certain of his arrival in Montreal on Christmas. He didn't want bad weather or mechanical difficulties keeping him from arriving at the appointed hour.

The flight went off without problems or delays, and at noon on Christmas Day Jimmie flew over the military airfield on the outskirts of Montreal in a salute to the Royal Air Force and their gallant efforts to defeat the Nazis. He landed shortly thereafter and presented the Lockheed Hudson bomber to a

CHAPTER TWENTY-SIX

colonel in the RAF. The bomber was graciously accepted and in return, two small gifts from London were bestowed upon the American flier.

His job complete, Jimmie called his family back in Burbank to wish everyone a very Merry Christmas and assure Dorothy he would be home by the 31st. He then spent the remainder of Christmas Day and the day after with his sister, Gertrude, and his nieces Naomi and Yvonne before heading south to New York to hopefully catch a plane back to L.A.

Due to the holiday, all flights from New York to Los Angeles were completely booked. After much searching, Jimmie found a flight to Las Cruces, New Mexico, with stops in Chicago, Denver, St. Louis, and Dallas.

When he finally reached Las Cruces, Jimmie found more crowded airplanes. There were no seats to the West Coast until January 2. That simply wouldn't do. Dorothy would kill him if he didn't get home until then.

Jimmie had no choice but to board a California-bound train. He bought two tickets, one for himself and one for the gifts he had received back in Montreal.

The train lumbered through Tucson and Phoenix, and finally, early on December 31, it pulled into the Los Angeles Union Passenger Terminal. Not too many hours later Jimmie was back home in Burbank with his mother, his mother-in-law, his wife, and his two daughters.

Everyone was overjoyed when he walked through the front door. And their joy grew to pure delight when they saw the two "gifts" squirming around in his arms—a pair of extraordinarily cute 12-week-old Corgi pups descended from Princess Elizabeth's Cardigan Welsh line.

One for Pattie.

And one for Joy.

The pups made for a very merry late Christmas.

Early in the new year, Jimmie received a very special gift of his own. The top brass at Lockheed gave him a brand-new assignment: lead test pilot on the P-38 Lightning, a high-altitude interceptor and tactical fighter.

For Jimmie, this job was a dream come true.

CHAPTER TWENTY-SEVEN

January 1941–September 1945

By the time Jimmie got the assignment as lead test pilot on the P-38, the twin-engine, twin-tail, high-altitude fighter already had a lengthy and substantial history. The Army Air Corps had sought a new fighter as far back as 1936. In February of 1937, the Air Corps delivered specifications to all aircraft manufacturers with an interest in submitting proposals. Lockheed went to work immediately on the project.

The two biggest challenges from the start were the Air Corps' insistence that the fighter have the capability of sustaining airspeeds of at least 360 mph and that it be able to climb to twenty thousand feet in six minutes or less. No fighter yet designed had been able to deliver this potent one-two punch of both sustained speed and climbing ability. Lead engineer Kelly Johnson quickly dismissed a single-engine aircraft, as he believed only a twin-engine, high-horsepower airplane could fulfill these criteria.

By early spring, Johnson and his team had settled on a unique design concept, even if all the particulars had not yet been hammered out. Originally called the Model 22—as it was Lockheed's twenty-second original aviation design—it quickly took on the moniker XP-38: X signifying "experimental," P for "pursuit," and 38 for the year construction began.

The Lockheed engineers chose twin booms to accommodate the tail assembly, engines, and turbochargers, with a center fuselage for the lone pilot and his armaments, which were substantial—they included up to a thousand rounds of ammunition for its rapid-fire 20-mm cannon and its two .50-caliber machine guns.

The airplane would be powered by two 1,000-hp supercharged Allison V-1710 engines, each with twelve cylinders spinning in opposite directions to counter torque and make the airplane both nimbler and more stable. It was a hefty powerplant, one that Johnson believed would be capable of sustained speeds up to 400 mph.

Additionally, the XP-38 Lightning would be the first American fighter to make extensive use of stainless steel and smooth, flush-riveted, butt-jointed aluminum skin panels. Massive in both size and weight compared to other American fighters of that generation—it tipped the scales at almost fifteen thousand pounds unfueled and unarmed—the XP-38 was nevertheless an extremely sleek and, at least on paper, maneuverable airplane.

In mid-June, Lockheed presented its concept to the Air Corps, and on June 23, 1937, the Air Corps declared Lockheed the winner of the competition. The company was awarded $163,000 to produce a prototype. Design and engineering went on for the next several months, and construction on the prototype began in the spring of 1938. In January of 1939, $761,000 later, the prototype was finished and ready for its first test flight.

The test pilot was Ben Kelsey. He took off from Burbank Airport's Union Air Terminal, flew out over the California desert, and put that prototype through its paces. He climbed and dove, flipped and rolled, and demonstrated to the boys on the ground just how quick and agile the big, powerful fighter could be with the yoke in the hands of an experienced pilot. After a week of testing, Kelsey flew the plane from Los Angeles to New York in a record time of seven hours and two minutes, not including two stops to refuel.

The success of the test flights and the subsequent cross-country flight led Gen. Henry "Hap" Arnold, chief of the Air Corps, to recommend to the Secretary of War and the Bureau of the Budget the purchase of several Lockheed P-38s. Arnold understood the plane needed refinement, but he trusted the engineers and pilots at Lockheed to keep tinkering with the P-38 until they had it perfect. Starting from scratch on a new aircraft was not feasible with the threat of war looming on the horizon.

CHAPTER TWENTY-SEVEN

On April 27, 1939, the Army Air Corps approved the purchase of thirteen P-38s at a rough cost of $134,284 per aircraft. One-point-seven-million-dollar contract in hand, Lockheed was off and flying, and hiring like mad. New employees arrived at the rapidly expanding Burbank plant almost daily.

The company would build more than ten thousand P-38 Lightnings before the Allies finally beat the Axis powers into submission. The plane would prove an integral part of the Allies' success.

But it was not all smooth sailing for the big fighter. The airplane went through considerable growing pains and all agreed the Lockheed test pilots did yeoman's work in turning the P-38 into a stellar aircraft and one of the finest and deadliest fighters of World War II.

Jimmie went to work at Lockheed just a few months after that initial contract was signed. He got his feet wet testing Hudson bombers and Venturas, but before long he took his first flight in a Lightning. From the moment of takeoff, it was like nothing he had ever experienced. Jimmie fell in love with the airplane on that first flight, and it began an affair that lasted until the end of the war.

Jimmie was just thirty-four when he went to work for Lockheed. And despite his vast experience and countless adventures in the air, including two around-the-world attempts, he had only been flying for a dozen years. In that time, however, aviation technology had climbed the equivalent of Mount Everest. Jimmie's Lockheed Vega, *Century of Progress*, seemed like little more than a toy compared to the P-38 Lightning. The Vega *pushed* its way through the sky, whereas the P-38 *exploded* through the sky.

Jimmie could not believe the power and rate of ascent.

The only bad thing about the P-38 Lightning interceptor was that Jimmie had to share it with the other test pilots. He wanted his own and he wanted it parked outside his house up in Wildwood Canyon.

But as Jimmie was first to admit, the plane was not yet perfect. It had problems, and those problems became more pronounced when the time came to hand the first airplanes over to the Air Corps. Lockheed's test pilots—accomplished aviators like Marshall Headle, William "Bill" Monday, Anthony

"Tony" LeVier, and Jimmie Mattern—were highly qualified professional fliers who had spent literally thousands of hours in the air. Plain and simple, they knew how to fly and just about nothing rattled them.

The trouble started when the young, green pilots of the Air Corps slipped into the P-38's tight cockpit, closed the hatch, and pulled back on the yoke. Many of these boys were simply not prepared for the power, thrust, and rate of ascent the Lightning provided. They took off like bats out of hell, climbed to 20,000 or 25,000 or even 30,000 feet in what felt like mere seconds, then leveled and began their descent.

At that altitude the air was thin, and with speeds rapidly approaching 350 to 400 mph, the airplane would inevitably begin to buffet. It would shake, sometimes severely. The tail especially would wobble mightily. This made the nose heavy and the plane would angle forward, and, if not immediately corrected, point straight down.

An experienced pilot knew to slow his ship, adjust the elevator trim, and patiently return to level flight. But these Air Corps boys—some of them not yet twenty years old and with only seventy-five hours of solo flight time, most of that in primitive PT-17 and PT-22 trainers; absolute toys compared to the P-38 Lightning—panicked when the nose grew heavy and their aircraft began to descend straight down at high speed. Unfortunately, far more than one P-38 crashed and exploded into a ball of fire before it ever reached combat.

Sometimes the pilot ejected safely, sometimes not.

Lockheed first addressed this issue, known as high-speed compressibility, by fitting steel spring-loaded servo tabs on the elevators to assist the pilot in pulling the nose up during a steep dive.

Test pilot Ralph Virden was sent aloft to put this fix into practice.

The fix didn't work. Virden, an extraordinarily accomplished pilot, crashed and perished, his P-38 destroyed.

More tests were done and eventually the shape of the wings was altered slightly and the size and strength of the flaps—which essentially act as brakes for a descending aircraft—increased. The changes helped but did not entirely eliminate the problem.

CHAPTER TWENTY-SEVEN

Of course, the test pilots—a completely dissimilar breed of fish from the engineers hunched over their blueprints—had a far different take on what was wrong with their precious Lockheed P-38 Lightning. They thought the plane was being flown by inexperienced pilots who didn't have a clue what they were doing.

Jimmie—a flier's flier without question—strongly supported this position. He'd been up in the Lightning and put the plane through the ringer enough times to know what the P-38 could do, as well as how to handle its eccentricities.

So when Lockheed put him in charge of the test pilot program in the spring of '42, Jimmie threw everything he had into tackling the problem. He studied the plane. He flew the plane. He flew the plane some more. A natural engineer, Jimmie put together a list of things that needed doing, of stuff that needed changing. It was a short list.

At thirty-thousand feet, a pilot needs oxygen or he passes out. The P-38 of course had oxygen, but in order to operate the air-to-ground radio, the pilot had to lift the oxygen mask off his face and speak into the microphone. This was absurd. Jimmie insisted they incorporate the microphone into the oxygen mask.

"Even an idiot," he quipped, "knows an unconscious pilot is not your best-performing pilot. Let's get these boys some oxygen."

Jimmie joked, but he knew full well the problems with the P-38 Lightning were serious problems. So, after much observation and reflection, he came up with what he hoped would be the perfect solution.

To get his plan implemented, Jimmie went to his boss at Lockheed, Vice President Carl Squires, and asked permission to visit military bases around the country where pilots were being trained to fly the P-38.

Squires gave the green light and off Jimmie went. In his own P-38.

What Jimmie found gave him cause for concern. Young pilots—some just eighteen years old, few if any over twenty-two years old—raw and restless and eager to kill Nazis and Japs, were learning how to fly by sitting in classrooms. Jimmie, who was by and large a modest guy who downplayed his aviation accomplishments, took the instructors aside and said, "Guys, I'm not here to tell you how to do your job, but dammit, I flew around the world in an underpowered airplane made of nothing but wood and grit, and I never spent ten seconds learning how to fly in a classroom. To learn to fly you need to FLY!"

Comments like these did not endear James Joseph Mattern to these flight instructors, but up the chain of command Jimmie climbed until he reached the office of Gen. Barney M. Giles, who was then commander of the Fourth Air Force. Giles liked what Mattern had to say and gave him his full endorsement.

Back at Lockheed, Vice President Carl Squires was not quite so excited. He reamed Jimmie out pretty hard for going over his head and concluded by saying, "I hope you're right, Jim, or we could lose a helluva lot of business."

Jimmie's plan called for getting those young, green pilots out of the classroom and flying in airplanes, specifically in P-38s like the ones they would soon be piloting in battles against the enemy over the Pacific and the Mediterranean and eventually, hopefully, over Berlin and Tokyo.

But before they got to fly, they had to sit and watch Jimmie fly. At military bases around the country, Jimmie put on demonstrations. The idea was not for Jimmie to show off his extraordinary flying skills, but rather for young pilots to see firsthand what the P-38, in the hands of a first-class pilot, could do.

Jimmie would climb to fifteen- or twenty-thousand feet, then put his P-38 into a steep dive, kill one of the engines during descent, and once down below a thousand feet, pull out of the dive just over the heads of his eager audience. And with one engine still dead he would put the Lightning through a series of rolls and spins, loops and tailslides.

It was aerial acrobatics at its finest, performed very close to the ground at high speed by a highly skilled professional pilot.

More than once, Jimmie practically touched a wingtip to the ground as he demonstrated the airplane's incredible dexterity.

And then, still with one dead engine, Jimmie would circle the airfield and come in fast and steep for a pinpoint landing, stopping right in front of those boys with their eyes wide and mouths agape. He'd climb out of the cockpit, stand on the wing, and shout, "If an old man like me can do it, I'm damn certain you boys can do it too!"

CHAPTER TWENTY-SEVEN

But all this was just a prelude to the real show. The prelude was just Jimmie being Jimmie, having some fun, putting his audience at ease. He'd been doing it for years.

The main event was something else altogether.

The Lockheed P-38 Lightning was a single-pilot airplane. The cockpit provided barely enough room for one average-sized pilot. No thought had ever been given to making room for a second pilot or a navigator.

Jimmie made room.

The communication equipment was housed behind the pilot's seat. Jimmie had the radio, the antennae, and all other superfluous equipment removed. In their place he inserted a wooden plank that would act as a rear seat. It was a difficult space to access and a cramped, uncomfortable place to sit, what with the cockpit hatch pressing against your neck and back as you hunched forward and peered over the pilot's shoulder.

But for these boys preparing to go to war against Japan's and Germany's flying aces, this was their new classroom. Jimmie dubbed it the "piggyback," as the person behind was all but sitting on the pilot's back.

One by one, hour after hour after grueling hour, day after day, week after week, month after month, Jimmie took those young, green pilots aloft and taught them how to fly the Lockheed P-38 Lightning interceptor. He showed them what to do and how to do it, all while instilling in them an aura of confidence and invincibility.

And then he took the next step. A big step. A courageous step. Jimmie changed seats with those boys. He pressed his no-longer-quite-so-slim-and-trim physique into that wooden piggyback seat and instructed from the rear. He shouted loud and clear so those novices would know what to do when the trouble started.

"More speed, kid, not less! More speed!"

"Pull back! Hard! You can't be afraid of that stick!"

"Fly the plane, dammit! Don't let it fly *you*!"

"Engage, pilot! Engage! Engage!"

Numerous times, those zealous young pilots, with Jimmie yelling in their ears, nearly crashed and burned and killed them both.

But no matter. After each close call Jimmie went aloft again.

And again.

And again.

He knew it was the only way those young men would be ready to fight the enemy and win the war.

This valiant and sustained effort was unquestionably Jimmie Mattern's greatest contribution to the war effort. In fact, it can be debated, but training those fighter pilots and preparing them for combat may have been Jimmie's finest hour and his greatest lifetime achievement, surpassing even his intrepid, record-setting flights around the world.

War is a great evil. Most wars are futile and fought for greed, vengeance, and ego. But the Allied war against Nazi Germany and Imperial Japan was clearly the exception to this rule. It was, on virtually all fronts, a necessary war to preserve decency and democracy and suppress tyranny around the world.

The pilots who flew the Lockheed P-38 Lightning in combat helped make the Allied victory possible. Jimmie Mattern trained a sizeable number of those pilots. He worked tirelessly during the final three years of the war to make sure every kid who climbed into the P-38 cockpit had both the skills and just the right amount of cockiness necessary to stay alive and kill the enemy. It was a nasty, terrible, brutal business, but as the cliché goes, somebody had to do it.

Jimmie crisscrossed the country dozens of times, often being away from Dorothy and Pattie and Joy for weeks on end. He believed his absence was a small price to pay to preserve the American way of life—and he well knew hundreds of thousands of American soldiers had been scattered across the planet and were separated from their families for not weeks but years.

Jimmie's contribution to the war effort was profound, to say the least. But the toll that effort would take on Jimmie physically, mentally, and emotionally would be even greater.

CHAPTER TWENTY-EIGHT

September 2, 1945–July 22, 1946

When World War II finally ended with the formal surrender of the Japanese to Gen. Douglas MacArthur aboard the USS *Missouri*, James Joseph Mattern was just forty years old. It seemed like he had done too much and flown too far to have only lived four decades. But forty he had turned, back on the 8th of March.

He had played his role and selflessly done his part, and few men in America could have been happier to see the war finally draw to a successful close. Beyond the obvious elation of a widespread Allied victory against the Axis powers, the war's end meant Jimmie could finally go home. For three solid years he had been on the road at military bases all across the country, rarely at home more than a day or two at a time.

Pattie and Joy were suddenly young ladies of seven and five. The last time he had really taken stock of his girls, Joy had been a baby squirming in his arms. One afternoon in the late summer of 1945, Jimmie took an extra-long look at his daughters and knew if he didn't slow down and take a breath, he would miss their formative years altogether and then suddenly find himself walking them down the aisle, wondering when they had grown up.

Jimmie took an extended, much-needed vacation. The family spent lots of time at the beach, usually in Santa Monica, sometimes up in Malibu. And in the fall, Jimmie went back to work, back to testing airplanes for Lockheed. But now he went to work in the morning and was always back home in time for supper. Lockheed still had military contracts to fulfill, but with those winding down, the company once again began designing and building commercial airliners and smaller airplanes for companies and individuals. Jimmie enjoyed flying a wide range of aircraft without the pressure of flying the P-38.

In the spring of 1946, soon after his forty-first birthday, Jimmie was invited to attend a meeting with the president of Lockheed, Robert Gross. At this meeting, Mr. Gross told Jimmie the company was building a brand-new airplane for corporate use. It would be a spectacular and innovative aircraft and Gross intended to show it off around the world.

"And I want you to fly it, Jim," Gross added. "I want you to be Lockheed One's primary pilot."

It was, Jimmie knew, an incredible offer and a great mark of respect. Essentially Gross was saying, "You're the man, Jim. You're our guy."

Jimmie thanked Mr. Gross profusely. But then added, "Before taking the job, sir, would you mind if I discussed it with my family?"

"Of course," replied Gross. "I wouldn't have it any other way."

Jimmie knew the job was a great offer and a terrific honor, and under normal circumstances he would have accepted on the spot. Unfortunately, there were certain complications, and Jimmie knew they needed addressing. The most obvious one was, of course, his family. He knew Dorothy would encourage him to take the job, but at the same time she would be incredibly sad to have the family torn apart yet again. Jimmie knew he would find himself halfway across the country or halfway around the world two or more weeks out of every month. It would not be as bad as the war years, but it would still be a major sacrifice.

But this was not his greatest concern. Jimmie's main apprehension, which he had thus far not shared with Dorothy or anyone else, was an occasional numbness in his left hand and wrist. This numbness was typically accompanied by a spasm that ran up and down his left arm. The arm felt jerky and the only way he could stop it was to hold it still with his right hand. It had been going on for several months, infrequently at first, but more regularly as of late.

CHAPTER TWENTY-EIGHT

Initially, Jimmie had thought it was probably just stress. He knew lots of pilots had physical problems related to stress. Why should he be any different?

But more recently he'd decided it was a pinched nerve or maybe a bad disk in his neck or upper back.

Not for a second did he fear anything worse.

Still, Jimmie knew he could not accept Bob Gross's offer until he found out what was going on and received a doctor's clearance to fly. Test piloting under the circumstances was bad enough, but at least flying solo he put only himself at risk. Taking command of an airplane with Bob Gross and maybe half a dozen other Lockheed executives on board was a nonstarter.

The next morning, he went to see Dr. Fenn Poole, an old friend and Lockheed's company physician. Much to Jimmie's distress, Dr. Poole, after hearing the various symptoms and doing an examination, made a call to a neurologist in Los Angeles. He made an appointment for Jimmie that same afternoon.

"It can't wait?"

"It shouldn't."

So Jimmie went into the city, saw the neurologist, and afterward, in a stupor, made his way back to the house on Harvard Road in Burbank. He found Dorothy sitting alone out back on the sun porch. Jimmie held it together long enough to learn the girls had gone out with Grandma Cleo for a few hours. Upon hearing this, the undaunted aviator, who had been through so many trials and tribulations, broke down.

"What is it, Jimmie?"

"I have some news."

He laid out the whole mess for Dorothy, who sat calmly and stoically and occasionally squeezed her husband's hand. Dorothy squeezed extra hard when Jimmie, nerves raw, said, "This neurologist guy, he thinks it's a brain tumor."

For several minutes neither of them could speak. Tears filled their eyes. All they could think about was their two little girls. Those girls needed a father. They needed two parents. This could not be happening. This could not be right.

Finally, Dorothy said, "Let's call Dr. Poole. Tell him what you learned. See what he thinks we should do."

Dr. Poole thought Jimmie should definitely seek a second opinion. And not just any second opinion but a second opinion from one of the foremost hospitals in the world.

The doctor immediately made arrangements for Jimmie to see several specialists at the Mayo Clinic in Rochester, Minnesota. And not only did he make the arrangements, he accompanied the Matterns on the trip east.

Pattie and Joy stayed behind in Burbank with Grandma Cleo. The travelers had to go by train, as even a year after the war's end most airline travel was restricted to government and military use only.

It turned out to be extraordinarily fortunate that Dr. Poole decided to make the trip. In the middle of the night, while sleeping fitfully in their sleeper car, Jimmie suffered his first seizure. The physician kept Jimmie calm and assured him all would be well.

When the train stopped in the morning at a small station in South Dakota, Dr. Poole raced into town. He located the local pharmacy and filled a prescription for phenobarbital. He grabbed the bottle of pills from the pharmacist, sprinted back to the train, and jumped aboard as it was pulling out of the station.

Dr. Poole immediately administered the drug to Jimmie.

The following day they arrived in Rochester. Jimmie was admitted into the hospital and Dorothy and Dr. Poole checked in at a nearby hotel. Several doctors soon stopped by to examine Jimmie and inquire about his condition. The lead neurologist was Dr. Timothy Adler. He ordered a spinal encephalogram, which removed the fluid from Jimmie's spine and replaced it with oxygen so they could capture images of Jimmie's brain.

The encephalogram resulted in a headache so severe, Jimmie begged Dorothy to put him out of his misery. The pain lasted almost twenty-four hours.

The following morning, Dr. Adler invited the couple into his office. He asked the Matterns if they had children. When he heard about Pattie and Joy,

Dr. Adler's expression turned sad. He could not hide his emotions. Still, he had to do his job. "We discovered a ruptured blood vessel deep in Jimmie's brain," he explained matter-of-factly. "That blood vessel has atrophied and is no longer carrying blood to the brain. And because it has atrophied it has started to press on the surrounding nerves, which can cause pain, as well as numbness in the extremities."

Jimmie and Dorothy took this information in, and after a few moments, Dorothy asked, "So what can be done to fix this, Doctor? Surely a ruptured blood vessel can be repaired."

"A repair of this kind is not so easily done deep inside the brain, Mrs. Mattern."

Dr. Adler went on to say that surgery could be performed but the procedure was complex, and, at best, a risky venture with a low incidence of success.

"I'd like to avoid surgery, Doc," said Jimmie.

"That's probably for the best."

"But without it, what's my prognosis?"

"I believe if you're careful, avoid stress, take excellent care of yourself, and don't strain yourself physically, you have an excellent chance of surviving for up to two years."

"Two years!" Jimmie and Dorothy voiced in tandem.

"Perhaps a bit longer. But starting now, this instant, you will absolutely need to modify your behavior. You will need to avoid getting overly excited or agitated." Dr. Adler turned to Dorothy. "Mrs. Mattern, you will need to do everything possible to keep your husband calm. When a part of the brain atrophies or is damaged like this, changes can occur. Personality changes. Mood swings. A shortened temper."

"Gosh, Doc," urged Jimmie, "just slow down a second. This is all a little too much to take in with one breath."

But Dr. Adler was the kind of man who spoke plainly. "Additionally, I am recommending a dose of Dilantin and a dose of phenobarbital daily."

"That's some powerful meds. For how long?"

"The rest of your life, Jimmie."

"Seriously, Doc?"

Dr. Adler nodded.

Jimmie took a moment to settle himself down, then asked, "Anything else?"

"There is one other thing. And this takes effect today. There can be no confusion about this, none at all."

"What's that?"

"The seizure you had on the train. It was just a prelude of things to come. Going forward you can expect seizures to crop up unexpectedly from time to time. Low stress, positive lifestyle changes, medications—these will all certainly help, but additional seizures with this condition are a foregone conclusion."

Jimmie swallowed hard. He could feel it coming now. He knew there was more. He could already feel the knot in the pit of his stomach. "Yeah, okay, Doc. I hear what you're saying. So what else?"

"Well, Mr. Mattern . . ."

"Give it to me straight, Doc."

"Well, sir, your days as a flier, as a pilot, are over and done. A seizure in the air would lead to disaster for yourself, your airplane, and for anyone else on board."

His days as a flier, a pilot, an aviator suddenly over? Just like that? Out of the blue? At the age of just forty-one? It seemed impossible. Ludicrous even. Like some kind of dream. A nightmare. Like something he'd wake up from and all would be well.

Jimmie had his whole life, his whole personality, really his entire self-image wrapped up in the moniker of flier, of daring aviator. Rob him of that distinction, of that identity, and what was left?

The lurid nightmare persisted. As the days passed, with more doctors and more tests and more results, the prognosis remained the same: two years to live, lots of medications, no flying, no fun, no hope.

"What the hell's the point of living?" he asked Dorothy one night, sitting in his hospital room feeling dreary and depressed and damn sorry for himself.

Dorothy had already quietly decided not to pamper her man. It would do neither of them any good. Love and kindness, yes, but no pampering.

CHAPTER TWENTY-EIGHT

"I guess you'll need to figure that out."

"Figure what out?"

"The point of living."

The next morning he found out the reason for his condition. During a routine conversation with several doctors, they got to talking about the Lockheed P-38. The docs knew Jimmie had been a test pilot, but they didn't know the extent to which he had flown the fighter over a protracted period of time. They became more and more interested as Jimmie went into great detail about the complex maneuvers he would put the P-38 through when teaching novice pilots to fly. He described the flips and rolls, flying upside down less than one hundred feet off the ground, the high-speed ascents and the steep, plunging descents at speeds approaching 400 mph, his entire body pressed back into the seat.

"And you did this for how long?"

"I'd say pretty much from the middle of '42 right up until the end of the war in the summer of '45."

"And how often did you perform these types of maneuvers?"

"Damn, Doc, I'd say just about every single day. Sometimes two or three or even four times a day. You know, there was a war on, and those boys needed a full understanding of exactly what that P-38 could do."

The doctors collectively whistled softly.

There was little doubt that the intense and relentless g-forces exerted upon Jimmie's body over a prolonged period of time resulted in the ruptured blood vessel in his brain. The speed, the flips, the rolls, the ascents, and especially those steep descents from twenty-five thousand feet over weeks and months and years had taken their toll on Jimmie's circulatory system until finally one vital vessel weakened and exploded.

Jimmie's compromised and potentially fatal condition came about in service to his employer, the Lockheed Aircraft Corporation, and more indirectly, though more importantly, in service to his country during a time of war.

Back in Burbank, things did not go as Jimmie had hoped. He assumed Bob Gross and Carl Squires and the rest of Lockheed's higher-ups would understand that "test pilot" was no longer a viable title for their guy Jimmie Mattern, but they would, of course, find another position for the man who had single-handedly saved the P-38 Lightning program.

Unfortunately, no offers were forthcoming, and for several long and excruciating weeks, a kind of silent stalemate existed between Jimmie and the company.

During this time, Dr. Poole, who had become a close friend, confided in the Matterns that Lockheed knew full well the specific cause of Jimmie's condition. But the company had no intention of taking responsibility or compensating Jimmie financially. Lockheed lawyers, in a classic case of corporate greed and malfeasance, feared if the company took either of these actions it would open the flood gates for dozens, if not hundreds, of lawsuits generated by test pilots and combat pilots with similar conditions.

So James Joseph Mattern, pioneer, original Hollywood stunt pilot, wildcatter, barnstormer, around-the-world adventurer, and savior of the P-38 fighter, was hung out—really no other way to put it—to dry.

And not only hung out to dry with considerable health problems and two young children to raise, but also handed a final paycheck out of the blue and summarily let go without explanation or even a last "job well done."

CHAPTER TWENTY-NINE

August 1946–May 1956

It is a testament to the man's greatness that he did not harbor intense bitterness for the way he was treated at Lockheed. Surely, he was angry, and no doubt Dorothy and close friends had to listen to windy diatribes in the days and weeks following his dismissal. But overwhelmingly, Jimmie kept any and all ire close to his vest, and he sent it packing as quickly as he was able. James Joseph Mattern was not a man to hold a grudge or feel sorry for himself for long. He had always believed in the ancient adage that life is short, and with his grim prognosis in hand, he embraced the maxim even more deliberately.

If he did not have long to live, Jimmie intended to enjoy what time he had left without self-pity or rancor toward others.

As for what was worth living for, the answer was obvious: his family. His wife, his mom, his two beautiful, curious, energetic daughters. Plus his sister and his brothers and their children. A man with a family, he knew, was a rich man.

And, of course, his friends. Jimmie had a deep reservoir of friends. He had his Hollywood friends and his flying friends, his social friends and his professional friends. A rich man without friends is a poor man, emotionally destitute. But a poor man with friends is wealthy beyond all measure. Jimmie, never a particularly philosophical man, pondered all of this in the days and weeks and months after his trip to the Mayo Clinic. He had lived through so many close calls and near tragedies, but here, clearly, he stood on the precipice.

He could wallow in disappointment and misfortune or he could continue to fly without ever climbing into the cockpit. Every important decision Jimmie had ever made and every important action he had ever taken suggested the man would travel the latter path.

And indeed he did.

Money was not an immediate concern. Jimmie and Dorothy, who liked the nightlife and the good things in life, had not saved for a whole lot of rainy days, but they were financially stable in the short term.

Jimmie applied to the military to have his commission reinstated, as this would provide him with a small but comfortable pension. This seemed a simple matter, but, in fact, the battle for that pension would drag on for sixteen years before Vice President Lyndon B. Johnson finally approved his commission as full colonel in the United States Air Force Reserve. This honor, however, would be bestowed without monetary benefits.

So in the end, his country, too, hung Jimmie out to dry, failing year after year to recognize and celebrate his efforts and achievements. But just as with Lockheed, Jimmie mostly kept a lid on any lingering animosity. Jimmie knew to his last breath that America was the greatest country on earth, and its military the finest to ever exist.

Besides, the small income from his USAFR commission would have put but a small dent in the Mattern family monthly budget. The family needed money, and with earning money as a flier no longer an option, they needed to forge fresh paths.

Dorothy, always up for a new challenge, went out and earned her real estate broker's license. With the Southern California postwar real estate market booming, Dorothy easily found a job in a local real estate office. Her pleasant, easygoing demeanor won her many sales and some excellent commissions. But more importantly, the job gave her access to land and homes that would soon be for sale.

With this knowledge, Jimmie and Dorothy decided to go into the real estate and land development business with Dr. Fenn Poole. They soon added another partner, Avery Black, who was an old friend of Dr. Poole's with money to invest.

Together they considered the purchase of a sizeable tract of land on the western edge of the San Fernando Valley in the small farming community of Northridge. In the late 1940s, Northridge had a mostly rural population of fewer than five hundred residents. The main street, Reseda Boulevard, was still a dusty dirt road.

All that was about to change.

Jimmie knew the area from his days as a stunt pilot working for Howard Hughes. Much of *Hell's Angels* had been filmed at Hughes's private airport just a couple miles southwest of the center of town. Jimmie convinced his partners that hundreds of thousands, if not millions, of Americans would be making their way to Southern California over the next ten years. They would need places to live.

A housing boom, he insisted, was coming, and fast.

Poole and Black agreed. Contracts were drawn. Money was put down. Land—flat, dry, open farmland—was purchased. Several hundred acres. Plans were presented to the local land use board and zoning office. Permits were granted. Roads built. Foundations dug. Houses framed. Dozens and dozens of houses. Mostly small, single-story, single-family houses. Most sold before they were even finished.

Southern California was the fastest-growing area in the United States.

Jimmie oversaw construction while Dorothy did the selling. Poole and Black, who had other professions, mostly sat back and counted their money.

It was, by all accounts, a very successful business enterprise that continued well into the 1950s, a time of unparalleled prosperity across the country.

During these years, Jimmie pushed forward with another enterprise. This endeavor kept his hand in aviation. The man who had twice tried to fly around the world in a small single-engine plane could not entirely dismiss the calling that had been the overriding passion in his life for well over twenty years.

With not even a high school education, Jimmie invented, designed, manufactured, and marketed a small device he called the "Jimmie Mattern

Course & Mileage Calculator." The device went through a variety of incarnations, with each new generation incrementally improving upon the last, but essentially, they all accomplished the same basic task.

During his P-38 years, Jimmie had spent large amounts of time flying around the country. He frequently needed to know the distance between two points or cities or air bases. He might be flying from Los Angeles to Fort Collins, and somewhere over Salt Lake City want to know how far he'd traveled and how far to his destination. The Jimmie Mattern Course & Mileage Calculator provided this information.

The calculator (in later editions, Jimmie would call it a "computer") was a handheld device that could easily be operated with one hand so a pilot would have his other hand free to fly the airplane, even at high speed or during inclement weather. It had two cardboard (later aluminum) swing arms that spread apart, similar to a drafting compass. Each unit came with charts of North America and Europe, and by applying the arms to the charts, distances between points could be accurately and quickly determined.

Each calculator also provided the pilot with other useful information that Jimmie squeezed onto the arms. There was an altitude and speed correction dial, a Centigrade/Fahrenheit conversion table, and a Morse Code chart. It was a pocket-size, ingenious piece of aviation equipment invented by a man who had quite possibly flown more air miles than any pilot alive.

Jimmie advertised in various aviation magazines and over the years managed to sell several thousand of his calculators. The fact that virtually every flier in the country knew who Jimmie Mattern was and what he had accomplished in the skies did not hurt sales. He probably could have put his name on anything from throat lozenges to board games and sales of those items would have soared.

But the truth was also this: Time was passing, and the country was moving at the speed of sound. Super-fast, super-powerful jet aircraft now crisscrossed the country in a few hours. The Golden Age of Aviation was quickly fading into the past. And with this passage went the names and accomplishments of so many of the fearless pioneers like Douglas Corrigan and A. C. Read,

CHAPTER TWENTY-NINE

Roscoe Turner and Fred Martin, Harriet Quimby and Florence "Pancho" Barnes, Frank Whittle and Jimmie Mattern.

A few—Lindbergh, Earhart, Orville and Wilbur Wright, Howard Hughes, Wiley Post—would go down in history and remain household names throughout the twentieth century and into the twenty-first.

In the eyes of many, the greatest single feat by a lone individual in the history of aviation was Wiley Post's solo flight around the world. But as this narrative has represented, that honor, shy of a few missteps and a bit of bad luck, could easily have been bestowed upon James Joseph Mattern of Freeport, Illinois.

Jimmie was far too busy to consider such things. In fact, he was so busy with his mileage calculator, the land development business up in Northridge, and his two beautiful, rapidly growing daughters that he forgot all about what the doctors at the Mayo Clinic had told him in the spring of '46—that he was supposed to be dead within two years.

Well, Jimmie roared past two years without so much as a hiccup. If not for the occasional bone-jarring seizure and the daily doses of Dilantin and phenobarbital, and, of course, the fact that he could no longer pilot an airplane, Jimmie might have forgotten all about being sick and living with a death sentence.

The 1940s disappeared in a flash. The '50s were a fast-moving blur of work and travel and old friends and new friends and lots of time with his girls. Jimmie worked from home during these years, and so was often on hand when Pattie and Joy left for school in the morning and arrived home in the afternoon. He attended most of their sporting events and musical concerts, and he never failed to be home when a new boyfriend showed up at the door.

"Hello, son," he'd say. "I'm Jimmie Mattern. Who are you and what do you have on your mind?"

But then, with the young man properly flummoxed and either Pattie or Joy standing in the background annoyed and embarrassed, Jimmie would flash his famous smile, pound the boy on the back, and welcome him to the house.

One warm and pleasant evening in the late spring of 1956, Jimmie and Dorothy sat in the kitchen before dinner, sipping vodka tonics. Ten years had passed since the Mayo Clinic scare and for the most part, beyond some stiffness and fatigue, Jimmie felt great. After experimenting with various dosages of his two meds, he had found just the right combination and had not suffered a seizure in several years.

Beyond the kitchen window, out on the back patio, Pattie and Joy laughed with a couple of close friends. Pattie was a high school senior and heading off to San Jose State in the fall. Joy was a rising junior at Hoover High School in Glendale with interests in horseback riding and drama. They were good kids, happy and healthy. Pattie was a bit more of an extrovert, similar to her father, and Joy, like her mama, was more reflective, more prone to analysis than to action. The girls had been brought up with love and affection by both parents, and they would take the security and stability of this solid upbringing into adulthood.

Being the child of not only a famous man but also a man endowed with the guts to attempt something so audacious as a solo flight around the world in a small, single-engine plane is no easy task, but the constant presence of both Mom and Dad in their lives smoothed and straightened this potentially hazardous path for Pattie and Joy.

That evening, Jimmie took a look at his two lovely, grown-up girls smiling and laughing out on the patio and a tear came into his eye and ran down his cheek.

"You want to know something, Mother?" he asked Dorothy, using the name he often called her.

"As long as it's something pleasant."

Jimmie smiled. "It dawns on me all of a sudden that the busted blood vessel in my brain had a silver lining."

Dorothy squeezed her husband's hand and waited for him to continue. She had recognized this silver lining years ago and had quietly waited patiently for Jimmie to do likewise.

"If I hadn't ruptured that blood vessel, what would I have kept doing?"

"What, Jimmie?"

CHAPTER TWENTY-NINE

"I would've kept flying, that's what. Flying and flying all over damnation. You know me. I never would've slowed down. Never would've sat still. I would've flown those Lockheed boys all over creation, and after that it would've been something else, and then something else after that and something else after that, right up until today."

"All true," agreed Dorothy.

"And sure, okay, it would've been swell, a great adventure. But I would've missed it."

Dorothy was smiling now, but still she asked because she knew he wanted to say it. "You would've missed what, Jimmie?"

"I would've missed the girls. I would've missed them growing up. And by God, what the heck is more important in life than being around while your kids grow up?"

Dorothy gave Jimmie's hand a firm squeeze. "Daddy," she said, using her own nickname for Jimmie, "I can't imagine anything being more important than that."

CHAPTER THIRTY

May 1956–July 16, 1969

The entire Los Angeles metropolitan area witnessed an economic boom in the 1950s, and that boom persisted into the early 1960s. Unfortunately, land in the San Fernando Valley became prohibitively expensive, so the small land development company of Mattern, Poole, and Black decided to close up shop.

Jimmie and Dorothy, still relatively young, wanted to try their hand at an entirely new line of work. They opened the Eldorado Travel Agency on Santa Monica Boulevard in Beverly Hills, just off the Golden Triangle. The travel agency business barely existed at that time, but it was about to explode as more and more Americans found themselves with disposable income and a sudden itch to see the world.

Dorothy became one of the first certified travel agents in California and only the seventieth to receive that certification in the entire country. Jimmie ran the business side of the agency while Dorothy handled the clients. The Hollywood/Beverly Hills crowd had plenty of cash, and the Matterns sent many of them off on far-flung adventures to Europe and South America, Africa and Asia.

The business did not make Dorothy and Jimmie wealthy, but it provided a steady income while Pattie and Joy studied and socialized their way through college.

During those years, they frequently vacationed in Palm Springs, and so in the spring of 1965, Jimmie having just turned sixty, the Matterns decided to sell their business and their house and move full-time to the desert. The house in Burbank was far too large, and with the girls now grown and Pattie married with two girls of her own and Joy engaged, it seemed like a good time to set off on a new adventure.

They bought a condominium in the foothills overlooking the Coachella Valley and adjacent to the Shadow Mountain Golf Club. They both took up the game, took lessons, made new golfing buddies, and teed off several times a week. Jimmie was not the greatest ball striker, but he enjoyed being outdoors and the camaraderie of the game.

Before long, Dorothy, still in her early fifties, grew antsy and began working at a local travel agency. Soon she and Jimmie decided opened their own agency first, as a franchisee of Peter Ueberroth's Ask Mr. Foster Travel, and eventually Mattern Travel in Palm Desert, just a stone's throw from their small condo. Business boomed and soon Dorothy had three full-time agents on staff. This allowed Dorothy and Jimmie to take advantage of the primary perk of being in the travel business: free travel. Cruise lines were especially eager to bring travel agents aboard and provide them with first-class treatment in the hope they would return to their agencies and book trips for their well-heeled clients.

Throughout the 1960s and well into the '70s, Dorothy and Jimmie enjoyed high-end trips to Honolulu, Tahiti, Tonga, New Zealand, Tasmania, Australia, New Caledonia, Fiji, Pago Pago, Samoa, and other ports in the Orient. They also cruised to Mexico, Panama, Columbia, Venezuela, Aruba, El Salvador, Brazil, Argentina, Chile, Peru, and Ecuador. Many of these cruises lasted six weeks or longer and the Matterns set sail three or four times a year.

During these long cruises, Jimmie was often asked to give talks about his days as an aviation pioneer and reminisce on his around-the-world flights. Jimmie, of course, enjoyed this tremendously as years and then decades slipped by and the adventures of his youth were mostly remembered only by old-timers.

Jimmie loved cruising—the vast oceans, the ports of call, the new friends he and Dorothy made—but without question his greatest pleasure during those years was his association with the Society of Experimental Test Pilots (SETP) as an Honorary Fellow.

SETP was founded in 1955 by six civilian test pilots who felt it was time for their highly skilled and extremely dangerous profession to have its own association. Membership grew rapidly and Jimmie was among a handful of early invitees. He loved attending meetings and indulging in a little "hangar flying" with his fellow pilots. But even more importantly, SETP brought Jimmie in contact with the pilot-astronauts of the National Aeronautics and Space Administration (NASA), who first journeyed into space by rocket.

One of those pilot-astronauts was Edwin "Buzz" Aldrin, whom Jimmie had known as a baby. Buzz's dad, after all, was none other than Ed Aldrin, head of the aviation division at Standard Oil, and without a doubt one of the men primarily responsible for making both of Jimmie's around-the-world attempts possible.

Ed Aldrin often told his young son stories about the early days of aviation. Some of those stories starred Jimmie Mattern, whom Ed called "one of the finest, most courageous pilots who ever lived." Buzz, who had dreamed of being a pilot from an early age, never forgot his father's words. Some kids have pictures of sports stars or famous movie stars on their bedroom walls. Buzz had pictures of famous pilots: Lindbergh. Post. Doolittle. Mattern.

It turned out another astronaut, when just a kid, had similar pictures on his bedroom wall—Neil Alden Armstrong.

Buzz and Neil would soon shoot for the moon, land, walk around, collect some rocks, and fly home safely.

Jimmie Mattern would have their backs.

The space program in general, culminating in Apollo 11's successful lunar landing and safe return to earth, was, in Jimmie's estimation, easily the greatest technological achievement in human history.

NASA was founded in July of 1958. Less than three years later, astronaut Alan Shepard was launched into space for fifteen minutes aboard a capsule powered by a Redstone booster. A year after that, astronaut John Glenn, aboard *Friendship 7*, orbited the earth three times. And just eight short years later, Armstrong and Aldrin left their footprints on the moon.

An extraordinary series of achievements in a very short time.

Jimmie Mattern was symbolically on board all of those Gemini and Apollo flights. He knew well the men who flew the missions—Buzz, Alan Shepard, John Glenn, Don Slayton, Scott Carpenter, Jim Lovell, Gus Grissom, Wally Schirra, Michael Collins, David Scott, and, of course, the indomitable Neil Armstrong.

Neil was not only a naval aviator and aeronautical engineer and Apollo astronaut, he was also a great student of aviation history. Being able to sit down and discuss those early years of flying with a man who had tried to circumnavigate the earth in a single-engine monoplane was one of the great joys of Neil's life.

"Going solo," he said more than once to Jimmie while shaking his head, "that's the thing that astounds. Having the guts to go it alone. Just you and your airplane. You paved the way, Jim. You made it possible for the rest of us."

One of their visits took place just before Neil embarked on the Gemini 8 mission, during which his spacecraft would orbit the Earth. As Jimmie was about to bid the astronaut farewell, he had an impulsive thought. He took off his one-of-a-kind, all-proof Wittnauer watch—the one he had worn on his solo flight around the world that had survived the crash and the cold and the icy water of the Anadyr—and buckled it onto the astronaut's wrist. Neil's eyes opened wide as he fingered the treasured watch carefully.

"It's for good luck," Jimmie said. Then added, with a wink, "But I want it back."

Jimmie came to know those early astronauts well, and for years he was like a father figure to them. They were all of the same ilk, cast from the same cloth, and so a strong bond formed between the early pioneer from the Golden Age of Aviation and these "astronauts" who strapped themselves into monstrously powerful rockets and launched themselves into outer space.

It was mad.

It was insane.

CHAPTER THIRTY

It was terrifying.

Of course, these were all the same pronouncements people had made back in the '30s when Jimmie had set off to fly around the world in a small single-engine plane made mostly of wood, wire, and fabric.

"What—are you crazy, Jimmie?"

"Are you out of your mind?"

"Do you have a death wish?"

No, Jimmie wasn't crazy or out of his mind. And no, he definitely didn't have a death wish. The man simply possessed a keen sense of adventure, a powerful urge to fly, and an overwhelming desire to explore new frontiers. Flying was exhilarating.

Those first astronauts were cast from precisely the same mold.

Jimmie had a strong kinship with the Gemini and Apollo pilots. He spoke with them before their flights and wished them all Godspeed. He and Dorothy flew to Florida on several occasions to watch and celebrate their launches. The Matterns received special invitations from NASA to attend the launch of Apollo 11, the first flight bound for the moon—Buzz Aldrin, Neil Armstrong, and Michael Collins on board.

Armstrong contacted Jimmie a week or so before the mission and told the aging aviator he wanted to carry something of Jimmie's to the moon. "Something important, Jim. Something special. Something that somehow ties all of this and all of us together."

Jimmie thought about it for several days prior to departing for Cape Canaveral and the July 16, 1969, launch. During a brief get-together with the three astronauts, Jimmie approached Neil and pulled something from his jacket pocket.

"I think this is what you should carry with you."

He handed a small leather portfolio to the man bound for the moon. In gold letters across the cover, it read "National Aeronautic Association of U.S.A." Below that, "Aviator's Certificate."

Inside the passport-sized book was Jimmie's original license to operate an airplane. It was one of the first licenses ever issued to any pilot in the United

States. Dated August 31, 1927, it was signed by the chairman of the National Aeronautic Association: Orville Wright.

Armstrong looked at it—stared at it—for several seconds. For several additional seconds he was speechless before finally breaking into a wide smile. "I tell you, Jim, I don't know what to say. I mean, Orville Wright for crying out loud. That's like having your Bible signed by Jesus."

Jimmie would later say that moment was easily one of the happiest and proudest of his entire life.

He squeezed Neil's arm and said, "You told me you wanted something to tie all of this and all of us together. I think this is just the ticket, Neil. I can see the headline now: 'Armstrong Hauls a Small Piece of the Wright Brothers to the Moon'."

"And back."

Now it was Jimmie's turn to smile. "That's right, son. And back."

EPILOGUE

Several weeks later, after Armstrong, Aldrin, and Collins had returned successfully from the moon and then spent three weeks in quarantine, Jimmie received a package in the mail. He opened it with no small amount of anticipation.

Inside, he found his watch and leather portfolio.

And inside the portfolio, he found a small addition to the original information. On page two, under his picture and his signature, in small block letters, it read: CARRIED TO TRANQUILITY BASE, MOON, ON APOLLO 11 JULY 16–24, 1969. And signed: *Neil A. Armstrong*.

On pages three and four of the portfolio—pages that requested in English, French, Spanish, German, Italian, and Russian that any civil, naval, or military authority finding this certificate to please aid and assist the holder—Jimmie found the signature of the second man to step onto the moon: *Buzz Aldrin*.

Time that elapsed between Orville Wright's first powered airplane flight on December 17, 1903, and Neil Armstrong's first step onto the lunar surface on July 20, 1969: a few months shy of sixty-six years.

It took more than twenty years just to build the Taj Mahal.

It took more than six years to build the 1,700-mile-long transcontinental railroad.

Almost fifteen years to erect the Brooklyn Bridge connecting Brooklyn to Manhattan, a distance of less than one mile.

And just sixty-six years to go from a flight of less than twenty feet across a windswept dune on the Outer Banks of North Carolina to the moon and back, a distance of almost half a million miles.

And James Joseph Mattern of Freeport, Illinois, was there in the cockpit just about every step of the way.

It is by no measure an exaggeration to say the history of aviation unfolded during Jimmie's lifetime.

Despite the dire predictions of those doctors at the Mayo Clinic back in the spring of 1946, James Joseph Mattern would live to the ripe old age of eighty-three, forty-plus years longer than those medical experts predicted.

His second act would not involve flying airplanes, but Jimmie would nevertheless live a full and active life, working, rearing his children and spoiling his grandchildren, and as often as possible, circling the globe over and over again, this time by ship.

And, as shown by his strong connection to NASA and the early astronauts, he continued to participate in the ongoing development of American aviation right up until the first lunar landing and beyond.

Jimmie was one of very few airmen who knew them all—Lindbergh, Post, Earhart, Howard Hughes, Louis Blériot, Eddie Rickenbacker, Dick Merrill, Jimmy Doolittle, Richard Bong, Chuck Yeager, Alan Shepard, John Glenn, Buzz Aldrin, Neil Armstrong. The first flights, transcontinental flights, transatlantic flights, around-the-world flights, in-air refueling flights, high-altitude flights, supersonic flights, flights to the moon—all of this happened during Jimmie's lifetime and on his watch.

Jimmie was celebrated for his aviation heroics. He was fêted in ticker-tape parades, lauded as the greatest flier of all time, granted audiences with four U.S. presidents. He hobnobbed with some of the brightest stars in Hollywood and posed for photographs with the most famous sports figures, entertainers, and politicians of his time.

But at heart, Jimmie was a flier. He loved nothing in life so much as climbing aboard an airplane, slipping into the cockpit, firing up the engine, checking his gauges, rolling down the runway, and lifting off into the clear blue yonder.

James Joseph Mattern passed away on December 11, 1988, in Palm Desert, surrounded by his wife, his daughters and their husbands, and his three oldest grandchildren, Shelby, Kelly, and Stephanie. He was eighty-three. Shelby and Kelly arrived in town late the night before and drove straight to the hospital. As they passed through the lobby toward his room, they saw a waist-high stack of newly delivered *Palm Desert Life* newspapers, the ink barely dry. A full-color photo of Jimmie graced the cover. The girls plastered the hospital-room walls with the newspapers, hoping their grandfather would wake up to see the colorful homage. The cover story lauded the local hero's lifetime achievements—a fitting and timely tribute to a man who gave so much to the world.

AFTERWORD

James Joseph "Jimmie" Mattern accomplished a great deal during his remarkable life. This narrative has chronicled those achievements. But the full breadth of a man's legacy must also be measured by the family he leaves behind—for those who come after may ultimately prove even bolder and more vital to mankind.

Jimmie's bride:
- Dorothy Harvey Mattern, February 14, 1913–February 1, 2002

Jimmie's children:
- Patricia "Pattie" Glee Mattern Scarbrough, September 5, 1938
- Joy Joan Mattern Garrison, May 11, 1940

Jimmie's grandchildren:
- Shelby Joy Scarbrough, April 23, 1962
- Kelly June Scarbrough, January 26, 1964
- Stephanie Ann Garrison Southwick, July 18, 1967
- Patricia "Tricia" Jean Scarbrough Corcoran, November 3, 1967
- Mitchell Allen Garrison, January 15, 1969
- Amy Elizabeth Garrison Olson, April 9, 1971

Jimmie's great-grandchildren and great-great-grandchildren:
- Ashley Michele Garrison, May 12, 1991
- Jaqueline Grace Southwick Pierson, June 30, 1995
  - Mabel Rose Pierson, December 20, 2021
- Kelsey Joy Southwick Crawford, September 12, 1996
  - Kannon Jackson Crawford, August 21–25, 2020
  - Judah Carl Crawford, September 28, 2021
- Casey Jean Garrison, March 3, 1997
- Ryan Timothy Olson, January 29, 1999
- William Taylor Corcoran, October 27, 2000
- Charles Jeffrey Olson, December 22, 2000
- Hannah Igera Olson, May 30, 2003
- Isabella Bliss Baccala, April 2, 2004
- Jack Gregory Corcoran, April 17, 2004
- Stephen "Stevie" James Garrison, August 26, 2004
- James Peter Olson, May 11, 2007

Jimmie, who so easily could have bought a ticket south in the Canadian wilderness or over the North Atlantic or outside of Minsk or along the Anadyr River in Siberia or in his P-38 or any number of other times while in the cockpit, was clearly a man possessed of nine lives. On so many occasions he could have died flying his airplane, having never fathered a child.

But he lived and went on to have two children who produced six grandchildren who produced twelve great-grandchildren who, as of this writing, have produced three great-great-grandchildren, with undoubtedly many more to come.

All of Jimmie's descendants will, of course, forever remember their patriarch who risked his life over and over to advance the potential of powered flight and to make the world a smaller, more civilized place.

But this flier, James Joseph "Jimmie" Mattern, should be remembered by all who desire an understanding of who we are and how we got here, as he was unquestionably one of the giants of the Golden Age of Aviation.

ACKNOWLEDGMENTS

The grandchildren of Jimmie Mattern (collectively "Garrison Scarbrough") would like to acknowledge the following people for their contributions to making this book a reality:

- Joy and Steve Garrison
- Pattie and Bill Scarbrough
- Elayne Wells Harmer
- Thomas William Simpson
- Merack Publishing
- Writing Nights

Most of all, we would like to thank you, the reader, for helping us honor the legacy of the extraordinary hero we knew as "Grandpa Jimmie."

TRIBUTES

"Jimmie Mattern was a pioneer in the truest sense of the word. [. . .] From his first flight in 1924, he was a trailblazer. [. . .] Jimmie Mattern was a giant. As we mourn his loss, we also rejoice in his life and legacy. Surely a special place in heaven has been reserved for this great and gentle man."

    Ronald Reagan, excerpt from a letter he wrote to Dorothy Mattern on December 16, 1988

"Jimmie Mattern is a pilot's pilot."

    Gen. James "Jimmy" Doolittle (led the Doolittle Raiders in the raid over Tokyo in WWII)

"What a full and marvelous career you have had in the air. It is only through the early achievements that the rest of us could follow. We are standing on your shoulders as we reach for the stars. My thanks to you for providing the paths and guidance."

    Astronaut Alan Shepard (Mercury 7, Apollo 14)

"The spectacular achievements of modern aerospace scientists and engineers are, in a large measure, due to the inspiration they received from you and your aviation brethren."

    Neil Armstrong (first man on the moon, Apollo 11)

"As one of the newcomers to the world of aviation, I thank you for helping to pave the way."

    John Young (shuttle pilot Columbia I, Apollo X, and Gemini flights)

Jimmie: "They must think I'm on the final approach when they make me Elder Statesman."

Goldwater: "When you are on your final approach, we'll all be out of the pattern."

    After Jimmie received the National Aeronautic Association's Elder Statesman of Aviation award in 1973

"Mattern's story is a thrilling tale of adventure and discovery. His legacy is one of dreaming and discovery, hard work and talent, tenacity, and bravery, and, above all, perseverance. Undaunted brings to life a truly American story of surviving and succeeding against all odds. It's the pioneer aviators of the Golden Age like Jimmie who inspired me to start our first XPRIZE for spaceflight."

    Peter H. Diamandis, MD and founder of XPRIZE Foundation

"James Joseph 'Jimmie' Mattern was looking forward with enthusiasm to being here tonight for a reunion with his many Texas friends. Though he was born in Freeport, Illinois, he spent much of his early flying career in Texas and considered himself a Texan. However, his flight plan to Texas this time was cancelled by a higher authority. On December 11, 1988, he took off for his loftiest and longest flight.

We could spend hours reciting his scores of flight accomplishments. Most of you have already received listings of his famous flights, many establishing records which remain unbroken. The most publicized was the first attempted around-the-world solo flight in a Lockheed Vega in 1933, which established new records for every leg until a clogged oil line forced a crash landing on the Siberian tundra 600 miles from Nome, Alaska. Injured, he survived for twenty-three days without food, until rescued by Siberian Eskimos.

His 30,000 flight-hour career included more than 3,000 hours in Lockheed P-38s, more than any other pilot. He developed and carried out the piggyback method of instruction in the P-38, which greatly reduced accidents, saved countless pilots' lives, and established the P-38 as one of the premier fighting aircraft of World War II. This accomplishment earned him the U.S. Army Air Force Scroll of Appreciation.

Jimmie was received at the White House by four U.S. presidents, and among the dozens of honors, accolades, and awards bestowed upon him during his illustrious career were decorations from six foreign governments. He was a colonel in the U.S. Air Force Reserve and was, as Jimmy Doolittle called him, "a pilot's pilot" who earned the title of National Aeronautics Association Elder Statesman of Aviation.

Though Jimmie has left us for a higher orbit and we will all miss him, his contributions will live on for generations to come through benefits that have accrued or will accrue for his followers.

We believe that Jimmie's character, empathy, and compassion are best exemplified by the letter he wrote to Neil Armstrong and David Scott after their harrowing experience when their Gemini VIII capsule spun out of control in space in March 1966."

> Tribute to Jimmie at the Texas OX5 Aviation Pioneer Day in Dallas, December 19, 1988

Jimmie's letter to Neil Armstrong and David Scott in the summer of 1966:

Dear Neil and David,

During the time when Gemini 8's thruster stuck open and the period until you regained control was almost unbearable for those of us whose every heartbeat and spirit rode with you. Then, the seemingly endless time of anxiety awaiting word that a satisfactory capsule re-entry attitude had been accomplished, the successful firing of the retrorockets and finally the bull's eye splash-down, was an emotional experience all shall not soon forget. Neil and David are safe.

There is more rejoicing in the heavens over one prodigal son who returns than the ninety and nine who are safe in the fold.

Neil Armstrong and David Scott, you did not fly alone. No, many invisible spirits rode with you; the spirits of all men, present, past, and yet to come, with their unconscious dreams of longing and pathos, deep feelings, half melancholy, the wish to rise above themselves, to master the air and space, to cover the surface of the sea and explore its depths, to stand on the highest mountain and have one's voice heard above the throng.

Neil and David, you did not fly alone with only courage by your side. A throng rode with you: the girls and boys, the fathers, and mothers, and yes, the grandparents, all castes, all colors, all creeds of all nations, as one, flew with you. When capsule control was lost, we worked with you. In those endless doubtful moments when you were doing all the right things at the right time, as only experimental test pilots do, calm, efficient, calculating and prompt to correct the situation, you thought not of your own personal safety, but the throngs did. When re-entry fuel was diminishing before stabilization was regained in that spinning, yawing, tumbling, erratic capsule, perhaps to leave you forever in space, we never left your side.

As you returned to this earth, we not only rejoiced, but something in ourselves returned also.

Neil Armstrong is a personal friend of this writer, who in another era attempted the first solo flight around the world. A takeoff from New York, a nearly disastrous Atlantic crossing, flying the entire breath of Russia in 2,000-mile consecutive hops. With success in sight, he too had trouble develop in his small, single-engine plane and crashed in Arctic Siberia. He knows the heartbreak felt by Neil and David for not being able to complete their flight. Now 33 years later, he dreamed and longed to go with Neil Armstrong and David Scott, thrilled at the thought of a walk in space or being the first man to step on the moon. But time has caught up with him.

So, as you come back, Neil and David, something in ourselves has returned, something we had lost for a while and found again. You are more than Neil Armstrong and David Scott; those are only identifications. You are the Spirit of Progress, and you did not ride alone with only courage by your side.

Sincerely,
Jimmie Mattern

Without realizing it at the time, Jimmie had written a prophetic letter. Just three years later, Neil Armstrong was the first man to set foot on the moon

JIMMIE MATTERN AVIATION RECORDS*

- First pilot (at age 24) for Cromwell Airlines (1929)
- First to fly a Ford Trimotor from the United States to Alaska (1931)
- First to perform a midair refueling over Fairbanks, Alaska (1931)
- First (with Benny Griffin) to fly nonstop from North America (Newfoundland) to Berlin (1932)
- Set a transatlantic speed record (with Benny Griffin) that stood until 1940: 2,000 miles in 10 hours, 50 minutes (1932)
- Set a speed record (with Benny Griffin) for flight from New York City to Berlin: 4,100 miles in 29 hours, 30 minutes, beating previous record (Post and Gatty in 1931) by nearly six hours (1932)
- Carried first airmail (with Benny Griffin) from North America to Berlin (1932)
- **First to attempt a solo flight around the world (1933)**
- Third person (after Lindbergh and Earhart) to fly solo and nonstop across the Atlantic (1933)
- First flight from New York to Scandinavia, in 23 hours, 55 minutes (1933)
- Carried first airmail from New York to Scandinavia
- Longest nonstop flight over open water—4,200 miles, from New York to Norway—breaking Lindbergh (3,600 miles in 33.5 hours) and Earhart's records (2,000 miles in 15 hours) (1933)
- First solo flight from New York to Moscow (1933)
- First solo flight across Russia and Siberia (1933)
- First U.S. Flying Ambassador for a World's Fair (1933)

- First aviator to have their own radio show: *The Diary of Jimmie Mattern* was broadcast on the Mutual Network (WLS-AM) on 72 stations, twice a week for 23 weeks (1934)

- First nonstop flight from California to Alaska; also set speed record, flying 2,600 miles in 14 hours 10 minutes from Oakland, California, to Fairbanks, Alaska, to join the search for missing Russian flier Sigizmund Levanevsky (1937)

- Held the record for most hours flown in a P-38: 3,000+

- First to have a document (official Aviation Certificate) taken to the moon (1969)

* Data gathered from newspapers of that era, aviation historians, and Jimmie's personal records.

JIMMIE MATTERN HONORS AND AWARDS

- Founder and president of California charter of the OX5 Club of America (1957)

- President of the OX5 Club of America (later named "OX5 Aviation Pioneers") (1960–1962)

- Named Honorary Fellow of the Society of Experimental Test Pilots (1964)

- Named "Honorary Citizen of West Berlin" for beating the speed record for a flight from United States to Berlin (1932)

- Received official welcome back to New York City by Mayor Jimmy Walker (1932)

- Honoree of parade in Oklahoma after setting transatlantic speed record and recipient of a special honor presented by Oklahoma City Chamber of Commerce and mayor (1932)

- Commissioned colonel on the military staff of the governor of Oklahoma, William H. Murray (1932)

- Honored by Fort Worth Chamber of Commerce and Mayor William Bryce for setting transatlantic speed record (1932)

- Commissioned lieutenant colonel on the military staff of the governor of Texas, Miriam A. Ferguson (1933)

- Honoree of ticker-tape parade in New York City after return from round-the-world flight (1933)

- Commissioned a Texas Ranger by Governor Ferguson (1934)

- Logged 20,000+ flight hours in twenty years (1926–1946)

- Awarded one-of-a-kind U.S. Air Force citation for his service in teaching young pilots how to fly a P-38 during WWII, using the revolutionary "piggyback" method (1949)

- Recipient of the Navy League Award

- Named Honorary Member, U.S. Navy Strike Fighter Squadron 151 (VFA-151), Naval Air Station Miramar

- Named Honorary Member, U.S. Navy Air Test and Evaluation Squadron Four (VX-4) Naval Air Station Point Mugu, California

- Named Honorary Signal Officer, USS *Enterprise* (CVN-65)

- Received at the White House in the Oval Office by four U.S. presidents: Herbert Hoover, Franklin D. Roosevelt, Dwight D. Eisenhower, and Lyndon Baines Johnson (1932–1967)

- Commissioned full colonel in the U.S. Air Force Reserve Command by Pres. Lyndon B. Johnson (1967)

- Received Elder Statesman of Aviation Award, National Aeronautical Association (1973)

- Wings enshrined on the "Famous Fliers Wall" of the Aviator's Chapel at The Mission Inn in Riverside, California (1974)

- Honored in the International Forest of Friendship, a memorial to the history of aviation and aerospace in Atchison, Kansas, birthplace of Amelia Earhart (1976)

- Named Honorary Pioneer of Alaska, Igloo #4, Fairbanks, Alaska (1977)

- Inducted into The Oklahoma Air and Space Hall of Fame for his contributions to aviation (1981)

- Named "Honorary Crop Duster," along with Gen. Jimmy Doolittle, by the California Agricultural Aircraft Association (1982)

- Inducted into the OX5 Aviation Pioneers Hall of Fame (1984)
- Received the OX5 Aviation Pioneers' Distinguished Service Award
- Featured in the "Golden Age of Flight" exhibit (1919–1939) at the Smithsonian National Air and Space Museum (1984–)
- Jimmie's Lockheed 12A was featured on the cover of the Smithsonian 1986 calendar
- Honored with proclamation of "Dorothy and Jimmie Mattern Day," City of Palm Desert, California (May 16, 1987)
- Scheduled to be the guest speaker and honoree at the Texas OX-5 Aviation Pioneer Day in Dallas on December 19, 1988, but passed away just two days before
- Featured in the Russian Transpolar Flight and Robert W. Stevens Alaskan Aviation collections at The Museum of Flight in Seattle, Washington (2004–)

Made in the USA
Monee, IL
18 July 2022

2ba09f19-9631-4efe-bd80-2abcc614958cR02